W9-CWW-861

THE LIVINGSTON INDIAN RECORDS, 1666-1723

BOOKS IN THE

AMERICAN INDIANS AT LAW SERIES

AMERICAN INDIAN LEGAL MATERIALS:
A UNION LIST
Compiled by Laura N. Gasaway, James L. Hoover, and Dorothy M. Warden

INDIAN NULLIFICATION OF THE UNCONSTITUTIONAL LAWS OF MASSACHUSETTS RELATIVE TO THE MARSHPEE TRIBE
by William Apes

LAWS OF THE COLONIAL AND STATE GOVERNMENTS, RELATING TO INDIANS AND INDIAN AFFAIRS, FROM 1633-1831 INCLUSIVE

LIVINGSTON INDIAN RECORDS
Edited by Lawrence H. Leder

THE CASE OF THE SENECA INDIANS IN THE STATE OF NEW YORK

THE LIVINGSTON INDIAN RECORDS, 1666-1723

Edited by Lawrence H. Leder

EARL M. COLEMAN, Publisher
Stanfordville, New York 1979

Library of Congress Cataloging in Publication Data

Livingston, Robert, 1654-1728, comp.
The Livingston Indian records, 1666-1723.

(American Indians at law series)
Reprint of the 1956 1st ed. published by the Pennsylvania Historical Association, Gettysburg.
Bibliography: p.
1. Iroquois Indians—Government relations—Sources. 2. Indians of North America—Government relations—To 1789—Sources. I. Leder, Lawrence H. II. Title. III. Series.
[E99.I7L5 1979] 323.1'19'7073 79-22246
ISBN 0-930576-33-0

This Earl M. Coleman edition of THE LIVINGSTON INDIAN RECORDS, 1666-1723 is a faithful facsimile reproduction of the first edition published in Gettysburg, Pa. in 1956.

This edition reprinted by arrangement with The Pennsylvania Historical Association.

Manufactured in the United States of America

THE LIVINGSTON INDIAN RECORDS

1666-1723

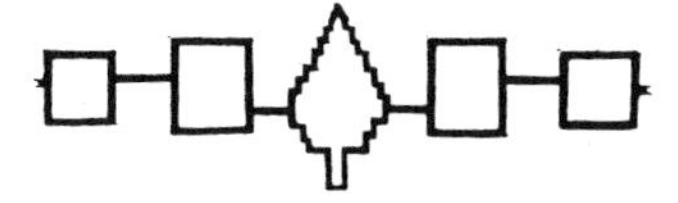

Edited by

LAWRENCE H. LEDER

THE PENNSYLVANIA HISTORICAL ASSOCIATION
GETTYSBURG, PA.
1956

FOREWORD

The mystery of the whereabouts of the Livingston Indian Records, which disappeared from public view 176 years ago, is at last resolved in these pages. The story of their vicissitudes is told by Lawrence H. Leder in his introductory article, "Robert Livingston (1654-1728), Secretary for Indian Affairs, and His Papers." The records themselves fill the pages that follow.

These documents, detailing Iroquois negotiations with English colonies from Massachusetts to Virginia, 1666-1723, are important for the illumination they give to a hitherto obscure corner of American history. They are of particular interest to New Yorkers, because the homelands of the Five Nations whose international relations are here unfolded were in northern New York. At the same time they are of special interest to Pennsylvanians, because it was under the Iroquois Tree of Peace that the Quaker colony had its birth and enjoyed so long an adolescence undisturbed by Indian wars.

We are accustomed to think of the Iroquois Confederacy as the foremost Indian power on the continent, as undoubtedly it was for a time. But in 1666, when the Livingston Indian Records open, the Iroquois enjoyed no such supremacy. At that time they were engaged in exhausting wars with both the Mahicans and Susquehannocks, the outcome of which no man could foretell. It was not until nine years later, in 1675 (peace meanwhile having been made with the Mahicans), that the destruction and dispersion of the Susquehannocks fully opened the Susquehanna Valley to the Iroquois, giving them access to new hunting grounds and hegemony over distant tribes to the south and west. Thereafter the Iroquois made free use of Pennsylvania's trails and waterways for their war parties and peace embassies, by which means they established the Great Peace over a territory comparable in extent to that embraced in the ancient *pax romana*.

In the Livingston Indian Records it is what happened at the far ends of Pennsylvania's war paths—in the principal Iroquois trouble centers of New York, Maryland, and Virginia—that receives the lion's share of attention. There is, however, much in these papers of special concern to Pennsylvania. For one thing there is the early map of the Susquehanna River, drawn in 1683, with comments on Indian travel. There are frequent evidences of trade rivalry among the English colonies. This was a time when New York, Maryland, and Virginia alike resented the intrusion of traders from upstart Philadelphia among the Indians of the Susquehanna and Schuylkill valleys. We learn from these pages something of the movements of the Shawnees both before and after the Iroquois gave them domicile in Penn's Woods. The picture, furthermore, of clashes between white settlers and Indians along the Appalachian border, whatever may be the immediate locale of particular incidents reported here, is as true of conditions in Pennsylvania as it is of conditions in the colonies on her borders.

The Pennsylvania Historical Association is happy to present to the readers of Pennsylvania History, and to others interested in the history of the Iroquois, the Livingston Indian Records, edited by Lawrence H. Leder, Penfield Fellow in History at New York University, and author of the forthcoming biography of Robert Livingston.

Paul A. W. Wallace
Editor, *Pennsylvania History*

TABLE OF CONTENTS

MAPS AND ILLUSTRATIONS

ROBERT LIVINGSTON (1654-1728)

First Lord of Livingston Manor.

Courtesy of Mrs. Herman Livingston of Oak Hill, New York, and the Frick Art Reference Library

ROBERT LIVINGSTON (1654-1728), SECRETARY FOR INDIAN AFFAIRS, AND HIS PAPERS

By Lawrence H. Leder

IN THE half-century from 1675 to 1725 two men, brothers-in-law, played key roles in Anglo-Iroquois relations. One of these was Peter Schuyler, the "Quider" of the Iroquois, who might well be designated the man of action; the other was Robert Livingston, the subject of this sketch, who might well be designated the man of vision.[1]

Born in Scotland in 1654, Robert Livingston was the youngest son of the Reverend John Livingstone, one of Scotland's most eminent Presbyterian divines. Outspoken in his opposition to Charles II's efforts to anglicize the Kirk of Scotland, the Reverend John Livingstone was exiled in 1663 by the king's ecclesiastical authorities. He fled to the more hospitable atmosphere of cosmopolitan Rotterdam where his wife and two youngest children, Robert and Janet, soon followed him. The resultant division of Robert's youth between Scotland and the Netherlands was a most fortunate occurrence. Not only did he obtain a sound training in the most advanced business community in the Old World, but he gained a mastery of the Dutch and English languages that was to prove invaluable in the New World.

After his father's death in 1672, Robert determined to try his luck across the Atlantic. Going to the colony of New York by way of Scotland and Charlestown, Massachusetts, he arrived in Albany in the early months of 1675. That frontier outpost was an ideal location for a young man possessed of ability, good train-

[1] There is no adequate biography of Livingston. The two published sketches provide the basic outline of his life, but neither have used the Livingston-Redmond MSS. deposited with the Franklin D. Roosevelt Library, Hyde Park, New York (hereafer cited as L-R MSS.), and both are inadequate in their interpretations of his career. Edwin B. Livingston, *The Livingstons of Livingston Manor* (New York: 1910); John A. Krout, "Behind the Coat of Arms: A Phase of Prestige in Colonial New York," *New York History,* 16 (January, 1935): 45-52. The generalizations made about Livingston in this sketch are based upon the present author's study of the L-R MSS. and other relevant materials for the life of Livingston that he is writing.

ing, a fortunate parental reputation, and but little else. New York had just been restored to the English, and the Duke of York's proprietary agents in New York City could make good use of someone with Livingston's qualifications as an intermediary between themselves and the Dutch burghers of Albany. The latter, in turn, appreciated someone who understood their desires and problems and could make them known to the English authorities.

In this fortunate setting Livingston quickly moved up the ladder of success. His first official position was that of Secretary to the Colony (or Manor) of Rensselaerswyck which he received in 1675 from Domine Nicholas Van Rensselaer.[2] Included in its functions were the duties of Town Clerk of Albany, second most important urban community in New York. His great personal charm, attested by numerous contemporaries,[3] soon won him the hand of young Alida Schuyler, widow of Domine Van Rensselaer, thus allying him with the powerful Schuyler and Van Cortlandt clans and insuring his success as a merchant.

By the mid-1680's Livingston's star was rising rapidly. With the approval of Governor Thomas Dongan he purchased two tracts of land, one of 2,000 and the other of 600 acres, on the eastern side of the Hudson River from the Mahicans. Then, in the vague manner typical of seventeenth century land grants in the New World, the obliging Governor converted the 2,600 acres into the 160,000 acre Manor of Livingston.[4] Further, when Albany received its municipal charter in 1686, Livingston found himself named to the offices of Town Clerk, Clerk of the Peace, and Clerk of the Common Pleas. To insure a comfortable income for Livingston, Governor Dongan soon thereafter added the posts of Sub-Collector of the Excise and Receiver of the Quitrents for Albany County to Livingston's accumulation of titles.[5]

[2] Wheeler B. Melius and Frank H. Burnap, comps., *Index to the Public Records of the County of Albany, State of New York, 1630-1894: Grantees* (12 vols., Albany, 1908-1911), 7: 4588.

[3] Wentworth Greenhalgh (April 19, 1678) and Charles Wolley (March 22, 1678/9) to Livingston, L-R MSS. These provide just a few examples of Livingston's reputation for winning ways.

[4] Dongan's patents of November 4, 1684, August 27, 1685, and July 22, 1686. Edmund B. O'Callaghan, ed., *The Documentary History of the State of New York* (4 vols., Albany, 1849-1850), 2:615-616, 620-621, 622-627 (hereafter cited as: *Doc. Hist. N. Y.*).

[5] Commissioners of Statutory Revision, *The Colonial Laws of New York from the Year 1664 to the Revolution* (5 vols., Albany, 1894), I: 206. Dongan's Report, c. 1686. Edmund B. O'Callaghan, ed., *Documents Rela-*

With this sound foundation of social position, business success, landed property, and local office, Livingston's horizons began to broaden. During Dongan's administration he took on the added task of victualling the troops stationed in New York, a function he performed on and off for the next twenty years. Not only did he become involved through this in the whole question of the defense of the Colony against the French in Canada, but he became deeply enmeshed in the Colony's finances. For a short time, under the aegis of the Earl of Bellomont, he became a member of the Governor's Council, and during the administrations of Governors Robert Hunter and William Burnet, he became a member of the New York Assembly and Speaker of that body, holding the latter post until illness forced his semi-retirement from public life in 1725.

The reader must not imagine, however, that Livingston's career followed a smooth path ever upwards. It was far from that, and its direction was rarely as clearly delineated as this sketch might seem to indicate. The greatest stumbling block in Livingston's path lay in his own personality. Coupled with his great personal charm, consciously exuded whenever it was to his advantage, was an unflagging righteousness regarding the obligations of his debtors to himself. (Such righteousness, however, did not extend to Livingston's obligations to his creditors.) At one time or another Livingston became embroiled in bitter clashes with almost every governor of New York. These altercations always centered about financial matters, for this was a period (until 1717) when the government was dependent upon the credit of private individuals, and Livingston was usually in the forefront of its creditors.

On two occasions his inability to achieve amicable financial settlements with the local authorities necessitated voyages to England where he placed his case before the Crown. On the first of these (1695-1696) he was nearly shipwrecked; on the second (1703-1706) he was almost captured by a French privateer within sight of Bristol.[6] A third voyage, in the period 1711-1715, was averted solely through the shrewd political bargaining of Governor Robert Hunter. When the Governor found himself unable to repay

tive to the Colonial History of the State of New York (11 vols., Albany, 1856-1861), 3: 401 (hereafter cited as: *Doc. Rel. Col. Hist.*).

[6] Lawrence H. Leder, "Robert Livingston's Voyage to England, 1695," *New York History,* 36 (January 1955) : 16-38. Robert Livingston to Board of Trade, July 9, 1703, L-R MSS.

Livingston's advances for the subsistence of the Palatine refugees settled in New York to produce naval stores, he offered instead a new patent for the Manor of Livingston which not only confirmed Livingston's title, but also gave him a seat in the Assembly, a "pocket-borough."[7] Later, Livingston, through his own efforts in that body, did obtain a sizable cash settlement,[8] but in the process he became one of the key political lieutenants of Governors Hunter and Burnet.

Of all the governmental posts held by Livingston, one of the most interesting was that of Secretary for Indian Affairs. Such a position had never existed prior to 1696, and its duties, never legally and fully defined, had always been performed by the Secretary of Rensselaerswyck and, after 1686, by the Town Clerk of Albany. During his first sojourn in England, Livingston decided to take advantage of the naiveté of the Lords of Trade and the Privy Council concerning intra-colonial administration to gain for himself an extra title and another salary. He convinced them that the Indian affairs aspect of the Town Clerk's office was so burdensome and time-consuming that a separate position should be established to cope with it. Livingston, however, was to hold both the clerkship and the secretaryship! A royal patent from William III was duly forthcoming which confirmed Livingston in his local offices in Albany and added that of Secretary for Indian Affairs at an annual salary of £100 sterling payable out of the revenue.[9]

When he returned to New York, Livingston found himself a political outcast. The Council and Governor Benjamin Fletcher, whose reputation Livingston had done his best to tear to shreds before the Lords of Trade, did their utmost to block the financial settlements he had arranged in London. Further, they denounced the office he had invented for himself: "the Allegacons upon Which the grant thereof is founded are false." It was probably the salary that most annoyed them, for he had been performing these tasks without recompense for nearly twenty years. In addition, this new salary was almost three times that which he was then receiving

[7] Hunter's patent of October 1, 1715. *Doc. Hist. N. Y.*, 2: 697.
[8] Commissioners of Statutory Revision, *op. cit.*, 957-989.
[9] Royal Commission of January 27, 1695/6. Public Record Office, *Calendar of State Papers Colonial Series America and West Indies* (40 vols., London, 1860-1939), 14: no. 2247.

for the more arduous office of Sub-Collector of the Excise. As though to substantiate this contention, Livingston was suspended from both the salary and the office and forbidden to perform its duties "otherwise than by virtue of his office as Town Clerk of Albany."[10]

Not until Fletcher was replaced by the Earl of Bellomont did Livingston regain his title and salary, though he continued to perform the Secretary's duties as Town Clerk. He was suspended once again by Bellomont's successor, Lord Cornbury, on the specious pretence that Bellomont had never formally lifted the initial suspension.[11] During his second visit to England, Livingston obtained still another royal patent for all his offices, this time from Queen Anne. It took two years before Cornbury grudgingly accepted it and restored Livingston to the post of Secretary for Indian Affairs.[12] From that time forward, however, the office was no longer questioned. When Livingston resigned all of his offices except the Speakership of the Assembly to hs eldest son, Philip, in 1721, he had the complete support of Governor Burnet who was instrumental in securing a royal patent for Philip.[13]

In accordance with custom and usage, the Secretary's duties were twofold: to maintain the records of the Indian Commissioners, and to assist at the Indian conferences. Both tasks were clerical in nature, but the second is in a way the more interesting. The blend of nationalities in New York necessitated the employment of three languages in the conferences. The original proposition of the Governor was usually prepared in English. Since those most familiar with the I'ndian tongue were rarely skilled in the subtleties of English, the document would then be translated into Dutch, usually by the Secretary. Finally, working from the Dutch version, the official interpreter would verbally expound the ideas in the Indian tongue. The Indians' replies would go through the same procedure in reverse. It is because of this complex mechanism that we have so few examples of the legendary oratorical prowess

[10] New York Colonial MSS. (New York State Library, Albany, New York), 40: 197 a(1).

[11] Robert Livingston to Board of Trade, c. 1704. *Doc. Rel. Col. Hist.*, 4: 1124.

[12] Livingston had presented his commission to Cornbury in October 1706, but it was not acknowledged until September 1708. New York Council Minutes (MSS. in New York State Library), 10: 45, 198-200.

[13] Royal Commission of June 30, 1721, L-R MSS.

of the Iroquois.[14] Their speeches simply could not retain any lyricism after being put through the wringer of three languages by interpreters more concerned with meaning than style.

But if the Secretary's duties were primarily clerical, why then did the office assume any importance? The answer, as is so often the case, lay not in the position, but in the man who held it. With almost every document pertaining to the Iroquois passing through his hands, the Secretary could not help but become intimately acquainted with all aspects of Indian affairs. A lesser man might have simply turned the office into a sinecure, but Livingston was of a different breed. It was an age when the concepts of public service and private gain were inter-twined, and Livingston used the knowledge so readily available to him to advance his own welfare as well as that of the English colonies in general and New York in particular. He became the confidant and adviser of those Governors—Dongan, Bellomont, Hunter, and Burnet—who, through the use of skill and imagination, were determined to extend English influence among the Iroquois and to maintain New York's dominant role in Indian affairs.

Indeed, one of the most important developments in Livingston's political career rested upon the firm foundation of his knowledge of Indian affairs. This was the ambitious program suggested by Livingston and implemented by Burnet to destroy the illicit Albany-Montreal trade and thereby subvert French influence among the western tribes.[15] The French, unable to compete with the English woolens in the Indian trade, had developed the practice, frowned upon by French authorities but persistently continued, of trading furs with the Albany wholesalers for woolens. Both Livingston and Burnet quickly grasped the fact that a blow struck at that trade would be a blow struck at French authority in the West and, conversely, would increase English influence, for the Indians highly

[14] "The art of public speaking is in high esteem among the Indians and much studied. They are extremely fond of method, and displeased with an irregular harangue because it is difficult to be remembered. When they answer, they repeat the whole, reducing it into strict order. Their speeches are short, and the sense conveyed in strong metaphors. . . . [The scene] cannot but impress upon the mind a lively idea of the ancient orators of Greece and Rome." William Smith, *The History of the Late Province of New-York, From Its Discovery, to the Appointment of Governor Colden in 1762* (2 vols., New York, 1829), 1: 54.

[15] Charles H. McIlwain, ed., Peter Wraxall, *An Abridgment of the Indian Affairs . . . From the Year 1678 to the Year 1751* (Cambridge, 1915), lxv.

prized English duffels and stroudwaters. This policy was first effected through an outright prohibition of the Albany-Montreal trade, but the wholesalers' subterfuges made it possible to evade the law. Next, a double tax was laid on the northern trade, while a single tax was placed on the western trade.[16] This means of discouragement and encouragement was much more successful in achieving its purpose. It was so successful that the Albany wholesalers, ever reluctant to abandon a profitable trade, pressured their English correspondents who, in turn, exerted their influence at the Board of Trade. The English authorities gave way to this pressure and the Crown disallowed these trade laws.[17]

Despite the ultimate collapse of these regulations, which might have extended English influence west to the Mississippi, Livingston left behind him another monument to his tenure as Secretary for Indian Affairs—the records of his office. As early as 1721 they were referred to as the "books of the Board where they keep the propositions made to the Indians & the Indians Speeches to them."[18] By the 1750's there were four such bound volumes, all of which were taken to Canada at the outbreak of the American Revolution by Colonel Guy Johnson, Superintendent of Indian Affairs, and eventually deposited with the Dominion Archivist in Ottawa during the nineteenth century. Sometime thereafter the first two volumes containing the records from 1677 to 1723 disappeared.[19]

The loss of this source material has distorted the historical treatment of the Iroquois. The only remaining records have served to perpetuate, for one reason or another, the undue emphasis placed upon their role in the Anglo-French conflict for North America at the expense of the equally important story of their relations with the various English colonies. Naturally enough, the French sources[20] largely concern themselves with the rivalry for the Indians' allegiance and, through them, control of the continent. Edmund B. O'Callaghan's monumental publication of New York's

[16] Commissioners of Statutory Revision, *op. cit.,* 2: 8-10, 281-287.
[17] McIlwain, *op. cit.,* lxxx.
[18] Burnet to Robert Livingston, c. January 1, 1720/1, see above, p. 228.
[19] McIlwain, *op. cit.,* lxxxvii-lxxxix.
[20] Reuben G. Thwaites, *Jesuit Relations* (73 vols., Cleveland, 1896-1901) and P. F. X. de Charlevoix, *History and General Description of New France* (trans. by J. G. Shea, 6 vols., New York, 1900) are two examples.

colonial records[21] contains a scattering of Anglo-Iroquois transactions, but they were taken from among those carefully selected and sent home by English Governors to illustrate the severity and significance of that rivalry. Cadwallader Colden's famous *History*[22] was written as an *apologia* for the Livingston-Burnet trade program and, therefore, falls into the same pattern. Peter Wraxall's *Abridgment*[23] was written as propaganda for Colonel William Johnson's appointment in the 1750's as Superintendent of Indian Affairs, an appointment intended to develop an imperial Indian policy during the final stage of the Anglo-French conflict.

While this "grand theme" of Iroquois history, which found its ablest exponent in Francis Parkman, has tremendous validity and importance, the story of the relationship between the Iroquois and the English, wholly neglected, is just as valid and important. With the publication of the present collection of documents—the Livingston Indian Records—we can further explore that relationship, restore some balance to Iroquois history, and remove from the province of supposition and legend some facets of early Iroquois activities.

This important collection is the result of Robert Livingston's delightful (as far as the historian is concerned) habit of retaining nearly every scrap of paper that came into his hands. As Secretary of Rensselaerswyck, Town Clerk of Albany, and Secretary for Indian Affairs he transcribed the conference minutes and other documents into the permanent record books from drafts or attested copies written in English, Dutch, or both. The drafts and copies he retained for his personal files. Now that the record books have disappeared, Livingston's file copies greatly aid us in filling in an important historical void.

This, however, is not the first time that these records have been made available. In 1780, when the State of New York was seeking proof of its claims to the trans-Allegheny West, these papers were brought into play. A committee was appointed by the Legislature to examine the records and validate New York's title. But the only source for such validation was the Iroquois title which, as it was claimed, had been transferred to New York in

[21] *Doc. Rel. Col. Hist.*

[22] Cadwallader Colden, *The History of the Five Indian Nations of Canada* (2 vols., New York, 1922). See especially 2: 1-59.

[23] McIlwain, *op. cit.*, cvi.

1701 by the Iroquois in a deed.[24] With the record books in Johnson's possession in Canada and the American Revolution underway, the committee could not perform its task until James Duane remembered that the first Robert Livingston's papers were in the possession of his descendant. Being a family friend, Duane secured permission to survey them, and his report was presented to the New York Senate and Assembly on March 30, 1780.[25] Since that time his report has lain forgotten among his papers in The New-York Historical Society, and the Livingston Indian Records, equally forgotten, have remained in the ownership of the Livingston family and have been placed in three different public depositories.[26]

Undoubtedly Livingston did not have a copy of every item that went into the permanent record books, and a comparison of this collection with the Duane Report indicates that some documents have vanished since 1780. But it can be safely assumed that the Livingston Indian Records contain the bulk of the two missing volumes. Indeed, they contain materials which could not have been found in those books—the records antedating 1677 which Livingston inherited from his predecessor as Secretary of Rensselaerswyck, William Schellyne.

In preparing these papers for publication, all items duplicating those already published in O'Callaghan's collection of New York records[27] have been eliminated unless there were marked variations. In the case of materials available in both English and Dutch versions, the former have been used. Where only a Dutch version existed, it has been translated into English by Miss Alida J. Kolk, and such translations have been individually noted. When, upon comparing this collection with the Duane Report, certain items were found to have been lost, that fact has been noted. Occasionally Duane prepared abstracts of some of the now-missing items and, wherever appropriate, these have been inserted in footnotes. Since

[24] *Doc. Rel. Col. Hist.*, 4: 909-911.

[25] James Duane, "Report of a Collection of Treaties &c with the five Nations remaining among the Papers of Robert Livingston & Philip Livingston Esqrs deceased; formerly Secretaries of Indian Affairs, in the hands of Col. Robert Livingston their Descendant and Heir at Law." Duane Papers, The New-York Historical Society.

[26] These records have been deposited first with the New York Public Library, then with The New-York Historical Society, and are presently in the Franklin D. Roosevelt Library.

[27] *Doc. Rel. Col. Hist.*

space precludes an analytical table of contents or index, these documents have been kept in strict chronological order. To guide the reader, italics have been used to distinguish the headings of documents and changes in speaker, time, and place.

No scholarly work can pretend to be the result of one mind or one set of hands. Among those who have made this volume possible and to whom the present author is indebted are: Mrs. William H. Osborn, owner of the Livingston-Redmond Manuscripts, and Mr. Herman Kahn, Director of the Franklin D. Roosevelt Library (depository for the papers), for their gracious permission to publish these materials; Mr. Stephen T. Riley, Librarian of the Massachusetts Historical Society, for his kind permission to publish the 1666 Iroquois transaction found in the unpublished Winthrop Papers; Mrs. Herman Livingston of Oak Hill and Mrs. Henry W. Howell, Jr., Librarian of the Frick Art Reference Library, for permission to reproduce the portrait of Robert Livingston; Mr. James A. Glenn for his permission to reproduce the portrait of Peter Schuyler; Miss Alida J. Kolk for her aid in translating the Dutch materials; and Mrs. Rose M. Leder for her invaluable assistance in typing much of the manuscript. It goes without saying, of course, that the present author assumes full responsibility for this work.

THE IROQUOIS:
A BRIEF OUTLINE OF THEIR HISTORY

By Paul A. W. Wallace

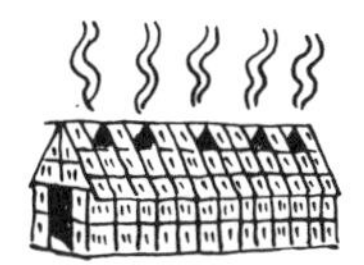

THE Five United Nations of the Iroquois called themselves "the Longhouse," a name that well describes both their geographical relationship to one another, and the government of their Confederacy. The Longhouse was composed of five independent peoples, each speaking a dialect of a common root language, seated in a line of villages on a trail stretching across northern New York from beyond Schenectady to the Genesee River. From east to west—as the names of rivers and lakes in that region remind us—they were the Mohawk, Oneida, Onondaga, Cayuga, and Seneca nations. The Mohawks were known as "Keepers of the Eastern Door," the Senecas as "Keepers of the Western Door." The Onondagas tended the central council fire. These were the three Elder Brothers. The Younger Brothers were the Oneidas (affiliated with the Mohawks) and the Cayugas (affiliated with the Senecas); later also the Tuscaroras and Delawares[1] when they were received into the Confederacy "on the cradle-board."

They had a federal council that met at Onondaga (Syracuse), presided over by the head chief of the Onondagas, Atotarho; but the political bond that held them was light. As in the typical dwelling of the Iroquois—a long frame house with roof and sides of bark and a corridor down the middle, inhabited by several related families, each group with its own separate fire—the nations of the League, though they sent representatives to the Onondaga Council, retained each its own sovereignty virtually intact. An ingenious system of checks and balances, together with a modified

[1] William N. Fenton, "The Roll Call of the Iroquois Chiefs," *Smithsonian Miscellaneous Collections,* Vol. 111, No. 15, p. 54.

form of the veto, made safe a maximum of liberty for each individual nation. At the same time the periodic meetings of the Great Council at which the common interest of all the member nations was discussed, and the impressive religious ritual associated with these gatherings, served to give the Five Nations an underlying sense of unity stronger than the many differences that divided them.

The course of Iroquois history, although to a partial view it has often seemed confused and unreasonable, may be comprehended easily enough if we first grasp its motivation and then follow its main movements. To attempt such a view, we must sacrifice here any close study of the innumerable filaments of Iroquois policy in order to see better the general drift of their history.[2]

For convenience, let us consider Iroquois history under five heads, these roughly corresponding with five historic periods: (1) *The Founding of the Confederacy;* (2) *The Coming of the European,* with the economic revolution that ensued; (3) *The Great War for Survival,* sometimes known as the Beaver Wars because of its origin in conflict over the fur trade; (4) *Balance of Power,* a period during which the Iroquois maintained their position of importance on the continent by observing a policy of neutrality between the English and the French; (5) *Dispersion,* many of the Iroquois migrating, after the close of the Revolutionary War, to Canada where they reestablished the Longhouse on the banks of the Grand River,[3] while others remained in scattered reservations in the United States.

There is no documentary record of the founding of the Confederacy, that event having taken place before the coming of the white man, probably about the middle of the fifteenth century.[4] But the founding is described in a legend that has been transmitted orally among the Iroquois.

[2] Certain of the main movements in Iroquois history have been individually treated in excellent analytical studies, such as the following: Charles Howard McIlwain's "Introduction" to Wraxall's *Abridgement of Indian Affairs* (Cambridge, Mass., 1915); George T. Hunt's *Wars of the Iroquois* (Madison, Wis., 1940); William N. Fenton's "Problems Arising from the Historic Northeastern Position of the Iroquois," *Smithsonian Miscellaneous Collections,* Vol. 100 (Washington, 1940); Anthony F. C. Wallace's "The Grand Settlement of 1701" (forthcoming).

[3] A number of Mohawks settled also at Deseronto on the Bay of Quinte.

[4] For a summary of the evidence on which this conclusion is based, see P. A. W. Wallace, "The Return of Hiawatha," *New York History,* October, 1948.

This legend, though undoubtedly in part a product of popular imagination and rationalizing, is important to us here both for the core of truth contained in it and for the influence it exerted in its elaborated form upon subsequent Iroquois history. It provided a patriotic incentive that helped to hold the Iroquois together, and gave to their wars something of the complexion of religious crusades.

Underneath the embroidery of myth, symbolism, and folk-tale, there is a foundation of honest historical broadcloth. The essential facts are there: the drawing together of five independent nations by slow degrees, through an intermediate process of local confederation, and against strong opposition, until under the influence of two great men, Deganawidah and Hiawatha, the union was completed and the Tree of Peace was planted on the shore of Onondaga Lake. The legend itself, with its wisdom and its poetry, seized the imagination of the Iroquois people, who took to heart the message it conveyed and derived from it a sense of national mission: to make the Tree of Peace *prevail.*

The Iroquois believed in the divine origin of the League. As the legend tells us, Deganawidah's mother was a virgin through whom the Great Spirit, in compassion for man, the victim of recurrent wars, incarnated his message of "Peace and Power." He converted Hiawatha to his ideal, and with the help of this disciple persuaded the Five Nations to organize effectively for peace. He left his people a body of laws which form the Constitution of the Confederacy.

The legend is full of vivid, unforgettable images, expressing man's perennial hope for a world in which, as a later Iroquois spokesman expressed it,[5] "The land shall be beautiful, the river shall have no more waves, one may go everywhere without fear." The Tree of Peace was not easily forgotten: a great white pine rising toward the sun for all men to see, with branches to shelter the war-weary, and white, healthy roots extending to the four corners of the earth.

What the Iroquois might have made of themselves if they had been given time to develop naturally under Deganawidah's laws, it is impossible to say. The coming of the European changed their whole mode of life and put them on the defensive. At first contact,

[5] Thwaites, *The Jesuit Relations* (Cleveland, 1896), Vol. 21, p. 33.

the Iroquois recognized the superiority of the white man's manufactured implements over his own stone-age tools and weapons. A brisk trade sprang up between the two races. Soon the Indian found himself dependent on the white man's goods, not for comfort only but for survival.

The Iroquois were an agricultural people and good farmers. Their cornfields were rich. But the white trader would not accept corn in exchange for the guns, powder, broadcloth, hoes and axes that the Indian now relied on for subsistence and defense. The trader demanded furs, especially beaver, for the European market. The Indian, in order to buy what he needed, found it necessary to devote his best energies to hunting and the marketing of hides.

The change in the end affected all Indians adversely. To the Iroquois it brought almost immediately near-disaster. Though their population was not large—never more than about twelve thousand men, women, and children—intensive hunting on a national scale soon exhausted their hunting grounds. By 1640 scarcely a beaver was to be found between the Hudson River and the Genesee. The Iroquois, to save themselves, had either to find new hunting grounds or to capture a position as middlemen (like the Hurons, whose country was also denuded of beaver) in the trade between the white man and the far Indians in the north and west, where the best hunting lay.

These were not pleasant alternatives. The Susquehanna Valley and the rich hunting territories westward to the valleys of the Allegheny River and the Ohio, with which the name of the Iroquois has been associated from Pennsylvania's earliest colonial days, were not in 1640 accessible to them. The Longhouse was hemmed in by powerful and suspicious neighbors. The Mahicans on the Hudson were pressing them hard. To the south were the formidable Susquehannocks, jealous of their trade with the Dutch and Swedes at the mouth of the Schuylkill River. To the north were the Hurons, a large and powerful people, the greatest Indian merchants on the continent, through whose activities as middlemen the French at Montreal held a monopoly of the trade with the Indians north of the Great Lakes. The Neutral Nation, immediately west of the Senecas, was allied with the Hurons. This was the tough market the Iroquois had to break into or perish.

The greatest obstacle was New France. For political as well as economic reasons, the French were determined to suffer no breach of their monopoly of the northern fur trade. It brought wealth to the colony, and at the same time kept France's Indian allies dependent on her. As long as she held the monopoly, she could control her allies by the threat of denying them trade goods. Repeatedly the Iroquois sought to make a commercial treaty with the Hurons. The Hurons themselves were not averse to it, but the French intervened and put a stop to it.

Desperate, the Iroquois took to piracy, as the English had done on the Spanish Main. They raided French trade routes on the St. Lawrence and Ottawa Rivers, ambushing Huron fur fleets. So successful were these raids that the French in alarm reconsidered their policy. In 1645 they, with their Huron allies, made peace with the Iroquois.

It was just such a treaty as the Iroquois had hoped for, containing the right commercial terms. Deganawidah in his laws had laid down the principle that friends eat out of the same bowl. Kiotsaeton, Mohawk spokesman at the treaty, made this explicit: the Hurons were now to trade with the Iroquois.

Next summer a Huron fur fleet of more than eighty canoes—"the greatest fur fleet in the history of New France"[6]—came out of the north-west and, unmolested by the Iroquois, descended to Montreal. The Iroquois were allowed no part in the trade, though the high prices paid for furs at Albany might have made it worth the Hurons' while to give Iroquois traders a middleman's cut. Twelve bales of furs which the French did not have merchandise enough to purchase, went back to Huronia. The Mohawks, enraged at this open breach of the commercial terms of the Treaty, sent war belts to the Senecas and Onondagas.[7]

Vis à vis the French, the Iroquois were in a strong military position. The Longhouse flanked French trade routes to the west, and, in case of French attack, they had at their backs a range of wooded mountains into which they might retire by paths inaccessible to the enemy. Within easy reach of them, too, were the Dutch (later the English) to supply them with guns and powder. But the French made up by diplomacy whatever disadvantage they

[6] George T. Hunt, *The Wars of the Iroquois* (Madison, Wis., 1940), p. 83.
[7] See Hunt's *Wars of the Iroquois* for a full description of this affair.

might have had in the matter of terrain. They tightened their hold on the nations surrounding the Iroquois.

In 1647 the Hurons made an aggressive alliance with the Susquehannocks, who agreed to lift the hatchet when the Hurons gave the word. It seemed to the Iroquois as if a trap had been closed about them. The Hurons went a step further. Taking advantage of the looseness of the political bond that held the Five Nations together, they sent an embassy to negotiate a separate peace with the Onondagas and Cayugas. Such a peace, if concluded, would have split the Confederacy apart, leaving the Mohawks and Senecas, at opposite ends of the Longhouse, to shift for themselves.

Thoroughly alarmed, the Mohawks and Senecas despatched forces to break Huron communications with the Onondagas and Susquehannocks, and together concerted further plans which took a little time to mature. The year 1648 passed with only inconclusive fighting. In the summer a large Huron trading fleet was brought successfully through the Mohawk blockade, with severe loss to the Mohawks.

In the autumn of that year, the Mohawks and Senecas quietly sent a thousand hunters up into the woods of Ontario. Some months later the hunters rendezvoused. At early dawn on March 16, 1649, they appeared suddenly out of the snowy woods before the Huron town of St. Ignace, stormed and took the place, and set it afire. Three of the inhabitants escaped, making their way to St. Louis, three miles away, where they gave the alarm. But by sunrise the Iroquois were before St. Louis, and by nine o'clock it, too, was in flames. A spirited Huron counter-attack decided the Iroquois not to press on against the principal Huron stronghold, Ste Marie. Instead, they returned to their own country.

But their work had been accomplished. Behind them, panic had overtaken the Huron people. They fled, burning fifteen of their villages as they went. Some spent a winter of near-starvation on Christian Island in the Georgian Bay. Others took refuge among the Petuns (Tobacco Nation), near neighbors to the south-west, or among the Neutrals about Niagara. A large number made their way to the country of the Eries. Some found shelter under the Tree of Peace, a whole village seating itself among the Senecas. Still another band made its way north to mingle with the Ottawas on Manitoulin Island. It was this last group, as we shall see, that in the end robbed the Iroquois of the expected fruits of victory.

The attack on Huronia was but the beginning. In the War for Survival, the Iroquois disposed of whole nations at a blow—not by massacring their people but by destroying their main centers of resistance and causing their dispersion. In this way the Petuns were destroyed in December, 1649, the Neutrals in 1650-51, and the Eries in 1654.

The wars with the Mahicans and Susquehannocks were a different matter. The Mahicans were good for the long pull. As early as 1626 they had driven the Mohawks from their lower Castle on the Mohawk River east of Schoharie Creek. The last great battle, at Hoffman's Ferry, in which the Mohawks defeated the Mahicans, did not come until 1669. Peace was not concluded until 1673.

The war with the Susquehannocks[8] dragged on for many years. Living in populous towns, well fortified, they seemed to be inexpugnable. They had a fort on the Lower Susquehanna River equipped with bastions and mounted artillery. Supported as they were with guns and powder from Maryland, and possessed of a strong military tradition, they were not to be destroyed with one blow. In 1663 they turned back a Seneca force of eight hundred men. They repeatedly raided the Iroquois country, and for years had the best of this desolating war. It was not until the Marylanders had turned against them that the Susquehannocks were at last dislodged from their riverbank stronghold. No adequate records have been preserved of this last Iroquois conquest. But we know with certainty about the dispersion, which was complete. Some of the Susquehannocks went south, only to suffer further humiliation at the hands of Maryland and Virginia. Others went north and were incorporated by the Iroquois, as some of the Hurons had been. A few were later allowed to settle in the Susquehanna Valley again, at Conestoga, near the present city of Lancaster.

The Beaver Wars, as we have seen, grew out of a struggle over the fur trade, but soon passed beyond that. As wars for survival, they were successful and decisive. The Iroquois emerged in 1675 as the strongest military power on the continent. They had won

[8] Also known as Conestogas or Minquas—White Minquas, the Eries being the Black Minquas.

title to a vast territory, including most of what are now the states of New York, Pennsylvania, and Ohio, as well as much of Maryland and Virginia. The Delaware Indians, formerly subject to the Susquehannocks, were now inherited as "props to the Longhouse."

As commercial ventures, however, the Beaver Wars as a whole were a failure. In particular, the dispersion of the Hurons did not give the Iroquois the expected middleman's share in the fur trade. The explanation is to be found in the activities of the Hurons who joined the Ottawas on Manitoulin Island and later moved with them to Michilimackinac. Hurons and Ottawas carried on as vigorous a trade as ever with the French, from a more distant and less vulnerable base.

Failing in their northern commercial objectives, the Senecas, after the defeat of the Neutrals and Eries, spread out into the west and developed a profitable trade in the Ohio and Mississippi Valleys. Whereupon the Susquehannocks, as yet unsubdued, raided Seneca trading routes, forcing the Senecas to despatch a large part of their warriors—as many as six hundred at a time—to escort their traders home.

The expulsion of the Susquehannocks in 1675 rid the Iroquois of certain dangers only to expose them to others. The opening of the Susquehanna Valley brought them into close contact with advancing English settlements in Pennsylvania, Maryland and Virginia, and confronted them with several difficult problems.

To begin with, there was the problem of the Virginia, or as it was sometimes called, the Carolina Road. The Virginia Road was a warpath extending from the Five Nations country, through Pennsylvania, Maryland, and Virginia, to the country of the Conoys (Piscataways), Tuteloes, Tuscaroras, Catawbas, Cherokees, and other tribes with whom the Iroquois were associated in matters of peace or war. Warriors travelled it to punish those who had harbored the Susquehannocks. Sometimes these war parties fell into conflict with the settlers. It was a maxim among the Iroquois that their warriors, when passing through friendly country, should "eat out of the same bowl" with the inhabitants. In other words, they expected to find victuals in Virginia. The settlers near whose farms the path ran, not understanding this point in international etiquette, refused food to passing war parties.

When the warriors helped themselves from the barnyard, the settlers took down their guns. At that point the natural law of reprisals took over.

To avoid such encounters, which the Five Nations deprecated as well as the Virginians and Marylanders, it was agreed in 1685 that the Virginia Road should be rerouted farther west, to the foot of the Blue Ridge. For a time all was well. Virginia discouraged settlement of the Piedmont in order to prevent trespass on the Indian highway. But, the path being still on the east side of the mountain, the westward thrust of population soon overran it, and the troubles began all over again.

Further negotiation resulted in the agreement of 1722, by which the Virginia Road was moved west of the mountain into the Shenandoah Valley, the Blue Ridge being accepted as the boundary between the English and the Iroquois. A similar problem beset the Pennsylvania frontier, where the Virginia Road, which for a time had run south through the lower Susquehanna Valley, was deflected ever farther west to avoid just such troubles as Virginia had had.

A more delicate problem for the Iroquois lay in the defenseless condition of the Susquehanna Valley after its former masters had been driven out. The crux of the problem was how to fill that vacuum before the English did, and to do it without bloodshed. The solution hit upon was to fill the valley with Indian refugee populations. It had long been a policy of the Iroquois, following Deganawidah's injunction to take strangers by the hand and welcome them under the Tree of Peace, to care for defeated peoples who appealed to them for sanctuary. We have seen them doing this with the Hurons and Susquehannocks. Now, in their time of triumph, the Iroquois had commiseration for Indians in the south who were having a rough time: the Shawnees and Conoys, for instance, whom the Iroquois themselves had been mauling; the Tuscaroras after the severe defeat administered to them by North Carolina in 1712; the Delawares driven by the Walking Purchase out of their homes in the Forks of the Delaware; the Nanticokes, who found themselves unwanted in Maryland. To all these dispossessed people the Iroquois offered asylum in the Susquehanna Valley. Colonies of them were placed at strategic points, usually at the junction of important trails or canoe routes. To superintend these "displaced persons," vice-regents or "half kings" were appointed, men like Shickellamy at the Forks of the Susquehanna (Sunbury) and Tenacharisson at the Forks of the Ohio. Sometimes—as when in 1766 a large band of Tuscaroras, with their sick and aged, came up from North Carolina to the Big Bend of the Susquehanna—the Iroquois despatched special agents to organize the removal and see to it that proper food and transportation were provided along the way.[9]

These little colonies or protectorates were moved up the river as the white settlements caught up with them, for the last thing the Iroquois wanted was a war with Pennsylvania or New York. Nevertheless these rearguard actions, though they were for the most part bloodless, were a reminder that the English colonies (whom the Iroquois, as they liked to tell them, had nursed through their infancy) had grown up to be dangerously acquisitive and importunate adults.

The Montreal Treaty of 1701, which marked a turning point in Iroquois history, came about as a result of the uneasiness felt by the Five Nations at the phenomenal growth and expansion of their English allies. They saw the need of a counter-balancing weight on the international scales.

We must go back a little in order to see more clearly the motivation of this treaty. In the year 1666 New France, in order to punish the Iroquois for their raids on her fur fleets, launched two expeditions under Courcelles and Tracy. The first was a failure; but the second, though it encountered few Mohawks (they having wisely vanished into the woods) burned villages and destroyed quantities of stored corn. Peace was made the following year, but it was soon broken. In 1687 Denonville's invasion of the Seneca country again caused little loss of manpower to the Iroquois, but the destruction of some 1,200,000 bushels of corn was crippling. In reprisal, two years later, the Iroquois secretly penetrated New

[9] See letter from the Moravian missionary, John Jacob Schmick, at Wyalusing: "On the 18th [November, 1766] two chiefs, Newollike and Aehkolunty . . . brought a message from the Six Nations for our Indian Brethren to this effect: The Six Nations have received news by a Tuscarora messenger that a number of their people are on their way, but they do not know how they are to make out and provide for themselves. The Six Nations, therefore, request the Indians everywhere along the Susquehanna to receive these poor Indians, send canoes from place to place for them, and provide them with corn. . . ." Bethlehem Diary, Archives of the Moravian Church, Bethlehem, Pa.

France to the gates of Montreal and emerged from the woods to devastate the country for many leagues about. The expedition goes down in Canadian history as the Massacre of Lachine, because the Indians, unable to reach and destroy the enemy's stores of food, as the French had done, killed or captured the crop producers, which came to the same thing in the end—injury to the enemy's economy. A few years later the French launched another punitive expedition into the Iroquois country; and so the pendulum swung, from reprisal to reprisal, each side continually getting hurt, though never mortally.

What the Iroquois wanted was not war but a better share of the fur trade. "In fine," wrote Lamberville of their war with the Miamis in the West, "they do not wage war save but to secure a good peace."[10] What the French wanted was freedom from Iroquois terror. "An extraordinary thing," wrote La Potherie, "that three or four thousand people should be able to make a whole new world tremble."[11] The Lachine affair had so frightened the Hurons and Ottawas that the French thereafter found them impossible to control. By this time the situation had reached a stalemate. The French had learned that they could not destroy the Iroquois. The Iroquois had learned that it would be unwise to destroy the French: they were a good counter-weight to the English. It was becoming apparent to both sides, French and Iroquois, that an accommodation was to be desired.

The English, getting wind of this *rapprochement,* did everything they could to stop it. They reminded the Iroquois that they were "subjects" of the King of England.[12] The merchants of Albany were apprehensive of losing their monopoly of Iroquois trade. The Province of New York feared losing Iroquois protection of the northern border. "Those Five Nations," wrote Governor Dongan, "are very brave & the awe & Dread of all ye Indyans in these parts of America, and are a better defence to us, than if they were so

[10] O'Callaghan, *Documentary History of the State of New York* (Albany, 1849), I, 133.

[11] Baçqueville de La Potherie, *Histoire de L'Amerique Septentrionale* (Paris, 1722), IV, 147.

[12] There seems to have been an honest misunderstanding here. The Iroquois, when they "gave" their country to the Governor of New York, meant only that they placed themselves under English protection in case of a French invasion, not that they had surrendered either their sovereignty or title to their lands.

many Christians."[13] The middle colonies, fearing war with France, did not want to lose the support of Iroquois manpower. "If we lose the Iroquois, we are gone," wrote James Logan, Secretary of Pennsylvania, in 1702.

In the summer of 1701 what the English feared came to pass. At Montreal the Five Nations made peace with the French and their Indian allies. The French invited the Iroquois to trade with them at Detroit. In return the Iroquois promised, in case of a Franco-British war, to remain neutral. But the Iroquois were not deserting the English. While one embassy was on its way to treat with the French in Montreal, another was, quite honestly, renewing the chain of friendship at Albany. At Montreal, in return for the promise of their neutrality, the Iroquois stipulated that the French should respect that neutrality and, in case of a war with the English should, as far as the Iroquois were concerned, "sit on their mats" (i.e., not breach the Iroquois borders).[14]

During the early years of the eighteenth century, Conrad Weiser in Pennsylvania and William Johnson in New York did much to confirm the "Antient Union" of the Iroquois and the English. The Joncaires, father and sons, strove to preserve Iroquois neutrality. When at last the French and Indian War broke out, the Five Nations, true to their treaty with France, remained neutral. There were, it is true, some scattered acts of partisanship, as when Senecas took part in raids on the English settlements, or when Mohawks danced the war dance and accepted the hatchet from William Johnson. But officially Iroquois neutrality was maintained, and, on the whole, it worked to the advantage of the English colonies. The Iroquois exerted judicious pressure on their wards, Delawares and Shawnees, who had joined the French and struck the English. The chastisement administered to Teedyuscung, leader of the pro-French Delawares, at the Easton Treaty of 1758, was decisive. That treaty ended the Indian War in Pennsylvania and made Fort Duquesne untenable by the French.

After the fall of New France in 1763, the Iroquois quickly learned how sound their policy of keeping the balance of power had been. The English, freed of the French menace on their

[13] September 8, 1687. O'Callaghan, *Doc. Hist. of the State of N. Y.*, I, 256.
[14] A full discussion of this episode is found in Anthony F. C. Wallace's forthcoming "The Grand Settlement of 1701."

borders, ceased to court the Iroquois or to right their wrongs. Gross land scandals were imposed upon them without redress. "The Indians need not to expect even moderate Justice in this Country," wrote Sir William Johnson.[15] They had to submit to hard treaties, whittling away their territories, like the Fort Stanwyx Treaty of 1768.

The American Revolution found the Iroquois divided. After a period of neutrality, the Oneidas and many of the Tuscaroras sided with the "Thirteen Fires," while the Mohawks, Onondagas, Cayugas, and Senecas, under the leadership of Joseph Brant, sided with the British. After the war came their dispersion. Many of them followed Joseph Brant to Canada. Their descendants may still be found on the Six Nations Reserve (the Tuscarora being the sixth nation) near Brantford, Ontario. There are between seven and eight thousand of them, representing all the nations of the Confederacy, with a good sprinkling of Delawares and others who came into the Longhouse on the cradleboard. Many have remained in New York and Pennsylvania: at Onondaga, St. Regis, Tonawanda, Cattaraugus, Tuscarora, Cornplanter. Still others have moved to reservations in the West. Many of the Oneidas are now in Wisconsin.

The last decades of the eighteenth century and the first decades of the nineteenth were the unhappiest years in the history of the Longhouse. Some of their fires had been put out and others had been scattered. Power in international affairs was gone from them. Their horizons had suddenly contracted. People accustomed to think in continental terms were overwhelmed by the nagging frustrations of reservation life. There was widespread collapse of morale.

Then came Handsome Lake, the Seneca prophet, with his visions. He had walked the Sky Road, he said, and had talked with three messengers from the Creator. The Creator was displeased with his *Ongwe-honwe* (Real People) for neglecting their Indian heritage and sinking so far below the spirit of their ancestors. Handsome Lake's words touched a chord among all the Iroquois, the vibrations of which have not ceased to this day. He had started a national religious movement that is still strong.

[15] Johnson to Gage, Feb. 14, 1765. *The Papers of Sir William Johnson,* Vol. XI (Albany, 1953), p. 572.

Under these and other influences the Iroquois pulled themselves together and set their shoulders to the long task ahead: without relinquishing their identity as *Kanonsionni,* People of the Longhouse, to join the rest of the world in clearing the path of brambles and briars for the advancement of all mankind. Their success is attested by notable contributions they have made in industry, the professions, scientific research, and the arts. They are the best structural steel workers in America, and for soldiering there are none to surpass them. Though their population today is little more than it was in the seventeenth century, they contributed to the armies of the United States and Canada during the Second World War more than twice as many men as they had assembled in their greatest days to crush the Hurons. The white man may well be proud to eat out of the same bowl with them.

The design on the title-page is made up of symbols of the Five Nations Confederacy. The geometrical figures are from the Hiawatha Belt (a piece of archival wampum now in custody of the New York State Museum at Albany), which the Indians believe to be a contemporary record of the founding of the Five Nations. The Tree of Peace, tended by the Onondaga nation, is in the center with the other four nations beside it. The open ends of the chain that binds them indicates, according to Indian interpretation, that the chain of friendship is not closed, the Five Nations hoping to bring other nations into the Confederacy. The Tree of Peace has four roots, extending to the four corners of the earth. Above the Tree is the Eagle That Sees Afar, placed there by Deganawidah to warn of approaching danger—a symbol of military preparedness. The men with clasped hands represent the Five Nations in so firm a union that even if a tree should fall on them it could not break them apart.

Intermingled with the text of the Livingston Indian Records in the following pages, is a picture version of the Legend of the Founding, done by Ray Fadden (Aren Akweks) of the St. Regis Mohawks. As far as possible the artist has depended on conventional Indian pictographs. When, however, he has had something to express for which no ancient symbols were available, he has tried to imagine what the old-time picture-writers would have done, and in that light made up his own characters.

THE LIVINGSTON INDIAN RECORDS

Edited by LAWRENCE H. LEDER

Proposal made by [ ] and some chiefs [ ] [ ] of the 8/18 February 1666[1]

Translated by Hille Couwenliche

1. Say: we pray you that you [ ], miss a covenant [ ] had promised last year in July [ ]
2. That the sacks with powder which they buy [should be bigger] than before which are too small.
3. Say, there are now four nations[ ] who have been here [who] have had alcoholic drinks [ ] nation should also [have] strong drinks [ ] by these proposals [ ] and an otter.

Present:
Captain Backer and all the commissaries but Van Bael
translated by Jacques Cornelissen

Proposals made by the Chiefs of the Maquas the 8/18 of July 1666 in the fort at Albany[2]

1° Brethren, you have our promise that we would warn you when the French were on their way. This is the warning which we now give you: the French are really coming now.[3] You forbade us (which promise we broke) from slaying them. When they came quite near to us, we were still on the defensive. Thus it happened that we have slain some handful of Frenchmen which was their

[1] Translated from the Dutch. Brackets indicate torn portions of MS.
[2] Translated from the Dutch.
[3] The Governor of Canada had sent out two detachments of 200 men each against the Iroquois. He recalled them before they engaged the Iroquois, but not before the Mohawks had learned of their departure from Canada. Tracy to Albany Commissioners, July 14, 1666. O'Callaghan, 3: 129.

This is the story of the founding of the Five Nations, the Iroquois Confederacy, and the planting of the Tree of Peace.

North of the Beautiful Lake (Ontario), in the land of the Hurons, was a village on the Bay of Quinte.

own fault. You spoke and told us also that we should stop bothering the Mahikanders, in which we obeyed you.

2° Say: we fear that we will get ourselves into much trouble, but we await the decision of our Brethren, for the French have let us know through the Senecas that they want to make peace with us. We do not believe this, for they come with all their might. If they really wanted or intended to make peace, they certainly would come to talk with us, but not with all their power, nor would they all come. Therefore, this is certainly a signal that they want to fight.

3° Say: Brethren, we do not know where we will see the French. Perhaps they will come to Schanegtade, which we think will be so. The country is in danger. We do not know how and where it will end. We did some things to you which have not been corrected, but that can be forgotten. Now you should quickly send us powder and lead so we may still fight the French.

4° Brethren, we do not wish to insist, but you cannot desert us now. You must help us with powder and lead as we requested.

5° Say: Brethren, we do not want to sleep on the hillside tonight, for we do not want to be killed by the Mahikanders. Leave the houses on the hillside for the Senecas who are coming in great numbers. Let them stay there.

Present:
the gentlemen except
Cornelis Van Nis

Answer to the proposal made by the Chiefs of the Maquas the 9/19 of July 1666[1]

1° Brethren, we thank you for the warning which you sent us that the French may be coming. As to your demand, we have looked the whole place over to buy powder and lead which we wanted to send to you, but could find very little. There is very little powder in the country and those among our people who have some do not wish to give it up. Also, we fear that the French might kill us too.

2° Brethren, you have now let us know from your side that the French are near you, or may be near Schanegtade. Now we pray you to let this be shown in haste to Corlaer. Then he can quickly advise us so that we can be on our guard also and keep good watch.

[1] Translated from the Dutch.

On the 9/19 of July 1666 paid to

Philip Pieterse for 6 lb. powder	fl. 50
Schermerhorn for 6 lb. powder	50
Captain Staets for 40 lb. lead	50
Borrowed from Captain Backer 3 lb. powder	

The above-written has been given to the Maquas Chiefs. It is still owed by Corlaer. Less the 32 florins wampum Schermerhorn had the other day, 18 florins are still due him.

Proposal 3/13 of August 1666
Captain Backer and Commissaries

Proposal and answers between the envoys from Canada and the Maquase in the presence of the Captain and Commissaries of Albany, some present and some absent, the 3/13 of August 1666[1]

After Mons. [Cousture] had read the letters of the Vice Roy[2] [of Canada] commanding either war or peace between the French and Maquase

[ ] by the Gentlemen, Captain Backer and the Commissaries, and the Chiefs of the Maquase is made known, and the opinion of the [ ] Vice Roy, on which the Maquase have answered that [ ] tomorrow being the 4/14 of this month will answer [ ]. On that date the Chiefs [ ] assemble to give answer to the [proposals] which have been made known to them [ ]

They answered as follows:

Translated by Jacques [Cornelissen]

1° Say that [they] thank the envoys very much that they [ ] have come from Canada to here [ ] has and they now understand quite well from his letters which have been brought here what the Governor of Canada means.

[1] Translated from the Dutch. Brackets indicate torn portions of MS.; material within brackets supplied from correlative or internal evidence.

[2] Cousture brought two letters with him. One advised that the two war parties sent against the Iroquois had been recalled; the other complained that the people of Albany had broken their pledge to keep the Iroquois peaceful. Albany Commissaries to Tracy, August 20, 1666. O'Callaghan, 3: 134.

Living in that village was a woman, a virgin, who in a vision was told that she was to give birth to a boy child, whom she must name Deganawidah. He was to be a great man who would plant the Tree of Peace and spread goodwill among the Indians.

2° Say that the war was not their fault and that they would very much like to see a good lasting peace made between them and the French.

3° Say now that three Maquase will go with as many of their male prisoners as want to go, but the greatest part will have to stay until our ambassadors retùrn and peace has been made, and until it has been determined that our people are not again locked up as has happened before. When they return safe and sound after brotherhood is settled upon, then they will try their best to return the women prisoners if there are any.

4° We have impressed upon our young men that they should not do any more harm and this they have promised [ ] also that for them this peace will remain [ ], and that no one should think [ ] and those Frenchmen who were killed [ ] also killed by their nation.

On this [the French envoys] answered (translated by Jan [ ]):

That if the Maquase Chiefs [ ] come to Canada that they doubt not that peace will be made with them and will be kept. As to the first Maquase who will now go to Canada with the male prisoners, no harm will be done to them. Thereafter, the Maquase who are prisoners of the French will be set free. This is on condition that then the rest of the female and male French people who are now among the Maquase will also be taken along to Canada safe and sound.

August 5/15. Proposals made by the Chiefs of the Maquase to Mons. Cousture[1]

1° Say that they are very glad that Mons. de Rolle is still alive and that the Viceroy will come and see them again. Do give wampum thereupon.

2° Say that they led the way, that they threw their guns away, and that they would not begin any trouble. The Maquase will keep the peace even though it might happen that the French would make war again with the Senecas. They will not participate in that. Do give wampum on this.

3° Say that they pray to have their prisoners returned and those who want to stay there, they may remain there.

[1] Translated from the Dutch.

4° Say that some are prisoners of the French and now that they have returned those whom the French wanted to be delivered.

Proposal of the ambassadors of Hartford and Springfield in Albany, 6/16 of August 1666[1]

Say that they learned that the Mahikanders accuse them of being the cause that their Sachems could not reach an agreement with the Chiefs of the Maquase, and that they want to end that accusation.[2]

Therefore, they came yesterday to relieve themselves of this accusation. The accusation does not hold since they have always done their duty towards their Indians. They want to come to a good and lasting peace. Gave wampum.

They pray for an answer

The Chiefs said that they would answer the above-mentioned proposal tomorrow.[3]

[1] Translated from the Dutch.

[2] Governor John Winthrop in Hartford, Connecticut, was attempting to bring about a peace between the Mohawks and the River Indians. Nicolls to Albany Commissaries, June 22, 1666. O'Callaghan, 3: 117.

[3] The following reply of the Mohawks is taken from the Winthrop MSS., 15: 10 (Massachusetts Historical Society):

August y[e] 7th 1666
Answer from the Cheife of the maquase to The Messengers from Hartforth & Springfeild don the 6th August 1666:

They Say Brothers you Sent for us yesterday that we Should give answer upon the proposishons you made to us. it is longe agoe that the Letter hath beene on the way, Since the Springe to the North
1. Given a band of Sewant. They Say Brothers. We have it alone that you tell us and We shall heare to it, in what you say to us. Therefore I tell you for an Answer. That we will keepe peace. But we cannot for the Other Indians to Witt Oniada, Onnundaga Cayuga Not answer for them. Butt I shall doe my Indeavor with the Other Nations that they shall take the peace.
2. Given 2 fadom of Wampum: They say to the 4 North Indians that are p[r]sent you See it Now you are Stuborne as one Stone had I Soe mutch eviell done as you have done, I had come here before now. They shall now kepe the peace, till that they have killed againe any of our men.
3. You must make haste to come hyther. We can give you Noe tyme because wee doe not know how longe you shall be on the Way.

The son was born, and the eyes of the Creator ever watched over him and guarded him from harm. By the Creator he was given special powers.

Peace between the Maquase and the Mahikanders. 31 August/10 September 1666
Proposals made by the Justices of Albany to the Chiefs of the Maquase and the Mahikanders.[1]

Translated by Gerrit Slichtenhorst, Gabriel Gomaz, and Hille Cornelisse

We say that you, the Mahikanders, and the other nations of Indians that from time to time most attacked our brothers, the Maquase, are now going to make peace with them. The Maquase, our brothers, have promised to make peace. Now you have come here and the Chiefs of the Maquase are also here. Now we pray you all, Mahikanders as well as other Chiefs who are present here, that you will now make a good, lasting, and true peace with the Maquase, a peace which cannot be broken. You people are thoroughly tired of all wars and hostilities and will dig a grave of forgetfulness and will put a heavy stone on the grave so that evil will not be able to come out of there again.

Answer of the Chiefs of the Maquase:

1° We thank you, brethren, that you have brought it so far that we have come to a good peace and will please watch from now on what will happen between us and the Mahikanders.
2° Say, let it now be certain that the Christians, English as well as Dutchmen, will stick to their word, and that we do not have to expect war from you or from the other nations of Indians, because the English have said that we and the others from the

4. The Maquase Says that the English and Dutch hath presented them with peace that they Should not prosequte their warr against North Indians, where they were intended to goe which p^{rs}entings for the with holdinge of our resolutions wee Except of.
5. Say urge the Maquase to the Assurance of a good peace betweene them & the Mohekanders. They Send two Messengers to the North to bringe ye North Indians Sackamakers hyther, ffor the confirmeinge of a fast peace, for the good of the comon Welth. Thurrow the Desires of the English & Dutch We are desirous to make a fast peace betwixt us and the Mehekanders. And if the Mehekand^{rs} will not make peace Nor keepe it then Shall the English & Dutch be bound to performe their promise that is that the Messengers Shall returne hyther in Good Safety.
In p^{r}sence of Captaine
and Comisaries

Wittnesse
W. Schellyne
Secretary.

[1] Translated from the Dutch.

Wajero will fight again and only because the Maquase 2000 years ago slew an old man from Wajero.

Answer of the Mahikanders:

Say that they thank us for the friendship that we made by acting as intermediaries in the peace between their people and the Maquase. Do give wampum.

Proposal made by the Maquase Chiefs to the Mahikanders and the other nations of Indians to the North:

1° We will put our heart now into yours, meaning by that that they will not have to distrust them any more. Do give wampum.
2° Pray that the Mahikanders will tell them where the heads are gone which they have cut off from their people in the North. Do give wampum.
3° All war and shedding of blood will now be put in a grave of forgetfulness and will not be thought of any more. Give wampum.

After the Maquase and Mahikanders reached an agreement, the Justices had the Maquase give wampum also to the Oneidas and Onondages to seal the peace with the Mahikanders.

Still other Maquase Chiefs gave wampum in gratefulness that they have listened to our counsel of peace with the Mahikanders and the other nations of Indians. The same was given by the Mahikanders with a recommendation to show a better conduct from now on towards the Maquase.

To seal the peace between them three shots have been fired from the cannon of the fort.

Present
Capt. Salisbury
Jan Everd van Bael
Gerrit van Slichtenhorst
Goossen Gerritse

Proposal made by the Chiefs of the Maquase in the fort of Albany, July 23, 1672[1]

Translated by Mr. van Slichtenhorst

1. Say that some Maquase had been in Trois Rivieres in Canada and that the French have told them that some Mahikanders and North Indians had been there and gave them 5 belts of wampum so

[1] Translated from the Dutch.

When Deganawidah became a man, he was honest and straight-tongued. He had a big heart. He never killed game for sport, but only when he needed food. He shared what he had with the less fortunate. Because of his kindness, the birds would light on his shoulders and animals would eat from his hand.

that they would again take up the hatchet with them against the Maquase.
Give thereupon 1 fathom wampum.
2. Say that the French stopped the belts and answered them [Mahikanders] that the Maquase are their children and live in one house, and that the English are their brethren and that you should not make war. You may accept or reject it as you wish. The English and Dutch have made the peace which they do not want to break.
Give thereupon 1 fathom wampum.
3. Say you people have made the peace between us and the Mahikanders, and we request that it may stay steadfast. You have taken the hatchets away from us and buried them. Now they bind the chain between us, the Mahikanders and the North Indians.
Give thereupon 1 fathom wampum.
4. Say we have accepted what you people have said and we have kept the peace, and our old men go fishing everywhere. We suspect that not one single Mahikander comes and that because there is still evil in their hearts.
Give thereupon 1 fathom wampum.
5. Say we have accepted the peace which has been made by you people between both of us. Speak with the Mahikanders so that they come and do as we do, so we can see that their heart is also good, and that they will hold to the peace.
Give thereupon 1 fathom wampum.
6. Say do not think that we will give any excuse to our enemies to do any harm, but we will keep quiet and wait to see what they will do. If it comes to pass that the Indians from the North come to do us some harm, what will you say then, you who have made the peace. Request clear brandy in their barrels as the same are small.
Give thereupon 1 belt wampum.

Answer to the proposal made in the fort of Albany, July 25, 1672[1]
Translated by Mr. Slichtenhorst

Present
Capt. Salisbury
Goosen Gerritse
Jan Everding van Bael
Jacob Schermerhorn
Gerrit Slichtenhorst

Brethren, it is agreeable to us that you come and tell us what had

[1] Translated from the Dutch.

happened in Canada, but we trust that that is not true, and we will look into this matter. Also, we will speak to the Mahikanders, or ask them what is happening. Also, we will take care that the peace will remain steadfast and force the Mahikanders to come here. And if they might come to slay one of you then they will see that they will have to deal with us and we will revenge it.

Proposals by the Chiefs of the Mahikanders, made in the Fort at Albany, the 14 February 1674/5[1]

Present:
The Commander, Knapton
Gerrit van Slichtenhorst
Adriaan Gerrits
Peter Tebinnen
Andries Teller
The Schout [Michael] Siston

Firstly: they regret the death of the late Mr. Rensselaer,[2] saying that they with their three nations mourn and cry. Give 5 faddom wampum to cover the grave. Since he is dead now they are afraid that the Maquase will come and do them harm, for he helped to make the peace between them and the Maquase.

Say that the English and Dutch and their people are now one, and thank us that we took the trouble to make peace between them and the Maquase and that we buried the axes. Give 7 bands of wampum, 1 of 13 high, 2 of 11 high, 2 of 10, 1 of 7, and 1 of 4 high.

Say that before they were strong of people and had power. Then the Dutch were but few, but they let them remain and live in peace. Now they are weak and are but few, and the English with the Dutch are now many. They pray to be able to live in peace among us and the English. Give thereupon 7 strings of wampum: 1 of 13, 1 of 12, 1 of 11, 1 of 9, 2 of 7, 1 of 2 high.

Say the English and the Dutch are now one and the Dutch are now English. Thus we Mahikanders, the highland Indians, and the "western corner" Indians are now one also. Thus they pray that they will not be exiled or destroyed by the English, something they have never done to the Christians. Give thereupon 7 strings of wampum: 1 of 12, 2 of 11, 1 of 9, 2 of 5, and 1 of 6 high.

[1] Translated from the Dutch.
[2] Jeremias Van Rensselaer.

One day he bade farewell to his mother and his grandmother. In a canoe of white stone he paddled across the Beautiful Lake toward the south wind (Little Fawn).

The wampum amounts to fl. 478: 12 in Zewant.
Say we are now all together the English and the Indians [brethren] and they intend to plant on Dutch soil, for their earth is very empty. Then the Dutch should not say that they, the Indians, eat too many "tatpoesjen"[1] as they said before. Do give 5 strings of wampum, 1 of 14 high, 1 of 12, 1 of 10, 1 of 8, 1 of 6 high.

Answer to the brethren, the Mahikanders

1° Brethren, we have seen how sad you are by the death of Mr. Rensselaer and that you cry loudly because he has been a friend of yours. Concerning your thought that the Maquase would now attack you because your good friend died, we say no, for you still have many friends who will take care of you. Concerning your statement that the English and Dutch are one, that is true for we are English now and the peace between you and the Maquase has also been made with the English government and the axe buried, which, we hope, never will appear again.
2° Concerning the brethren being afraid because they have but few people and we are stronger than you, be assured that we will not treat you but as good friends. If it happened that some Englishmen or Dutchmen did you wrong, you should come and complain to us about it and we will punish the persons in question. We hope that you will not give any cause thereto.
3° We are glad that the brethren in the three existing nations are so closely unified and tied together, for neither do we like to see that they are warring and living together amidst quarrels. Therefore the brethren can plant their soil in peace on Dutch earth, and can eat as many "taspoesjens" as they can get from the landowner.
For the wampum they gave has been bought:

25	(Dutch) pounds of powder	fl. 100:-
50	pounds of lead	fl. 40:-
	good smelling tobacco	fl. 60:-
½	a barrel of beer	fl. 15:-
	packages for powder	fl. 2:-
1	bushel of peas	fl. 4:-
		fl. 221:-
	misc. costs	fl. 25:-
		fl. 246:-

[1] Probably a local term with no modern equivalent.

Arnout Cornelisse Interpreter

Proposicons made to the Mohekandrs and other River Indians by Major John Pynchon and James Richards Genten Commissioners from ye Colonies of Mattasshusetts & Cannatticut in ye Court house at Albany ye 24th of Aprill 1677:

Wie are informed yt you these river Indians haue not engaged in ye late unhappy Warr against ye English,[1] but yt you have satt still according to ye Comand of ye Honble: Governr of New Yorke &c. And wee being of ye same naton, under ye same Prince, and soe as one With ye sd Governr; Wee doe therefore acknowledge these River Indians or freinds and Neighbours, expecting well from you to carry it towards us as frinds & good neighbours and soe demeaning of your selves. Wie looke yt you should timely discover any attempte of Mischeif yt you may heare of agst ye English, and yt you doe not henceforward harbour or Entertaine any yt shall remain or enemies, and yt have evill designes agst us, and in all things act as good and true freinds to ye English naton, and wee shall bee and remaine ye same to you, and desire yt ye sd freindship may be With these Indians among us; Doe prest 2 Belts and some Zeawant

True Coppy Attests /S/ John Pynchon
/S/ James Richards

The Mahikanders and other River Indians Sachems Answer upon ye Prop: of Major Pynchon &c: in ye Court 24 April 1677

1. The Christians and wee many years ago have always been freinds & brethren and now of Late years ye Govr. Genl: is become or father, we being now butt a very few, and ye Christians of ye North are our Bretheren & wee are glad to see each other att this present time for to speak & give Presents on to ye other. do give a hank of Zeaut:
2. Wee are glad Brethren to see yu in friendship and do thank

[1] The attack by the Eastern Indians on the settlers in the Kennebec area of Maine. Andros' "Short Account of . . . New-York," c. 1678. O'Callaghan, 3: 255.

He crossed Lake Ontario and went up the Oswego River. Then, crossing Oneida Lake, after a short carry he paddled down the Mohawk River until he reached a village of the Flint People (Mohawks). As was the custom for travelers at that time, he made a fire near the village and waited for an invitation to enter.

you heartily, for wn: we were formerly in warr, (pointing towards ye West where ye Masquasse live,) yn Major Pinson did as it were Take us in his armes & *p*tected us, Wee see now again yt his heart is good, & so is ours likewise, wch: shall always remain so do give a Belt of Zeaut.

3. The Brethren have told us now yt we shall nott harbour or entertain any of theire enemies, wch wee engage to doe & do *p*mise to continue in peace & friendsp. and there shall be no shrubs or rubbish grow along ye Rivers Shewing by a belt which he had in his hand that all was Clear, meaning therby to keep ye Rivers Clear even quite downe to N. Yorke. doe give a Belt of Zeut.

Answer to the proposal made by the Maquase sachems to Daniel Jans and Jaques Cornelis, June 4, 1677[1]

Firstly, the Maquase sachems were shown the harm their people have done and told that they should not expect to receive a gift therefor.[2] The more so since they should give satisfaction, and they were told that the sachems of the last castle would be called here, which was done, to free the prisoners without any molestation being done to them.

On the 5th: toward evening the other sachems came here, paying strict attention to all matters, and showed their thorough alarm.

On the 6th: about 11 o'clock two runners arrived saying that they had obtained 18 Indians, all women and children. But nine of these Indians are prisoners, two had lived here beforehand but had run away and now belong again to their owner, and the others will come to them by themselves. In the afternoon the Chiefs arrived with the prisoners.

About 2 o'clock the sachems assembled and having held a council, called us in, making the following proposal:

Firstly: Do give a string of wampum 10 high for this reason: they acknowledge the bad side of their people who go against

[1] Translated from the Dutch.

[2] The Mohawks had "robbed and captured Mahicanders and North Indians at Philipp Pieters [Schuyler's] bowery and at the Half Moon; also that they have killed some of Uncas men." *Cal. N. Y. Coun. Min.*, 29.

their commands. Hope and pray that the agreement made before this which was renewed in intent should not be broken, that they will not be made the laughing stock of the other nations, and that this evil could be forgotten. We will hand over immediately all the prisoners as we have been commanded and desired, except one that has been sent to the second castle and those who have been handed over on the way here about whom they do not have to bother. Giving for this the reason that while we are indeed sachems, we cannot simply turn our backs on our soldiers, for they are our protectors and have to fight for us since we are old people.

Secondly: give a string of wampum 12 high, meaning that here we loosen the prisoner's bonds and leave it to the Governor to dispose of them. But we should be treated with good will and politeness because we return these prisoners, and for that we should receive something.

Thirdly: give a string of wampum 13 high, for which we say that the Governor will not be angry about this and that no quarrel will arise from it because the harm has been done to a friendly nation, for no one was killed. Many times in the past our people and the Dutch have been in a fight of man against man and have been slain or badly wounded for a long time, but that all this has been cast into the well of forgetfulness. We hope that that will also happen again, and that the Governor will turn away his anger over that affair and will not hold it against us, so that our country may remain in peace as it always was with the old Corlaer who, to our regret, died in that cause.[1] Until now Corlaer has constantly worked with us to our great pleasure, and we hope that the same will continue.

Finally they are told that they will have to take care not to do it

[1] Arent Van Curler came to New Netherland in 1630 and was instrumental in founding Schenectady. He was drowned in 1667 while crossing Lake Champlain to visit the Governor of Canada. Highly regarded by the Indians, they took his name as a symbol for the Governor of New York. O'Callaghan, 3: 156fn.

The chiefs of the village sent a messenger to invite the stranger sitting by the fire to enter their village. There Deganawidah spoke to the council of the Flint People.

again, that this should not happen any more, and that they should punish it. Towards evening Jaques rode to the second castle to retrieve the one Indian, but did not get him. The owner was willing to return him if the Governor came and definitely wanted to have him.

Daniel Janse
Ackes

Copy of a certain proposal made by Gwuadzery that he has done his utmost duty with the sachems and that he has also presented a string of wampum to warn the Indians which is not charged to the Governor. He is not given anything for his trouble, but placed at the direction of the Governor who wanted to punish him for these troubles as they would not have happened but by the trader's activities.

Copia Vera
Ex Copia

Propositions off Coll: henry Coursey Esqr; Authorized by Charles Lord Barron off Baltamore, Lord Proprietor of Maryland, to ye maques & other Indians Westward as far as ye Sinnekes, New Yorke ye 30th of June 1677.[1]

Being informed yt ye maques Sineques &a are of this government, & faithfull & Constant friends to ye English under our great king, I am come from my Lord Baltamore Lord Proprietor of maryland and all his Majs Subjects of Virginia and maryland, to see and speak wt you here.

Though throw mistakes, some discontents or Injuries may have happened, between us heretofore, Now upon ye good Report of you, which I finde, Wee are willing that all what is Past, be buryed & forgott, you takeing care, (as we shall one our Pairts) that your Indians, nor none liveing among you, or comeing through your Countrey, doe for ye future Injure any of our Persons (Piscataway or other our Indians liveing wt us) or goods, and if any ill Person should doe any harm, that there be Present full Satisfaction given, for all Injuries or dammages,

The above being observed, so yt no Injury or dammage be done, or Satisfaction given for ye same, we shall alwayes Esteem and treat you as our good Neighboures, and friendes.

[1] This was probably prepared in New York City by Coursey with the collaboration of Governor Andros, but it undoubtedly was delivered in Albany on July 20. See the Indians' answers which follow.

To each nation a hundred & fifty gilders white Strung wampam, in 3 Pairts, fifty Each

Sic Subscribitur

This is a true Copy Examined by

W Niccolls

Perrused by me

Robt. Livingston Secr.

Mr Gert van Slichtenhst Interpreter

The Onnodagoes Ansr To ye propasitiones made to ym the 20 of July 1677 By the honnod Collnell Henry Coursy Authorized by Charles Lord Barron of Baltimor Lord properitor of Mary Land In the Court house of Albany ye 21 of July 1677

The Names of ye Sarchems are
Carachkondie who was Speaker
Tanonaniachita
Sienonkachvi
Oneyichkaron

1. They say, wee are sent for by a Belt of zeawant to Speak wth his honnor ye Governr Generall, here, and Afterwards a Belt was Sent to us by Collnll: Coursay, Authorized by MaryLand and Virginia that we might make ye greater haist to com down, wch we have and he Sayeth yt soe noe man living amongst us shall for ye futur Injure any of thar persones or goods Wharupon wee ansr and promise yt for ye futur wee shall not Injur or doe any damnage to ye peopell of MaryLand or Virginia, and doe Thank ye Gentleman thar yt they doe exhort us to ye peace for we are so mynded, bot doe acknowledge yt wee have killed of yor christians & Indians formely wherof Jacob Young[1] Alias my freind was a great occasione yr of, Bot wee desyre now yt all wch is past may be burried in oblivon and doe make now ane absolut Covenant of peace wch we shall bind wth a chayn for the Sealing of ye Same doe give ane band of Therten deep.

2. They do agane reharse yt Jacob Young was a great Leader

[1] Jacob Young, whose name appears often in the relations between the Iroquois and the Virginians and Marylanders, was an Indian interpreter at the head of Chesapeake Bay. Brodhead, 2: 328fn.

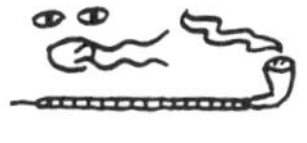

He told them of his mission, to speak the will of the Creator and establish the Great Peace among the Iroquois. Their nations should no longer kill one another. They must smoke the Pipe of Peace and Friendship together.

and Capt: agst: ym. whereby ye warre haith bein continued Butt Even as ye Gover of Cannada had ware agt us and yr upon a good peace ffalowed, so it is Now with us, To wch peace we desyre yt God Allmichty who dwells in heaven may give his blissing yr into, and Suppose that any difference should aryse hearafter betwixt us, and you, and yor Indians, wee desyre yt we might give one anoyr Satisfaction and not Immediatly fall in warre and doe give thre Beavers.

3. Wee doe Let you Know that ther is of our four Castelles of ye Senikars out a fighting aganst the Susquahannas you may yrfor waren yor Indians That thar may be no Injuryes or damnages done hereafter and so to continue ye peace and doe give two Beavers.

This is a true Coppy
Translated Compared &
Revised *p* me
R. L. Secr.

Mr Cort van Slichtenhorst Interpreter

The Onneyads Ansr to ye Proposito Made to them the 20 July by ye hon Colnell Henry Coursy Esqr Authorized by Charles Lord Burron of Baltimor Lord propritor of MaryLand In the Court house of Albany the 21 July 1677

The Names of the Searchems
Sweryse
Sarachtoa
Canachyndia
Cannanthaeve

1. They Say wee doe absolutely approve of that wch the Onndagoes haith now Said calling them thar fathers as they doe Lykewyes the Christians of this Goverment and are willing and readie to obey the Command off The Great King Charles who Liveth over the great Laike meaning our Soverng Lord The King of great Brittan &a and doe present ane belt of Zeawant.

2. Wee doe recomend that yea will tak Care (as wee Shall in our pairts) yt ye propositn yt yea maid yesterday be Punctually observed. Thar is formerly one of or Indians wounded by you wch occasioned or plundring of yr houses, Wee most alsoe aknowledge yt we have killed som hoggs and beasts to Eat when we were hungry bot never to have Killed any Christians doe present two otters.

31y. Wee are now Com togither to mak the Covenant and doe

agane absolutly approve of yt wch ye Onndagoes hath done Bot doe Lett you Know yt thar are Twentie of our Indians gone out to ffight agt ye Indians of yor Nation Wee desyre yt if they doe any harm that it may be excused this tym, becaus it is unknown to them, and if wee for ye futur Efter or peopell are com home, Shall use any hostility that way, then you may think wee doe not according to or promise but wee are not so mynded, and doe give two Beaver.

This is a true Coppy
Translated Compared & Revised
p me Robt Livingston
Secr.

NB The Oneydes were Present wn ye Prop. were made to ye Onnondages, and when they gave there answer.

Interpreted by Akus Cornelise who was assisted by Arnout Cornelise Viele

The Maquesse anser to the Propositio made to ym The 4th of this Instant by ye Honnored Coll: Henry Coursey Authorized by Charles Lord Barron of Baltimor Lord propritor of Maryland In ye Court house of Albany 6 August 1677

The names of ye Searchems ar
1st: Castell Canneachko
Aihagari
Roote
2th: Castell Cassenossacha
3th: Castell Cannondacgoo who was Speaker
Odiana
Tagansariggo
Semachegi

1. They Says with a presnte wee are glad yt ye Kinges Governors of MaryLand and Virginia have sent you hither to Speak with the Maquess as Alsoo yt ye Gover: Genll: hath bein pleased to destinat & appoynt this place to Speak wth all Nations in peace finding this fitt place for ye Same, ffor wch we doe return his honnr hartie Thankes, Especially yt his honnor hath bein pleased to Grant you ye Priviledge for to Speak wth us heir Seing that the Govr: Genll: & wee are one, and one hart and one head, for the Covenant that is betwixt ye Govr: Genll: and us is Inviolable yea so strong yt if ye very Thunder should break upon ye Covenant Chayn it wold

---

The Head Chief of the Flint People agreed that Deganawidah's words were good. But he demanded proof that Deganawidah was the one appointed by the Creator to plant the Tree of Peace and establish the Great Laws of Friendship.

not break it in Sunder, wee are Lykwyes glad that we have hared you Speak and now we shall ansr. yt in case yt any of or Indians Should Injur any Christians or Indians in yor parrts or yor Christians or Indians doe any damnage to or Indians wee desyre yt on both Syds the mattor May be Compossed, and that wch is past to be burred in oblivion. They Say further that ye Seneks war upon thar Jorney to com hither wth six hunderd Men Bot ffor fear Turned back agane Bot wee ware not affrayed to Com heir doe give thar upon ane drest Elk Skin and one Beaver.

2ly. wee have heard you Speak and now wee shall ansr Unto yor propositiones, you have said that all wch is past formerly Shall be burreid and forgott wch wee doe Lykwyes Holding or Selves Inocent of any Injure done to any of the Nations of MaryLand or Virginia bot have alwyes Spoke wth one another in frindship & have lykwys Recaived many favors bread and oyr provisions for wch wee humbly thank you and if any doe accuse us of having done any Injure or damnage thar, they doe belye us we haveing bein bot twyse thar and doe give thar upon two Beavers.

3ly. if any difference should aryse betwixt you yor Indians, and or Indians wee desyr yt thar may not Immediatly a Warre aryse upon the Same bot yt ye matter may be moderat & compossed betwixt us, and wee doe Ingage for or parts to give Satisfacn to you for any Eveill that or Indians might happen to doe and doe give thar upon two Beavers.

4ly. They Sing a song after thar maner being thar method of a new Covenant: maid wch they doe undertake to hold firm beeing ye first tym they have Seine any Authorized from MaryLand and Virginia, and Say further wee are glad and doe welcom his honnor the Collonll: wth a Beaver and ane drest elk Skine for his Troble in coming so fare a Jorrney.

5ly. They doe Sing ane oyr Song The meaning whereof is yt ther people might not forgett what is past betwixt ym and the Collonell: bot might be allwyes myndfull of what is done in ye house ordeined to that end by the gov: genll and if ye Senekes now or any time herefter, should appoynt any oyr place for to Speake wth you In ther own Cuntry or else wher Wee desyre yt it may not be accepted off bot that this be & remane the only appoynted & preffixed place. And all that was proposed by you the 4th Instant wee desyre yt it may be punctually observed upon yor Syd (as wee shall upon ors), And if you have a mynd hereafter to Speak wth us, we desyre yt it may bee heir and no wher else doe give thar upon ane drest Elk Skine.

6ly. They Say wee doe return you harty thanks for the relasing of the Two Sones off Canondondarwe ye cheef Sachim of ye maquase and lykwyes yt you beheaded ye Searchem of ye Susquannas named Acknaetsachawey who was the Cause of ther being taken prisioners and doe present 5 Beavers.

This is a true Coppie Translated
compared & revised pr me

The Sinnondowannes & Cayouges anser To ye propositio made to them the 22th August 1677 By the Honnored Coll: Henry Coursy Authorized by Charles Lord Barron of Baltimor Lord Proprietr of MaryLand In the Court House of Albany ye day and yeir abovewritten

Brethren wee are now com Upon yor Sending for

1°: Wheras wee have alwyes had ane firm Covet wth this Goverment wch haith bein faytfuly Keeped by this Govr: Genll: (for wch wee doe give him harty thankes, whom wee have taken to be our greatest Lord,) for hee haith putt asyd all mistakes wch haith hapned; Wee nevor have had warres wth this Goverment bot with yours, and Now you ar Com from MaryLand & Virginia to Speake wth us in his presence. And Lett yt which you have proposed to us bee as fast and firm as ye Covt: we have wth the Govr: Genll: wee humbly thank you yt you have Sent for us to Speake wth us in this goverment and doe present hare ane Beaver.

2ly Yea ar com heir to Speake wth us off good thinges & wee will give you ane good Ansr thar upon doe give one bever.

3ly Wee thank you yt yea doe bury & forget all former discontents or Injuryes as wee doe the sam, and never mor to be remembred, for wee know very well yt or peopell have bein offensive unto you, Wee desyre & recomend unto you the continuation of ye Covt: now mad betwixt us, as yt wch wee have with the Govr: Genll: doe give a Beaver.

Near the village was a high cliff overlooking the Lower Falls of the Mohawk River. On the top of this cliff and overlooking the rough waters was a tall tree. Deganawidah said he would climb the tree, and that then the people were to cut it down and let it fall with him into the waters below. If he lived, that would be the proof they needed.

4ly In caise any of yor Indians, doe any hostility to us, we shall acquaint you tharwith, before wee tak up the axe agt: them, and wee desyre the lyk of you, and the resone that wee plundred the Inglysh thar, was thar Interteining of those Indians yt wer our enemyes bot wee promise never to doe the lyk, and doe give a Beaver.

5ly Wee doe thank you for the presents Given to us, and we shall punctiously observe that wch you have proposed to us, desyring the lyk upon yor Syd. It is concluded in or Castells, that all the Searchims shall com heir the nixit Summer about ye moneth of Juny to make propositiones and it is thar desyre to see Conll: Coursey heir or Som oyr Authorized from his Goverment and doe give a Beaver.

1°: The Cajougoes Searchims Say as ffoloweth Wee Thanke you for yor sending for us and for the wagon wee had from Skennechtida hither Though the Smalest Belt of Zewaut was sent to us.

Yett wee doe Thanke you, and or heart is good and give a small Beaver.

2ly. Wee doe absouletly approve & Confirm the Synndowannes ansr for or resolution was taken togidder and doe give two Beaver.

3ly. They repeat the ansr agane, and shall observe that wch be propounded to ym, and doe say we thanke you kyndlie that you have buried all former discontents or Injuryes, as wee doe the same, and give two lapps.

4ly. This is the first tym wee have Seen any authorized from yor Goverment and doe thank you for yor propositions, and In caise any Mischeif doe hapen befor you com home that most not bee Acompted, for So Shoon as wee com hoom wee shall publish thiss, bot If any harme be done to yor Indians by us for the futur, wee will make you Satisfaction to ye full, desyring the Lyke of you. doe give 2 bev:

5ly Wee doe Thanke you lykwys for ye propositiones yea have mad, and for ye presents given us, and doe give 5 lapes.

Propositions made by Col: Wm Kendel agent for ye Contry of Virginia to ye Maquase in the Court house of albany ye. 25th of Septemb: 1679

I am come from Virginia upon occasion of some of your Neighbours doeing of mischeeff or harme in our Contry[1] wh. upon ye Interposition and Perswasion of ye Governr here, wee have wholly Passed by and forgive, & being Inform'd you'r not Concerned therein, but disowning Such action, Wee did desyre to see you, and to Lett you know, that Continueing the Like good Peaceable Neighbourhood, you shall find us ye Same, and willing to doe you frindship at all times, but must acquaint you, that wee have a law in our Country, that all frindly Indians comeing there near any Christians must Stand Still, and Lay down there Armes in token of frindship, and there Receivd and treated accordingly, otherways may be Destroyed as our Enemyes, wh. wee desyre you to take notice of, there being many of our People abroad & in ye Woods, was given

f. 150: Z

/S/ Wm Kendall

11 ells duffells
3 vatts Rom
3 Rolls Tobacco
25 Wheat Loaves
10 do Brown

Maquas ansser upon the propositiones made by Coll Wm Kendell authorized by the Govr & Councill & burgers of Virginia at the Court house of albany ye 26 Septr 1679.

After that the presents wer given said Wee are glad to See and Speak wth you heer whom wee have never seen heer before & have well understood yor propositio Thanking you for yor presents and shall give you ane ansr in ye Afternon.

Post meridem

Brethern

1. You have had no Small Trouble to com heer from Virginia being so Long a Jorney & having Sent for us, wee are upon

[1] The rupture of the 1677 peace treaty with Coursey by the Senecas was noted by Governor Andros in September 1678. O'Callaghan, 3: 271.

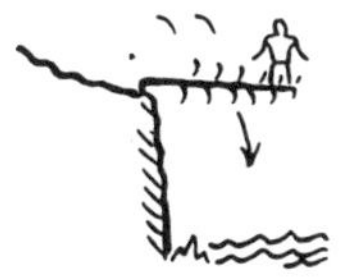

The people agreed, for the cliff was high, the rocks were sharp, and the waters were rough. They knew he must surely drown if he were not what he claimed to be. Deganawidah climbed the tree, and it was chopped down. He went beneath the waters and vanished.

yor desyre & or Govr Genll Consent come heer In this appoynted house to heer you Speak & to give Ansr

Wee doe not ansr yet upon yor proposito but doe make the preffixed house clean & in ordr to Com to or propositio meaning by cleaning of the house, that they will ansr uniformally and wth ane upright hart doe give ane fathom of Zewt.

2ly. wee Spake Just now of yor Long jorney which undoubtedly haith not been wthout a great deale of Trouble Especially yea being ane old man as I am, doe give a fathom of Zewt to Mitigat yor hard Jorney.

3ly. I't is Told us in the preface & wee doe very well remember the Covenant made wth Coll: Coursy in presence of his honnor wch Covenant wee have keept heetherto and shall continue yrin Inviolably, and are very glad to see you here to renew the Covenant yrin you doe exceed ym of ye East meaning ym of n England who did lykwyes mak a Covenant with us but have not Seen ym heer yet to renew ye Same. doe give a fathom of zewt·

4ly. Wee have now Spoke of the Covt: made wth Coll: Coursy and lykwyse now understood yt wee must continue the lyk good peacable Nighborhoods wch we shall Not only perform, But keep the Inviolable chayn clear & clene, meaning the Covt: chayne & yrfor desyre yt you may doe the Same. doe give a belt zewt 12 deep.

5ly. Wee have understood that the Mischeif and harme or Nightboors have done to you in yor Contry as upon the Interposition & perswasion of our Govr: wholy passed by and forgiven by you, for which wee ar very glad, Lett it be burried in oblivion, for if any mischef should befall ym we should not be free of it Seeing wee are one bodie. we approve of yt Law wch you have in yor Cuntry Concerning Laying down of our Armes as a Token of ffreindship which wee doe Undertak to perform, doe give a belt 14 high zewt.

6ly. It is made known to us befor the propositions yt ye oyr authorized from Virginia (meaning Coll: Litelton) is dead for which wee ar very Sory and doe Lament & bewaile his death, but doe admire yt upon the making known of the death of Such a person nothing is Laid down, according to our

Custom meaning present. doe give a blak belt of zw[t] 13 deep to wype of your Teares.

This is a true Copy Translated
Compared & Revysed *p*[r] me

R. Liv: Secr.

Message from the Sachims of Onnondage to Col. Wm. Kendall agent of Virginia Sent by one of there Sachims calld Othonoenis accompanyd wt his Sonne and another Indian in ye Court house of Albany ye 6 of Octob 1679.

We are sent by our Sachems to lett you know thatt wee have Rec[d]. the Belt long agoe w[h]. was Sent by you to us (by y[e] Gov[rs]. Consent), wherby you desyred that wee Should come here

It is not Long Since wee were here to Renew our covenant & to keep y[e] Covenant chain clean & clear Likeways all things are wel in our Country & have no Bad heart

But y[e] Reasons why our Sachims are not come are these vizt.

1. That it is Propounded to them 2 Year agoe w[t] Presents of Strung wampum by Jacob Young alis my frind in y[e] Presence of Col. Coursey after y[t] y[e] Propositions were ended in y[e] Prefixed house (meaning y[e] Court house) at s[d]. Courseys Lodging, that they of y[e] Southern Parts should come y[e] Spring following into our Country to Speak w[t] us, but would take another way then come hither directly from there Country to our Land, whom we did expect last Spring and doe dayly

2. And now afterwards, Receiving a Belt of y[m]. of y[e] Southern Parts, Sending for us (w[t] y[e] gov: approbation) to come hither, are not come, But if y[e]. gov: had sent for us in his name, to speak w[t] us, Should have been here long agoe, But seeing you are come this way, may take your Journey to our Castles, the way being good and here are Store of horses; and there speak w[t] us according to y[e] Col. Coursey saying. Interpreted by Jacob my frind.

3. And again y[e] Sicknesse of feavor and Small Pox Reigning soo

Next morning some warriors saw smoke rising from the smoke-hole of an empty bark house near the village. There they saw Deganawidah, alive, smoking a pipe while cooking his morning meal. Then the Flint people knew Deganawidah's tongue was straight, and that he was the one appointed by the Creator to plant the Tree of Peace.

Violently in our Countrey hath been likeways a great obstruction to our Comeing—doe give a Belt of Zewt 10 deep.

Coll: Wm. kendall agent for Virginia his answer upon a Certain message Sent to him by ye Onnondages Sachims wt one of yr Sakamakers called Othonoenes in the Court house of Albany this 6 of Octob 1679

I Received your message wt a Belt of Zewt of ten deep
1. The Covenant made wt Col. Coursey at ye. Court house of albany at that time, I come now on ye Like occasion to speak wt you and ye other nations here without alteracon of this Prefixed Place.
2. The Covenant you speak of made wt Col. Coursy in Private, I know nothing of it; The Articles you made wt said Coursey doth absolutly appoint this Place for Virginia & MaryLand Agents, to treat wt you & non else which doe admire you doe not Exactly observe
3. You Pretend the Small Pox hath alsoe been a hinderance of yr coming wh. I take to bee a weak Excuse, & ought not to have been an Obstruction of yr Journey hther of a Bussinesse of soe great Importance, and doe give a Belt of Zewt of 10 deep.

/S/ Wm Kendall

The Govr: Genl. Message to ye. Onneydes
[*Albany, October 12, 1679*]

To acquaint them that he is arriv'd at alby: & brougt wt. him ye. oneyde Squa, & they haveing not yet been to Speak wt. Col: kendall, upon his desire ye. govr: hath sent to know if they are comeing, or will not come.

Propositions of Col. Wm. Kendall [and Col. Southy Littleton][1]*authorized by the Governour, Councell, and Burgesses of Virginia at an Grand Assembly held in James City to the oneydes in ye Court house of albany this 30th day of Octob: 1679*

I am come from Virginia being as all these Countreys under our

[1] There are several drafts of this document, the earlier one making reference to Littleton who died at Albany on September 26 before the conferences began. The final copy is dated and mentions only Kendall. The latter has been used as the basic text. In order to indicate the changes in attitude and emphasis that occurred in its preparation, those items included in the earlier draft but omitted in the finished copy have been retained in brackets; the material included in the finished copy but not in the earlier draft has been italicized.

great King Charles, to speak to you, upon occasion of some of yours haveing entred our houses, taken away and destroyed our goods and Poeple, and brought some of our women and Children Captives in your Castles contrary to your faith and Promises, and is alsoe a breach of your Peace made wh. Col: Coursey without any Provocation or Injury in the Least done by us, or disturbing you in your hunting trade, or Passing untill you were found takeing our Corne, out of our filds and Plundring and burning our houses.

Thogh your Actions already done, are Sufficient Reasones to Induce us to a Violent war against you wh. might Engage all our Confederatt English neighbours, subjects to our great king Charles, yet upon the [great Respect wee have too & ye Perswasions of the governour here whom we finde your great frind, & ye] Informacon the govr: here hath given us, that you have quietly and Peaceably, delivered to him, the Prisoners you had taken from us, Who are alsoe Returned in Safety to our Country, and your excuseing ye Same [& Inclination to Continue Peaceable without Injurying us for ye future], We are therefore willing and have and doe forgive all ye Dammages you have done our Poeple (thogh very great) Provided you nor any Liveing amongst you or comeing from you, for ye future doe not offend or molest our Poeple or Indians Liveing amongst us, *Which if it shall appear that you do not truly Perform, then wee Expect full Satisfaction for all ye Injuryes that you have already done us to ye utmost farthing.*

And one of your Squaes being taken alive in our Countrey, and now Returned here, being freed, I Return her to you.

And whereas you have still a Christian Girle of our Parts with you, doe expect, that you likeways free & Return ye Same.

Wee have a Law in our Country, that al Indians comeing neer Christians any where, must Stand Still, and lay down there Armes, as a token of there being frinds, otherwise are Looked upon and

---

It was a time of great trouble among the Iroquois. The People of Flint (Mohawks), the People of the Upright Stone (Oneidas), the Hill People (Onondagas), the People of the Mucklands (Cayugas), and the People of the Great Mountain (Senecas) were continually at war with one another and with outside nations. Many were killed.

taken or destroyed as Enemies, and haveing many of our Poeple in ye woods abroad every way, *wee doe acquaint you (therewith) that if your Poeple shall goe to warr towards our Parts against any Indians not in frindship wt us that you forbear to come neer our Plantations.*

was given f. 150:–:–Z
11 els duffels
3 fats Rom
/S/ Wm Kendall 3 Rols Tobaco
25 wheat loaves
20 do Brown

Propositions made by the said Agent of Virginia to ye Maquase and other Indians westwards, as far as the Sinnekes (oneydes Excepted) in the Court house of Alby. this [(blank .... *c. October 31, 1679*)]

Wee are come from Virginia upon occasion on some of your Neighbours doeing of mischeef or harme in our Country, wh. upon the Interposition and Perswasion of ye. govr. here, wee have wholly Passd by and forgive, and being inform'd your not concernd therein, but disowning Such action, wee did desyre to see you, and to Lett you know, that Continueing the like good Peaceable neighbourhood, you shall finde us the Same, and willing to do you frindship att all times, but must acquaint you that wee have a law in our Country, that all frindly Indians comeing there near any Christians, must Stand still and Lay down there armes in token of frindship., & there Recd. and treated accordingly, otherways may be Destroyed as our Enemyes, wh. wee desyre you to take notice of, there being many of our Poeple abroad & in the woods.

Twas given to Each nation that came f 150 Z
11 ells duffels
3 vats Rom
3 Rolls Tobacco
25 wheat loaves
20 do Brown.

The Sachims names are
Doganitajendachquo
Speakr.
Toderassee
Interpreted by Aernt Corn:

The Oneydes Answer upon the Propositions of Col. Wm. Kendall agent for ye Contry of Virginia in the Cort. house of albany this 31 of octobr 1679[1]

Brethren of ye Virginia:

It was askd us Yesterday (before ye Propositions) whither wee had Received the message, to come here in the midle of Septembr Last, which wee have Recd. as all ye Indians our way and yr is a Second messengr. sent afterwards to ask us if wee would come or not,

Wee answer, that it is not done out of Contempt or disdain that wee are not come Sooner, but have been hindred by ye Small Pox and other Sicknesse.

It is Represented to us yesterday ye dammage that wee have done in Virginia, in destroying your goods and Poeple, & in takeing of your women and Children Captives &a. wee Confesse to have done soe But there is a Covenant made 2 Year agoe wt. Col Coursey in the Presence of his honr. ye govr: that wee might freely come towards your Plantations, when wee went out a fighting to our Indian Enemyes to Refresh our Selfs if wee wer a hungry, & wee came there, & gott nothing, then wee took Indian Corn and Tobacco, whereupon the English comeing outt shott some of our People dead, and afterwards wee defended ourselfs out of which these disasters are Proceeded, You say that it is our faults, and we think that ye fyreing upon us is ye Occasion.

Brethren of Virginia, & Brothr Corlaer meaning the govr:, and our frinds ye Maquase that are Present here hear.

Yesterday it was told us, that that wh: is already Past is forgiven, for wh. wee doe thank you, Yea wee thank you hertily, and Confesse that ye Pale or Stake of unity hath been fallen, but now Reared up again; Lett all that which is Pasd not only be forgotten but be Buryed in a Pitt of oblivion, yea I say in a Bottomlesse Pitt where a Strong Currant of a River Runns throw, that that wh.

[1] Colden declares that this answer was not found in the Indian Affairs Records. Colden, 1: 32.

In the country of the Hill People, near the village on Onondaga Lake, rose the smoke of a lone campfire.

is now thrown in't, may never appear more, let that wh. is done yesterday be kept I'nviolably as a fast chayen, which is keept smooth bright and shyning like silver or gold, doe Present 5 fad.
2. Wee have understood Yesterday, that if wee come nigh any Christians in your Contry, that wee must Stand Still, and lay down our armes. tis good, wee accept of it, But let it not bee of soe badd a Consequense as Col Coursey saying was, for he said Likewayse, that wee might come there as frindes, when wee went out a fighting against our Indian Enemyes, Butt our goeing thither did bring these disasters, Lett us have Victalls when wee goe a fighting agst. our foresd. Enemys but ye Susquehannes are all destroyed for wh. wee Return you many thanks, doe give 3 fad: *Z.*
3. Wee thank you for ye Duffells you have given us. doe give 4 fad: *Z.*
4. Wee doe thāk you for ye Rom & Tobacco that you have given us. doe give 4 fad: Z.
5. We were obedt. to his honr. ye govr. when he sent ye twoo messengers to our Contry last winter to demaund the Christian Prisoners, & did deliver ye Same,[1] not upon any Such Condition that ye Govr Should give this Squae in lue again, but did Referr that to his Prudent care, and shee is now come agn. for wh. wee are Verry thankfull.
6. Wee are thankfull for his honr. ye Govr: troble concerning ye freedom of ye Squae, You speak of a Certain Christian Girle which wee have in our Country, to deliver ye Same. But that lyes not in our Power, seing shee is brought there by dispersd Indians Calld Canistoges or Susquehannes, and not taken by our Nation, we shall not only Speak to ye Squae that hes ye Christian girle, but ye Sachims shall sitt about it, and doe there endevour in it, and be glad when shee shall have attaind to her liberty. doe give a Belt Zewt. 20 deep.
Wee have done, Pray let ye frindship betwixt us Continue, and if our Indians goe out to fight against our Indian Enemyes, be frindly to them, for it is better to be in Peace, then in warr, and then it will be as it is here.

[1] Colden dates this as February 15, but claims that the purpose of the message was to remove the Indians' fear of an English plot against them. This proposition, plus the bills which follow, indicate its primary purpose to have been the return of English prisoners in the hands of the Oneida. Colden, 26.

haveing done, it was askd them why they do not answer to ye Last Pointe of ye Propos: whereupon they Said,

Wee had forgot to answer upon ye last Point of your Proposition, about forbearing to come near your Plantations, when wee goe to warr agst. our indian Enemys not in frindship wt you, all which we undertake, as wee doe ye bovesaid.

A true Copy Transl
p me Rot. Livingston
Secr.

An Accompt of Presents given to ye Onneydes Sachims upon ye Country of Virginia Acct. at ye delivery of ye 6 Prisonrs.

A°. 1678/9 At ye delivery of Mrs. Prokter & 2 Children

feby. 17	To ye Sachims in Zewt	f. 500: –:–	f. 690:10:–
	And in Provision Bread & meal meat Pork, a hogg, Rom &a at ye Propos:	f. 190:10:–	
May 27	To ye. Sd. Sachims when they Brought Mrs. Thackery and her 2 Children 30 Bevrs in Zew.	f. 723:12:–	f. 792:12
	And in Provisions meal Tobacco & Rom	f. 69: –:–	
			Z f 1483: 2:–
July 8	To 12 kans Rom to ye messengers that was sent to Sinnondowanne by arnout, when he was in ye Sinnekes Land		f 48: –:–
			Z f 1531: 2:–

It was the fire of Adodarho, the terrible war-chief of the Onondagas. This evil man was feared alike by his own people and by other nations. His body was twisted in seven crooks. His long, tangled hair was a mass of living serpents.

To 2 hogs and 1 Shepl. Pease when ye Indians brougt ye Prisoners	f. 148: –:–	f. 148: –:–
Arnout ye Interpreter accts. comes		f 1000: –:–
in wampum, each gildr is 6 d.		2679: 2:–

Accompt of Charges Expended upon ye Christian Prisoners, to witt 2 woomen & 4 Children weh. came from Oneyde, being taken from Virginia

A°: 1679

Month	Day	Item	Amount
April	25.	Paid to Daniel Johnson for his Journey wt Arnout to ye Sinnekes land as pr. his Receit	f. 600: –:–
	28	To Ro: Story for goods deliverd to ye Christ: Pris: as p bil	f. 24: –:–
		To Staffel Janse for serge for sd. Prison: as p bill	f. 84:15:–
	29	To Joh: wendel for 1 Piece of Linning	f. 24: –:–
May	6	To frans Pruyn Tayler for makeing ye woms. Clothes	f. 31:10:–
	21	To Phil: fredriks for cloathes for Mrs. Prokter as p bil	f. 72: –:–
	26	To ands. Teller for a Piece of Linning for idem	f. 24: –:–
		To ands. Teller for more linning for ye Prison:	f. 78: 9:–
	27	To ye widw. goose for necessaries for ye Pris:	f. 74: –:–
		To Stoffel Janse for goods deliv'd to ye Prison	f. 156: 3:–
	30	To gert. Banker for Linning for ye Prison	f. 72: –:–
		To Jeronimus Wendel for Shoes for ye Prison	f. 27: –:–
June	4	To Mr Pretty for a Blankett for ye Prison	f. 24: –:–
	5	To Mrs. Parker for sewing ye Prison: Linning	f. 47:18:–

7	To Frans Pruyn for makeing the Prison: Cloathes	f. 54: -:-
		Z f. 1393:15:-
	To Ro: Story for linning & a pr bodys for ye Pris: as p Rec:	f. 58: -:-
		Z f. 1393:15:-

The above sd. Bills I Paid p his honrs order
here in alby as pr yr Receits
quod attestor
/S/ Rot: Livingston

Propositions of Col: Wm Kendall authorized by the Governr. Councill & Burgesses of Virginia at a grand Assembly held in James City to ye Onnondages in the Court house of albany this 1st day of Novemb 1679

I am come from Virginia, being as all these Countreys, under our great king Charles, to speak to you, upon occasion of some of yours haveing entred our houses, taken away and destroyed our goods and Poeple, Contrary to your faith and Promises, and is alsoe a Breach of your Peace made wt. Col: Coursey without any Provocation or Injury in the Least done by us, or disturbing you in your hunting trade, or Passing, untill you were found takeing our Corne out of our fields and Plundring and burning our houses. Thogh your Actions already done are Sufficient Reasones to Induce us to a Violent war against you, which might Engage, all our Confederatt English Neighbours, Subjects to our great King Charles, Yet because of your being Sorry for (and excuseing) ye Same, by ye Informacon the govr: here has Given us, Wee are therefore Willing, and have and doe forgive all ye Dammages you have done our Poeple, (thogh Verry great) Provided you nor any liveing amongst you, or comeing from you, for ye future, doe not offend or Molest our Poeple, or Indians liveing amongst us.

His crooked hands always held a war-club. He was the cause of much hatred and many feuds among the men of the Five Nations. He had great power, being a master of witchcraft, which he used to kill many people. Every attempt to destroy Adodarho met with disaster.

Wee have a law in our Contry, that all Indians comeing near Christians any where, must Stand Still, and Lay down there Armes, as a token of there being frindes, otherwyse are Looked upon and taken or destroyd as Enemyes, And haveing many of our People abroad Every way, wee doe acquaint you (therewth.) that if any of your Poeple shall goe to warr towards our Pairts agst. any Indians not in frindship wt. us, that you doe forbear to come near our Plantations, was given

/S/ Wm Kendall. f. 150:–:–Zewt
11 ells duffels
3 fats Rom
3 Rolls Tobacco
25 wheat loaves

The names of ye Sachims
Carachkondie
Otrewachte
Cachisuhtoe
Onuerachton & 5 Souldrs.
Interpreted by Aernt. Corn. Viele

The Onnondages answer upon the Propositions of Col. Wilm Kendall agent for ye. Contry of Virginia in the Court house of Albany ye 1st of Novemb: 1679[1]

Brethren of Virginia

Wee are come here in the Prefixed house where we are used to make Propositions, and have understood that which is by you Represented; All our Indians (meaning there Souldiers) have been distracted or wtout there Senses in Committing of this fact agst. ye Christians in Virginia, for it is done wtout our ordr. and agst. our will, they have been like a Childe who haveing a Ax in its hand, is not sensible what it does wt it, & cannot discern betwixt good and Evill.

Tis made known to us by you the dammage that our Poeple have done in Virginia in Plundring your houses &a

We doe Confesse it, but doe say again as above that they have done Verry Wickedly, Wee have likeways understood, that when our Yong Indians come neer any Christians must lay down there armes as a token of frindship, It is Likeways told us, that if any of our Poeple shall goe to warr towards your Pairts against any Indians not in frindship wt. you, That they shall forbear to come

[1] Colden states that this answer was not found in the Indian Affairs Records. Colden, 1: 32.

near your Plantations, all which wee absolutely undertake and doe thank you that you have Propounded ye Same.
Wee have likeways understood that by ye Informacon his honr. ye. govr: here hath given you, you have forgiven that wh. is past, for wh. we doe thank you hertily, You are Poeple of Understanding, but wee are Brutish Blinde and wtout understanding, as we have said above, And wee are thankfull & glad that you Impart or Communicate some knowledge to us, and if our Young Indians come amongst you, be frindly to them for they goe agst. there Enemyes ye Dowaganhaes. doe Present a Belt of Zewt. 20 deep.
2. We thank them of Virginia and commend or Prais there Understanding, that they shew such favour to ye Oneydes our Children, & Include them in such a frindship, doe give 6 faddom Zewt.
3. When our Joung Indians goe out a fighting against there Enemyes Lett them be well used, and doe not look soe Narrowly upon a litle Indian Corn or Tobacco but let us live like frindes, as for ye Burning of ye houses it is unknown to us, but the Plundring of some goods and ye killing of a Beast wee doe not deny, as for ye killing of horses wee have no hand in't, but ye Oneydes, Pointed to some of them yn Present, have Shott 4; And when we come for Indian Corne or any Provision, doe not Lett our gunns or armes be taken from us, seeing it was ye beginning of these Last Troubles, wee doe Thank you for yor Tobacco & Rom: doe give 7 faddom Z.

This is a true Copy
Translated ℘ me
Robt: Livingston Secr.

My Lord Baltimores Commission to Col. Coursey & Col. Loyd, 15 May 1682

CHARLES Absolute Lord and Proprietor of the Province of Maryland and Avalon Lord Baron of Baltimore &c. To or. Trusty and well Beloved Coll. Henry Coursey and Coll Philemon LLoyd of Talbett County in this or. said Province of Maryland GREET-

The Onondaga people hated Adodarho, but they obeyed him because they feared his sorcery. At last, however, they could endure him no longer. The council asked one called Hiawatha to clear the war-chief's mind and straighten his crooked body.

ING in or. Lord God Everlasting KNOW YEE that wee Reposeing Speciall Trust and Confidence in yor. ffidelity Prudence And Circumspeccon Have Ordained Constituted Authorized and Appointed And by these Prsents Doe Ordaine Constitute authorize and Appointe you the said Coll. Henry Coursey and Coll. Phill. LLoyd or Either of you to be or Embasadors or Embasador Agents or Agent Envoys or Envoy to ffort Albany in the Dominion of his Royll Highs the Duke of Yorke, for us and in or name to Treate with and Confirme a Peace with the Siniques and other the Severall Northern Nations of Indians for all his Maties. Loving Subjects as well as of and within this Province as Alsoe those of Virginia And all Neighbouring or ffriend Indians under or Protection According to or Articles wth them formerly Made by you the said Coll. Henry Coursey att the said ffort Albany wherefore you and Either of you are wth. all Convenient Speed soe soone as you and Either of you Can Possibly have Prepared for the Same to sett forward on yor Journey to N: Yorke with Such Necessary Provission and Attendance As you and Either of you shall thinke ffitt and Apply yor Selfe or Selves att yor or Either of yor. Arrivall there to the Governor. Generall or Other Commandr in Cheife under his Royll Highs. there for the time Being Desireing Leave to Passe through those Terrytories in Order to you or Either of you Comeing to A Treaty with the said Indians for the more Easie and fully Effecting whereof you or Either of you are Alsoe to Request (if need be) the assistance of that Governmt. in Procureing A firm and Lasting Peace with the said Indians as well for or Selves And all Other his maties Loving Subjects in the Collony of Virginia as Alsoe for the Piscattawayes And all other or Neighbouring and ffriend Indians in Peace and Amity with us and Under or Proteccon According to the Tenor of yor Instruccons Herewith Given you which you or Either of you are Dilligently to Observe Perform ffulfill and keepe in this and all Other Points Relateing to yor or Either of yor Negotiacon AND WEE Doe hereby Request and Desire that Due faith and Creditt may be given to you the said Henry Coursey and Phill. LLoyd or Either of you and that According To the Law of Nations you or Either of you be Received Creditted and Believed in all Parts and Points of this yor or Either of yor Negotiacon Hereby Promissing And Engageing to Rattifie Confirme and Approve off (as Good) whatsoever shall be by you or Either of you Donn in the Prmisses Pursuant to this Commission And yor said Instruccons as fully Amply Largely and Effectually to all I'ntents and Purposes as if the same were Imeadiatly Donn by or Selfe. GIVEN att or Citty of st. Maryes under the Greate seale of or said Province of Maryland the 15th Day of May in the Seventh yeare of or Dominion &c Anno Domini 1682:

BALTEMORE

Examined
John West Cl.

Anthony Brockholes to Col. Coursey and Col. Lloyd

Honoured Srs

Being Received wth that Honr. & Respect, the Authority yo bring & ye Persons meritt, We have considered yr Proposalls, and in Answer thereto think fitt to acquaint yo of what wee allready have done and still are ready to doe to serve you.

We have Ordered strict Enquiry to be made amongst all our Indians Northward: if possible to discover ye Murtherers wch find cannot be done. But the Maaquess and Senakes Sachems have been at Albany, and declared their sorrowfulness: for the wrongs they heard were done in your Province; much excuseing them-selves as innocent thereof.

And by that we find the Indians so willing & Ready to prevent the like Violations and to rectifie and confirm a peace wch may be attained wthout much dificulty and shall order yo all Assistance possible therein.

My Ocasions will not Admitt me to wayte on yo in Person but wt Desired in the four Articles: hath alwayes been the effect of our Treatyes, and may be reiterated as often as oportunity.

Wee willingly Consent that yo see & speak with the Indians at Albany for wch shall give orders for yr furtherance therein: & to be

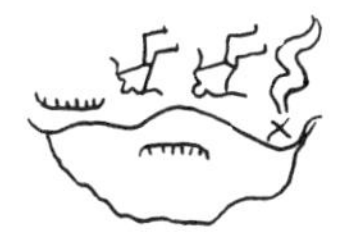

In canoes the people attempted to cross Onondaga Lake with Hiawatha to Adodarho's camp. When they were in the middle of the lake, Adodarho shouted his terrible war-cry. The canoes were upset and many were drowned.

served with ye best Interpreters: Expecting yo will have all due Regard, in yr discourses wth them to the former Peace, made wth Collonell Coursey and that all be done in Publick: In wch Wee wish yo A happy Issue & good Success

New York June 13th 1682 — Anthony Brockholes

this is a true Coppy transcribed from the originall pr me Robt Burman.

Propositions to the Commissaryes at Albany

1. That you would use the most Expeditious way yt yo can think of, to make known to the severall Nations of Indians: that you are lately informed, that they have suffered severall of their Troopes, to goe down into Maryland & Virginia contrary to the Order of the Governr that they must now forthwth send to call them back again, soe that no Mischeif may be done to the Christians; if they expect to make their peace wth Maryland or Virginia, or to hold their peace wth this goverment.

2dly After their great men, are come down to treat wth us: That yo then tell them, unless they comply wth us, and keep and observe the severall Articles of Peace that they formerly made wth us: or that shall now be made, yt they must not expect any longer to tread at Albany, & hold peace wth this govermt. but on the Contrary that the People of this govermt. being the Subjects and Children of the same King, as they of Virga & Maryland, must declare and make War upon them, and yt yo deliver this to them as a Proposition, and give a Present, for wch we shall be at the Charge.

June 27th 1682 — /S/ Henry Coursey
/S/ Phil Loyd

Col: Henry Coursey and
Col: Phillemon Loid

Hond Srs

The Commissaries of albanie, haveing understood your Proposalls yesterday, concerning what you desyre should by them be Propounded to ye Indians, after that you Shall have made a Peace wt them

Whereupon wee have Resolved to acquaint ye Indians after yt you shall have Trated wth them, that ye Christians of Maryland and Virginia are our Neighbours and his Majest: Subjects as well as wee And yt they take Care to prevent there young mens going out a fighting to ye Southward for fear of makeing any Incursions on the Christians there For in Violateing ye Covenant made wt them now, cannot Expect any Relieffe or assistance from us—Actum in albany Court house ye 13th: day of July 1682

By Ordr of ye Court.

Proposal made to the Mahikander and Esopus Indians, otherwise called Warrenacockse, and to the Catskill Indians by Col. Philemon Lloyd and Colonel Henry Coursey, for the right honorable Lord Baltimore, Lord Proprietor of Maryland, and all his Majesty's subjects of Virginia and Maryland, in the Courthouse of Albany, the 19th of July 1682.[1]

Having been informed by His Majesty's subjects of this government that you have behaved civilly and that you have placed yourself under the protection of our great King Charles, we have come from Lord Baltimore, Lord and Proprietor of Maryland under our great King, and for all his Majesty's subjects of Virginia and Maryland and all Indians at peace with us, but especially the Piscatawa Indians, to see you and to speak with you.

1° We say that we heard that some of your Indians have been fighting together with the Maquase in our country against some of our friendly Indians, which we hold very much against you, being contrary to the promise made by the sachems of the Mahikanders to Colonel Henry Coursey when he made them brothers five years ago. And therefore, we have come to tell the Mahikanders, the Warrenacokse, and the Indians of Catskill that they cannot come anymore to Maryland or Virginia to disturb

[1] Translated from the Dutch.

Again the people prepared to approach Adodarho and reason with him. This time they walked. Adodarho was ready with his magic power. He caused Akweks, the eagle, to fly close to the heads of the people, shaking his wings and loosening many prized eagle feathers. In the rush to gather the feathers, blows were struck and people forgot their mission.

any of His Majesty's subjects there, or the Piscatawa Indians, or any other Indians at peace with us, nor to go together or join with any other nation under any pretext whatever to make war on us or on any Indians at peace with us. Our great governor will forgive and forget this time what has happened, when all these things have been done and all these directions have been followed. We wish to esteem your people and keep you for our very good friends. If not, you can expect that we will make war against you.

given to them
3 kegs of rum
3 rolls tobacco
3 dozen pipes

Wednesday, the 19th
of July 1682

Translated by me, Robert Livingston
Secretary.

Answer of the Mahikanders & Catskills Indians upon the Propositions of Col: Phillemon Loid and Col. Henry Coursoy agents of ye Right honrble. the Lord Baltemore, Lord and Proprietary of maryland, and all his Majs. Subjects of Virginia and Maryland in the Court house of albany the 19 of July A° 1682.

Doe Say That they doe thank ye Gentlmen ye agents of maryLand for there Presents, & yt. they have Esteemed them worthy to Propose unto them, and doe lett them know that they are Very Small, and a Litle Poeple, & shal never doe any harme to ye Christians of Virginia and maryLand, nor to ye Indians Liveing in frindship wt. them; and shall never Joyne wt any Indians to doe them any hurt, or Prejudice, For they are necessitate to hide themselves or Lurk under this Govermt. & Shall answer further upon ye Propositions tomorrow.

The Esopus Indians

Say That they Confirm that wh. ye Mahikanders & Catskill Indians have now Said, and that they are also few and a Smal Poeple, and good friends of ye Christians, and Shall answr To morrow wt Said Indians

Names of ye Mahikander Sachims
Wickepee
Joris
Machanuk
Watt hawitt
Puhketay a Squae
Snotee &
kehomahak
The Cattskills Sachims
Skermerhoorn
Mataseet
kochkotee a Squae
Jan d Backes
Tatamshait
The Esopus Indians
Culpuwaan
Camirawechak
Mamaruchqua a Squae
Interpreted p *m^{r}. Gerret van Slichtenhorst*

The ffurther answer off ye Mahikanders, Catskills and Esopus Indians, upon the Propositions made to y^{m}. yesterday by Co^{l}. Phillemon Loid and Co^{l}. henry Coursey agents of ye Lord Baltemore Lord and Proprietare of Maryland, and for all his Maj^{s}. Subjects of Virginia and MaryLand in ye Court house of albany ye 20th day of July 1682

Do Say That they thank the Gentl^{n}. of Maryland and Virginia, that they are Come so farr a journey, to Speak Soe frindly w^{t}. them, and that they are all one heart w^{t}. them. doe give 2 faddom Zew^{t}.

2. Wee have been in good frindship and amity w^{t} ye Christians whilst they have been here, and desyre that ye Same may Continue and that there may be a good and upricht heart betwixt ye Christians and them. doe give a Belt of Zew^{t} 13 deep.

3. Doe give a Belt of Sewant or Peag which they call an Obligacon whereby they doe oblige themselvs, that when there Indians goe out a hunting, shall doe no harm or Prejudice to them of maryland or Virginia, nor to ye Indians in amity w^{t} them, or onder there Protection.

4^{ly} When wee goe out a Bev^{r}. hunting, wee Shall not come to MaryLand or Virginia, but shall goe more westwards, doe give a Bev^{r}. because they are goeing out a Bever hunting.

5. Doe thank y^{e} Gentlemen of MaryLand and Virginia that because they being a great Poeple, have thought them soo worthy that are a Small Poeple as to Speak to them and doe assure them

The people were to try three times before giving up their attempt to win over the war-chief. A Medicine Man told of a vision. He said that Hiawatha alone could not conquer Adodarho. But there was a great man who came from the north and traveled to the east, and this great man and Hiawatha together could win over Adodarho. Hiawatha must go to the Flint Country to meet this man.

yt they have a good heart, as they of Maryland & Virginia have now Show'd to them, doe give a Belt of Peag 8 deep.

Present
Mr. Cornel: van Dyk
Mr Dirk Wessells

Propositions of Sd Indians to the Commissaries here datum ut Supra

They give 2 Belts of Peag that ye Commis: shall be wittnesses of ye Bonde of frindship which they now have made wt ye Agents of maryland, for them and Virginia, and desyre that the Commissaris may take Cognisance of it, & yt ye 2 Belts may be a Remembrance of ye Same.

Quod attestor
Rot. Livingston
Secr.

The agents of maryLand Proposalls to Capt. Anthony Brockholls Commandr in Cheife Alby pmo aug 1682[1]

Hondr Sir

Those severall applications mad yesterday wee have Caused to be drawne up into these heads and humbly desire that noe negative detrmination may be made to any article wthout giving us a hering to Reploy to such matters as shall be objected therto.

Imps That yu Please to grant us yor Counsell and Asistance in demanding & Procuring satisfaction for thoes murders Robberyes Commited upon the inhabitans of Maryland last fall by the northerne nations of Indians

2. That yu please (after a fayr Complyance therein [by] those nations whose people ware Guilty of yt fact) To put us into the best Rules of Ratyfing and Confirming The peace last made, and in Such maner as may best secure us from Such violations as have beene two lately Committed one their Parte in order whareto wee have Considered of Some Expedient wch wee offer for yr Honrs approbation.

1. That yu Please by yr Selfe ore some Person Commisionated by yu to Declare to those severall northern nations of Indians in leage and amytie with his Majestie in his Royalle Highnes The Dukes Goverment that ye Inhabitants of Maryland and virginia are alike Subjects To the King of England as yr selves of new Yorke.

[1] The conference with the Iroquois that resulted from this request may be found in O'Callaghan, 3: 321-328.

2. That in having made a peace wth the subjects of the King of England att new yorke They must undrstand it includs all ye Kings Subjects of Maryland and virginia
3. That if they Commit any murders or Robberyes upon the Prsons or Estates of ye inhabitants of Maryland or virginia They must not Expect any longer to hold the Trade at Albany or Continou in the amytie and frindshipp of the Inhabitants of this Goverment. And that this may Make the Deeper impression upon those Indians and Consequently tacke the better Effect for Preservation of his majestyes Subjects in all theese Govermments. That youe Please at ye next Ratification yor oune Peace which wee understand is done yearly to add an Article To that Purpose for wch noble and Christien like service noe doubt bot yor Honr will have his Gratious majesty Royall Favor and Thankes.
1. In Order to ye Effecting whereof and making a Peace for our Severall Nayboring frinds indianse without which wee Cannot Expect to be free from Robberyes and Spoyles when these northerne Troppes Come Downe upon them, wee Desire Prmission to treat with thees severall nationes at Albany.
2 To have such interpretrs asigned to us as we shall Conseve may prove most serviceabll and ffaithfull for Caring on the prmises
3 That wee may have Liberty to manadge our discourses with thees Indiones in such maner and forme as may best mack oure proposiones apier Raetionell nesesery and Excepable To Them.

finis

This is a true Coppy attested
p me Robert Burman.

Draught of ye Susquehannes River & how soon ye Indians westward can come there

This draugt is taken from 3 Indians, 2 Cajouges called ackentjaeken and kaejaegoehe and 1 susquehannes that Live amongst ye onnondages, in ye Court hous of albany this 7th of Septembr 1683
It is one days journey from ye maques Castles to ye Lake which

Hiawatha had seven daughters whom he greatly loved. The Onondaga people tried to get Hiawatha to go to the Flint Country, but he refused to leave his daughters. The people knew that so long as he had his daughters, he would never meet Deganawidah. Some of them decided to kill Hiawatha's daughters through sorcery.

is the head of ye Susquehannes River, and then 10 days journey downe the River til ye Susquehannes castle, in all 11 days.
From oneyde by Land 1½ days journey to yt creek that Runns into ye Susquehannes River, and by water one day in ye Creek & att ye mouth of ye Creek where ye Susquehannes River is Entred 7 days to ye Susquehannes Castle, in all 9½ days.
From onnondage ½ days journey by Land & 1 days journey by water before you come to ye River & then 6 days journey down ye Rivr
From Cajouge 1½ days journey by Land and 1 days journey by water before you come to ye River and then 5 days journey down ye River
From ye Sinneks 4 Castles by Land 3 days and by water 2 days before you come to ye Susquehannes River and then down ye River before you come to ye Castle 5 days in all 10 days journey, which is verry easy they carrying ye burthens in Canoes downe ye River
The Indians asked why so Exact an account of ye Susquehannes River was demanded, and whither any People would come and Live there;
The Indians were asked whether itt would be acceptable to them if People should come and Setle there; The Indians ansurerd they would be verry glad if People should come and Setle there because it is nearer them then this place; and much Easier to transport themselfs and Burthens by water, whereas they muste carry all to this place upon there baks; and said further that People from hence ought to goe and Live there, they would be gladd off itt, they would then come and Trade there.
NB: that in Returning from ye Susquehannes Castle one must be as Long again goeing up ye River as comeing downe.

Instructions for Arnought ye Interpreter to be by him followed to ye Senecas, Magques, Onnondages, Oneydes & Cayouges [*c. July 1684*]

You are to informe them I have had an account from Virginia that in August last thier young men which they Said were out and would take Virginia in their way home but would doe us no harme made great distruction att the head of Rappahannock River of Cattle killing off one plantation 200 head of Cattle & one hundred off severall others & at last proceeded so far as to kill five

1683 Sept 7

Hudsons River

This draught is taken from 2 Indians, 2 Cajouges called Ackentjaakon and Tassaagodhe and 1 Sasquehannes that lives amongst ye Onnondagos, in ye Court house of Albany this 7th of September 1683 —

It is one days journey from ye Maques Castles to ye Lake which is the head of ye Susquehannes River, and then 10 days journey downe the River till ye Susquehannes castle: in all 11 days

From Oneyde by Land 1½ days journey to ye Creek that Runs into ye Susquehannes River and by water one day in ye Creek & att ye mouth of ye Creek where ye Susquehannes River is Entred 7 days to ye Susquehannes Castle in all 9½ days

From Onnondage ½ days journey by Land & 1 days journey by water before you come to ye River & then 6 days journey downe ye River

From Cajouge 1½ days journey by Land and 1 days journey by water before you come to ye River and then 6 days journey down ye River

From ye Sinnekes 4 Castles by Land 2 days and by water 2 days before you come to ye Susquehannes River and then down ye River before you come to ye Castle 6 days in all 10 days journey, which is very easy by carrying ye Bathons in Canoos downe ye River.

The Indians asked why so Exact an account of ye Susquehannes River was demanded, and whether any People would come and Live there. The Indians were asked whether it would be acceptable to them if People should come and settle there. The Indians answered they would be very glad if People should come and settle there because it is nearer them then this place, and much easier to transport themselves and their Goods by water, whereas they carry all to this place upon their backs, and said further that People from hence ought to goe and Live there, they would be glad of it, they would then come and Trade there —

NB: that in Returning from ye Susquehannes Castle one must be as Long again going up ye River as coming downe —

The Lake at the head of ye Susquehannes River

1 day by land to ye Lake from each Castle

The Maques Castles

East

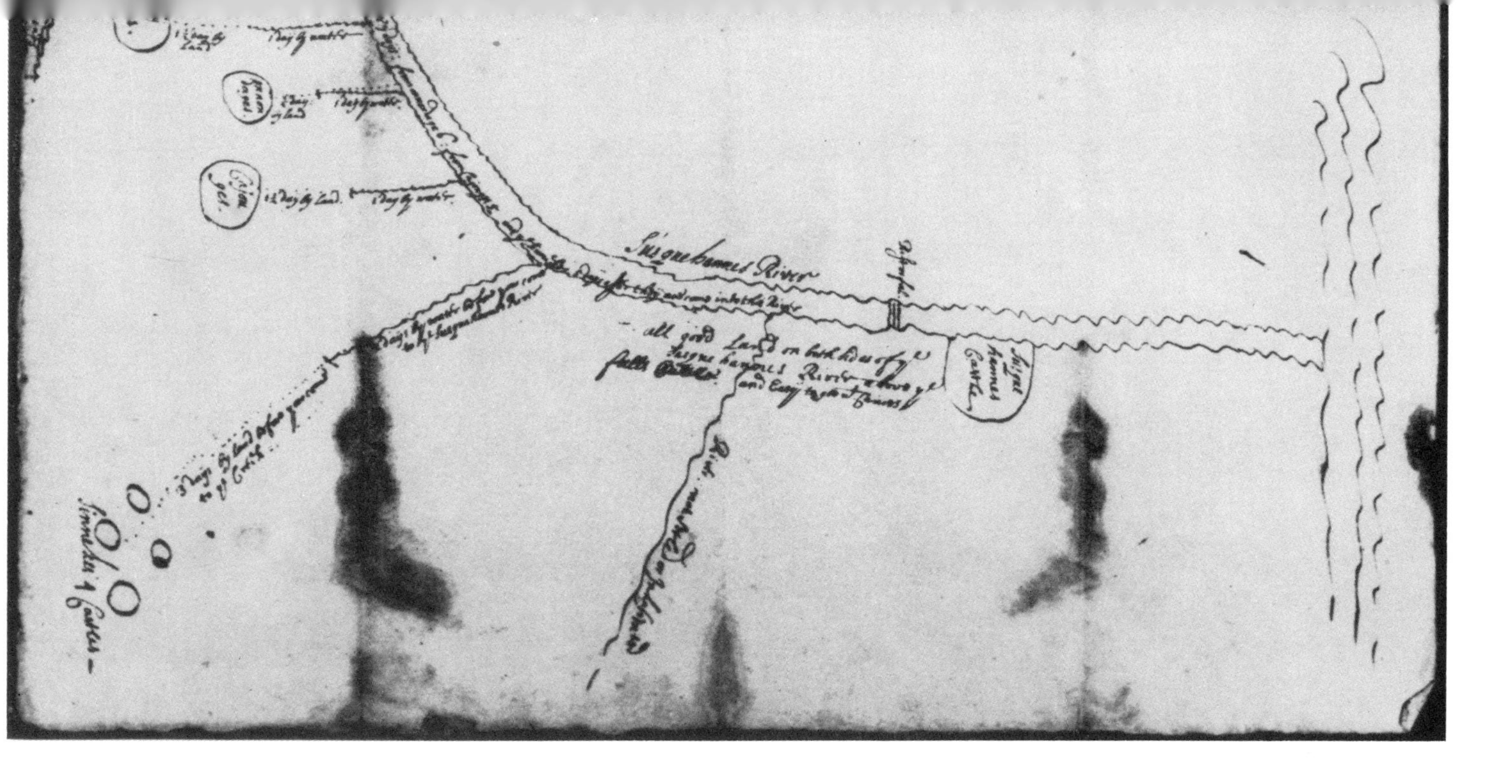

"DRAUGHT OF YE SUSQUEHANNES RIVER
& how soon ye Indians westward can come there."

September 7, 1683.

Courtesy Franklin D. Roosevelt Library

or six English inhabitants which made them fire on them againe and killed two or three of the Indians which was only in thier owne defence, for our english knowing that I came to make peace with the Severall nations would not take any advantages against them and tho they were acquainted with that, yet would they not desist from thier hostility: which let every nation know.
You are to acquaint them that I doe not take this to be a breach of the peace we have so lately made, provided they forthwith call home thier young men and make a new path when they goe to war & not come nere the Virginia and maryland plantations according to the Articles of peace; let that be related particularly to each of the nations.
The young men told our English they would be there againe when the Turky Cocks gobled which is in March according to thier Phrase which if they doe I cannot Judge they are so carefull to keep the chaine of freindsp. so bright & Strong as they Said they would, Let them know I send this only to acquaint them wt was done yt they may call home thier young men, & take care that the chaine of freindship be not broken for the future. for if they come againe we shall not take them for your Indians but as enemies & destroy what we can of them. it shall be carefully & honestly preserv'd by us which acquaint them severaly from

/S/ EFFINGHAM

Propositions made by the Right honble. Lord My Lord Howard, Baron off Effingham Governr. genl. off his Majes. Dominion of Virginia, to ye. Maquase Onydes onnondages, & Cayouges Sachims; in the Court house off albany the 30th day of July 1684.[1]

It is now about seaven yeares Since you (ūprovoaked) came into

[1] Colden is apparently confused concerning this conference. He dates it as July 13, and then gives a lengthy series of Iroquois answers. Colden, 1: 34, 39-45. Those answers, however, are more likely the ones made by the Indians to Dongan and Byrd on September 15, 1685 (see below). There is an Onondaga and Cayuga answer of August 2 which, while it does not appear to answer Effingham's complaints, may be a portion of the total Indian proposition. O'Callaghan, 3: 417-418.

Ohsinoh, a noted shaman, was employed to do this. Ohsinoh climbed a tree near the lodge of one of Hiawatha's daughters, and imitating the cry of a screech owl he sang a powerful witch song. In three days, the daughter died. He did this in turn to all of the daughters of Hiawatha.

Virginia, a Contry belonging to the Great king of England, and Committed severall murthers and Robberies, carryeing away our Christian women and Children Prisoners into your Castles all which Injuries we had deSigned to have Revenged on you, but by the deSyre of Sr Edmond Andross then Governr. Genll. of this Country, wee Desisted from DeStroying you, and sent our agents Col. Wm. kendall, & Col. Southy Litleton, to Confirme and make sure ye Peace that Col. Coursey of MaryLand included us in, when first he treated with you, but wee finde that as you quickly forgott what you Promist Col Coursey, soe you have likeways willfully broake the Covenant chaine which you Promist our Agent Col. kendall should be both Strong and Bright, if wee of Virginia would Bury in the Pitt of oblivion the Injuries you had then done us, the which upon Governr. Andross Intersession and your Submission, wee were willing to forgett, but you not att all mindeing the Covenants then made, have Every yeare since com into our Country, in a warrlike manner under Pretentions of fighting with our frind and neighbour Indians, which you ought not to have done, our agent haveing included them in the Peace, but you not only Destroyd and tooke Prisoners many of them, but you have alsoe killd and burnt our Christian Poeple, Distroying of our Corne and Tobacco, more then you made use of, killing of our horses, hoggs, & Catle, nott to eate, but to Lett them Ly in the woods and Stinke, this you did when you were not denyed any thing that you said you wanted.

I must also tell you, that under the Pretence of frindship, you have come to our houses, att ye heads of our Rivers, where they have been forted, with a white Shirt on a Pole (for a Flagg of Truce) and have laid downe your gunns before the fort, upon which our Poeple takeing you to be frinds, have admitted your great men into there forts, and have given them meate and Drink what they desyred, after the great men had refreshed themselfs, and desyreing to Returne, as they were Lett out of ye fort gates, the young men Rushed in to ye fort and Plundred the house, takeing away and Destroying all the Corne, Tobacco bedding and what Els was in ye house, and when they went away they took severall sheep with them, and killd severall Cowes bigg with Calfe, and Left them behinde them cutt to Peeces, and flung about, as if it were in Defyance of ye Peace and Dispyseing of our Frindship.

These and many more injuryes that you have done us, hes caused me to raise forces, to send to the heads of our Rivers to Defend our Poeple from your outrages, till I came to N: york to Col Tho: Dongan your govern^{r} gen^{l}. to deSyre him that as wee are all one kings Subjects, to assist me in warring against you, to Revenge the Christian blood you have shedd, & to make you give full Satisfaction for all the goods that you DeStroyed, and taken out of our Country of Virginia, butt by the mediacon of your Govern^{r}. I am now come to albany to Speak with you, and to know the reason of your Breaking ye Covenant chaine, not only with us & our neighbour Indians but w^{t} Maryland who are great king Charles Subjects for o^{r} Indians have given great K Charles there Land and Pay him tribute. therefore I ye Governor of Virginia will Protect them, as yor Govern^{r} under ye great Duke of York & Albany will henceforth y^{u} when ye chyne of frindship is made between us all.

Now that I have Lett you understand that I am Sencible of all ye Injuries you have done us, by the DeSire of y^{r} noble Govern^{r} Genl. I am willing to make a new chaine with you for Virginia Maryland & o^{r} Indians that may be Stronger and more Lasting, even to ye worlds End, soe that wee may be all Brethren & great king Charles Children;

I Propose to you

1. That you forthwith call out of our Countrys of Virginia and Maryland all your young men or Souldiers that are now there
2. Thatt you doe not hinder or molest our frind Indians from hunting att our mountaines, itt haveing been there Country and none of yours for they never goe into your Contry to Disturbe any of you
3. Thogh the Dammages you have done in our Country be verry great, and would Require a greatt deal of Satisfaction, which you are bound to give & Satisfy, yett wee assure you that only by the Perswasions of your governour, who is att a vast deal of trouble and Charge for your wellfare which you Ever ought to acknowl-

The grief of Hiawatha was great. He walked in a daze, but not one of his people came to give him sympathy or comfort. When no one punished the shaman, he said he would leave Onondaga and become a wanderer in the forest. Lightning flashed as he left the village and headed toward the south.

edge, I have Past itt by and forgiven you, upon this Condition, that your People nor any liveing among you, never Committ any Incursions on our Christians or Indians Liveing among us, or in Maryland and for ye Better Confirmacon of ye Same, & yt ye Peace now concluded may be Lasting, Propose to have Two hatchets to be buryed as a finall Determinacon of all warrs and jarring between us, the one in ye behalf of us & our Indians, and ye other for all your nations united together, that ever did us any Injury or Pretended to warr against our frind Indians or Maryland.

And that nothing may be wanting that might Contribute to ye Confirmacon hereof, if you desire itt, wee are willing to Send Some of our Indian Sachims wt an agent next Summer about this time, thatt they may Ratify this Covenant with you here in the Prefixed house, where you may see and Speak together as frinds.

4. That ye Covenant now made betwist us in this Prefixed house, in ye Presence of your Governr may be firmly kept, and Performed on your Parts, as it always hath been on ours, and yt you doe not break any Link of ye Covenant chain for the future, by your Poeples Comeing near our Plantacons, but when you march to ye Southward, that you keep to ye foot of ye mountains, & not come nigh ye heads of our Rivers Therr being no Beavour hunting therr, for wee Shall not in ye future (though you Lay downe your arms as frinds) ever trust you more, yu having so often deceyved us.

Twas given to each nation 20 yds duffels
1 doz: Stockings
40 gl. wampum
1 fatt Rom
1 Roll Tobacco

The Same Proposition was made to ye Sinnekes & ye Like Present as to ye other nations

Quod attestor
/S/ Robt Livingston.

Proposals to the Indians to the West which Arnout the Interpreter will make for and in the name of the Governor General, Colonel Thomas Dongan[1]

That his Honor thanks the Maquase and the Senecas that they did

[1] Translated from the Dutch.
For the story of Arnout's success with the Mohawks and Seneca and failure with the other three Nations, see Colden, 1: 60-63.

not go to the Governor of Canada when he ordered them to come.[1] That his Honor is displeased with the other three nations since they made a peace without his Honor's consent, after they had submitted themselves to this government and had promised that they would not do anything without his Honor's advice, he, who has been to so much trouble and labor to keep the English from making war on them, who would be a worse enemy than the French. And his Honor is sad that they are saying that the weapons of the Duke of York would not be able to keep the French back. They are very mistaken, for it is not the peace they made nor anything else they have done, but those same weapons which have rendered it impossible for the French to go on.
His Honor will not say much more to those nations but to order them to call their young Indians back home and forbid them to go to Virginia and Maryland. His Honor presents his service to the Maquase and the Senecas and assures them that they will not regret that they were so true to this government. His Honor thinks to visit them next year.

Albany, October 2, 1684 By the order of his Honor the Governor General
Robert Livingston

Pray be exact and sure to write down the Indians' answer
Firstly, instructions of my Lord, as well as above-mentioned proposals, and then that apart.

Propositions made by some messengers sent from ye Maquase Sachims in ye Toune house of albany ye 3d. day of February 1684/5.

Brethren

1. Wee come here in our Prefixed house where wee are wont to

[1] De La Barre was determined to create divisions within the Five Nations. On September 3, 1684, he had succeeded in coming to terms with all the Nations but the Mohawks and Seneca, the latter "not daring to come in order not to displease Colonel Dongan." De La Barre's Report, October 1, 1684. O'Callaghan, 9: 239-243.

On the third sun he came to a place where there were many round jointed rushes growing. He cut these into small lengths, thus making beads. He said that if he found a person bowed with grief like his, he would try to comfort him by use of the strings of beads. The strings would become words to lift the clouds from his heart.

come, Pray take care of us. doe give a Belt of wampum

2. Take care thatt wee may live in Peace & quietnesse in our Country. doe give a fad: of *Z:*

3. Doe your Endevour, & take graet care that no harm befal us —doe give a faddom of wampum

4. Doe give a Belt of wampum 11 deep, and desyre to know some news

5. Desyre that ye Chain of Peace & frindship may Remain firm, & that none Pull out yr hand out of ye chain, & Pointing to Mary-Land & Virginy sayd, that by all means they might keep the Covenant. did give faddome of wampum.

6ly. They Desyre again Informacon if there be any design to kill them; whether now by this Snow, or in ye Spring or 6 months hence when ye Indian Corn is thus high, did give a Belt of wampum 12 deep.

Were answered

As for news that ye Brethren seem to be Soo Inquisitive after, wee know of none, but on ye Contrary can assure ye Brethren that wee have Recd. a Lettr. from ye govr. Genl. that you need not to be affrayd, but freely goe out a hunting, for ye Reports you hear are false, & therefore you must by no means be Surprized att Such Storyes wee shal send doune your Propos: to ye govr Genl. by ye first occasion, was given back again wampum & bread to ye value of 12 S.

This is a true Copy Translatd
pr me Rot Liv.

Present
Majr Gert Baxter
Pr Shuyler
J: Wendel
Wm Teller
kajarawaago Speaker

Propositions made by four Sinnekes To ye Commandr & Justices of Peace in ye Court house of albany ye 29 June 1685

1. There is news Brougt us in our Country by 4 Indians of a nation called kighquakis Roene our frinds wt Presents & they tell us that ye Govr. of Canida is Intended to Destroy us, which Tideings is gone throw to ye maquase Castles, Broyr Corlaer wee come to acquaint you herewith, & desyre that you wil take care that no mischieff befall us, this is ye DeSyre of ye old men & doe give 2 beer.

2. The gov^r of Canida's design is kept verry Secret, & as itt were Smotherd in a Pott that is coverd, but neverthelesse tis broak out as far as our Country & wee are acquainted w^t itt, Now Corlaer It is your Goverment and wee are your Subjects; & therefore wee DeSyre that you would be Pleased to order that our Young Souldiers doe not goe out a fighting; but Stay at home to Defend there Country; if it should happen that ye french should Come & fall upon our Country, for wee are Informed that he Design to be ther about 3 months hence. doe give 2 Bev^rs.

Answer to ye fors^d. Propositions-

Wee have heard your Propositions and Perceive that you are fearfull of ye french which you ought not to be, nor give any Creditt to Such Stories, for your haveing Submitted your Selfs under this goverm^t. and obeyeing ye gov^r. Last year in not make-ing a Peace w^t ye french without his Consent and approbacon You need not doubt but ye gov^r will take all fitting care to PreServe you and your Country; in ye mean Time you must Tell your young men from ye gov^r. That they are not to goe out a fighting against there Indian Enemies but stay at home till ye time of ye Bev^r hunting approaches, w^h. will be in the fall, and then you are to Pursue & follow your hunting as formerly, & Bring your Bev^r hither where you finde you are Civily Treated, and have all Sorts of goods verry cheap.

were Presented w^t 30 gild^rs. white Strung *Z*
To ye Interpreter 12 s.

Present
Maj^r Ger: Baxter
P. Shuyler
Dav. Shuyler
Joh: wendel
M. gerritse
W^m: Teller
kil v: Renselaer

Propositions made by the north Indians that are come from Canida being about 56 in number besides: 100: women & Children there Sachim is called Sadochquis accompanyed with the Indians of Schaghkook in y^e Court house of albany y^e 1st: of July 1685

Brother Corlaer

1. Wee were here in this house last year & Spoke w^t the gov^r. who deSyred us to come here & wee did then Promise his hon^r

---

On the tenth sun he made a fire outside a village, and over a tripod pole hung his wampum strings. He repeated his words that, if he found a person bowed with grief, he would take the strings and they would become words of comfort. A scout overheard and reported to his chief.

to come and live in this goverm^{t}. & wee are now come: doe give 4 Bev^{r}.
2. Wee have formerly been Sick even to death but you have Planted a great Tree for us under which Shadowe we shall live in Peace dou give 4 Bev^{r}
3. When Sadochquis our Sachim came t Canida to live ther The gov^{r}. of Canida did Embrace them as his Children never the lesse our thoughts & Inclinations when we Rose in ye morning were always to come hither & to live at Skachkook doe give 3 Bev^{r}.
4. Br: you See Sadochquis and his People sit here you^{r} Christian have much wisdom as come from ye heavens above have a good heart & Courage and support us that are mean in knowledge & understanding, doe give 3 ps. Bev^{r}.
Br:
5. Wee are Somewhat affrayd for there is a gov^{r}. att Canida & he will look up and ask where are they gone & will may be come here to look for us butt there is a govern^{r} here likewise lett ye Path be Shutt thatt he doe not come here for you have great understanding, doe give 3 ps. Bev^{r}.
6. You: have always well treated wamsachko ye Sachim of Skachkook wee are now come & are one body w^{t} him & itt is always Said that ye Christians & ye maquase are in a good union & Covenant chaen be soo Small as your litle finger butt Verry thick & Strong. doe give 3 Bev^{r}.
7. his hon^{r}: hath been Pleased to order that Skachkook Shall be the Place of our habitacon for which wee are Verry Thankfull & if any of our Indians Should absent themselfs doe not think where is he gone? for wee are fully Resolvd to live and dye att Skachkook & there to be buryed. doe give 4 Bev^{r}.
8. DeSyre y^{t} the Christians may ont evilly tratt them butt be kinde to them & Shew: to them all Civility. doe give 3 Bev^{r}.
9. Wee are ashemed & have butt few Bevers the kills & Creeke from whence wee come being very bare of Peltry our Creditors say wee have Bev^{r} & wee have none lett nott: them force us wee Shall make amens for ye future. doe give 3 Bev^{r}:

Answer to the S^{d}. Propositions
2 July 1685

Wee are very glad to see you here & that you have so Readily obeyd the governours Commands and therefore in his Behalf wee doe bidd you hertily wellkom to this Place and the govr haveing orderd Skachkook for ye Place of your abode amongst the Rest of your nation you may freely goe and live there and your Children after you: in Peace and quietnesse and never fear off any Persuit of ye french for ye govr will take Such care to Secure & Protect you that you may wholly Rely upon itt and Sleep att quiet as your Broyr Sachim wamsachko and his People have hitherto done therefore desyre you to acquaint the Rest of your nation that are Still at Conida of ye good Entertainment you have here and send them this Belt of wampum as a lettr from ye govr who Promises them all favor and Protection and you are to use all means to Perswade them to live at Skachkook for there yr is land Eneugh and it shall be for you & them and Posterity after you & you need not to doubt but a firm and Strong Covenant chain Shall be kept unviolable on our Parts between us and all oyr of your nation that shall come & live under this government So long as they behave themselfs well and as for your Credrs. you: nead not fear them In ye least for there shall be all Care taken to Prevent any of them from molesting & troubleing you

was given them	4 fatts Rom	£: 1:16
	4 half fatts Beer	£: 1:10
	4 Rolls tobacco	£: –: 8
	[200 loaves] Bread fer	£: 1:10
This is a true Copy	white *Zewt* to ye value	£: 6: 6
Translated & Compared	Belt wampum	£: –:16
pr: Robt. Livingston		£ 12:16
	To ye Interpreter -	12

In Presence of
Major Baxster
mr David Schuyler
dito Johanes Wendle
& Wm. Teller
& Garet Banker
& Mar: Gerrisen
& K: V: Renseller

Albany 3:Augst. 1685 Propositions made by the Sakemaks of the Sinekes[1]

[1] This document exists in both a Dutch and an English version. The former contains only nine propositions with a list of numbers from ten

The chief sent the scout to invite Hiawatha to the village. He was asked to sit at council. For seven suns Hiawatha sat at council, listening to debates, but during all that time, although he was a chief, his opinion was not asked.

1. Brother Curler wee have past through all the Indian Castells to this place and have renued ower peace with them in Love & frindship. wee had order from Curler not to goe by the English plantations in Virginia & Meryland but to goe round about, which ordr. wee have Observed where upon prsent 4 peeces of Beavrs.
2. Brother: last year Aeskis Cornelisen was in ower Cuntrey and delivered a Lettr: to us from Curler to deliver to Governr: Labarr: and to no bodey Else but to him Selfes & Since ye Sd. govr. came no further then Unnadagoe Wee not being there had no accation to deliver it, and have now brought it with us. & deliver it now to You: and prsent: 3: peeces Beavr:

3. Brothr Curler: This is the Useall house where wee all wayes make ower proposistions (there younder) mening New Yorke is the house of Curler alsoe. But this is the house of proposistions which must be Kept Clene: & neat that no foulenes grow in it. Our hart & minde is as our mouth Speakes & we know certainly yt his honr. hart & mouth is one, for wee are his people & he hath done good to our nation, & Preservd our Country & give 3 peeces Beavr.

4. Brother: I said Just now that this Covenant house should be Kept Cleane and Neat: Curlers fire is ower ffire whereby wee warme our Selves in peace. and give 3 peeces Beavr.

5. Brother Just now I Spoake of the ffire That is so acceptable a fire. I did not Speake alone off ourself but our whole Country to past from our Castles hither which is ower Useall Custom: in Speakeing about this Covenant, and doe give 3 peeces Beavr.

6. Brother doe not thinke that wee have any thoughts in ower harts that wee should turne from Curler to the Governr of Canida: & give 3: peeces: Beavr:

7. Brothr Last Yeare wee tould you, that wee should come downe through all the Cuntrey to this place with prsents as wee doe: & give 3 peeces Beavr.

8. Brothr Curler: here is Curler prsent mening him that Reprsents his parson there are foure armes which wee lock together in a Covenant Chaine. That is ower whole Cuntrey. my Lord howard

through sixteen, while the latter contains the sixteen given here. Whether the last seven propositions were noted elsewhere in Dutch or were translated immediately into English cannot be stated with any certainty.

Governr of Virginia, and my Lord Baltemore govr of Meriland Let the Chaine be Kept Cleane & bright as Silver that the great tree that is can not break it a peeces if it should fall upon itt. & give 4 ps. Beavrs.

9. Brother; wee sit under a Cloath of frendshipp: where wee are all Covered in peace. & give 4: ps. Beavrs.

10. Brothr. wee *p*sant againe a great Tree off wellfare so Hey that it may be seene in ower Cuntrey; ye Roots whereoff grow under ground, as far as our nation, lest no weeds grow near It yt wee may live in Peace under itts Shadowe, & yt itt may grow So thick yt itt cannot be moved, doe give 4 Bev. Skins

11. Wee doe give you a Potion to Purge your hearts of all evill humors, if you should have any evill thoghts of us, doe give 3 ps bevr Skins

12. Brethren lett ye Lovely Sonne Shine upon us & you, on yr Children & our Children, & no dark cloud Prevent or hinder itt, doe give 4 Bevr. Skins.

13. Wee doe come & make our Propositions here; lett us see you kome throu ye. maquase Country, oneyde, onnondage Cajouge & Sinnondowanne, yt our children may hear & see what is Said & Spoke, doe give 3 bev Skins

14. Wee Said but now of your comeing to see all our nations, itt would be to hard a journey for you, but you have horses & can Ride, wee doe Rubb or greese yr Leggs; doe give 3 ps bev. Skins

15. Brethren: Lett yr Shipps be Strong & well fitted yt they may come Safe over, yt our People may Rejoyce att yr arriveall. doe give 3 Bevr.

16. Brethren, ye Mahikandars yt are Come from Canida to live in your Government, Receive ym. in yr Protection for they are worthy & they are our frinds frinds to witt ye maquase frinds. Lett your Ey be upon ym for good, doe give 3 ps Bevr

---

On the eighteenth sun a runner came from the south, telling of a great man who had come from the north and was now in a Mohawk village at the Lower Falls. He told of a vision that another great man was to meet him at Ka-nin-ke-a-ka, Flint Land Village. There the two men were to meet and together establish a Great Peace.

Propositions made by the River Indians that live at Skachkook, in ye Court house of Albany ye 4th of august 1685

Present
Majr Baxter
Capt wendel
Wm Teller
gert Banker
kelian van Ranselaer

Brethren

There hes been some of our Indians at Pinnekook in N: England to whom ye Sachims of those Indians said, that they heard yt Wamsachkoo and his People liv'd verry well & Peaceably att Skachkook, & yt ye governr was inclined to draw ye Indians to this government, & whereas ye north Indians that were att Canida for whom a Belt of wampum was given us to Send for ym. hither, are come to Pinekook by there brethren & frinds; we sent ye Belt of wampum thither to Pinekook, to invite ym unanimously to come and live wt us, & they will Probably Resolve to come, Butt Since you are Christians and can doe more then wee wee desyre Earnestly that may bring itt to Passe that they may come & live at Schachkook, for wee are verry deSyreous yt yy come and live amongst us— doe give 4 Bevr

Answer To ye Sd. Propositions

Since you Inform us that ye north Indians that wee sent ye belt of wampum too, are come from Canida and gone to Pinnekook in new England, Probably to Visite there frinds & Relacons, being of ye Same nation, you are again to acquaint them, yt ye govr desyres them to come and live wt you at Scachkook in this government where they shall be Protected, & Civilly used, & have Land Eneugh to Plant upon; & if any of yr frinds or acquaintance are minded to come along wt them, they shal have ye Same kindenesse Shown ym as you have, ye Path being open for all Indians yt are willing to come and live Peaceably under this government: was given a Belt of wampum of 25: gild
& in white Strung wampum 24:
14 wheat loaves 4:18

f 53:18

This is a true Copy Examined ꝑ me
Robt. Livingston

Proposities made by three mariland Indians to ye Commandr & Commissaries of albany ye 7th day of aug: 1685[1]
The names of ye 3 Indians aforsd. being Piscatwa Indians: kanhia
Pasinsiak
Achsaminnis

1. Wee are come here from maryLand To ye house of Corlaer where usually Propositions are made, & where ye Covenant fyre burns, to Speak wt al ye Indians westward about ye Covenant, doe give a Belt of 10 deep.
2. Wee are come to Stay here in Corlaers house till ye Indians as far as onnondage come here to Speak wt us about ye Covenant, and desyre yt arnout ye Interpreter may goe & fetch ym. doe give 4 faddom of wampum to greese his horses leggs.

Proposals made to the Sachems of the nations of Indians to the west who have been in New York at the Honorable Governor General's by the Mayor and Aldermen in Albany, the 8th of September 1685[2]

We have asked the brethren to come here to welcome them after the trip to New York where, we heard, they have been received most cordially by his Excellency, the Governor, who has sent up information about the proposal he has made the brethren, of which the most important is to send their prisoners, the Indians from far away, back to their home again with 28 of our people, who, to this end, will go there with his Excellency's authority, of which group Johannes Rooseboom will be Captain to convoy them. This we recommend most cordially to the brethren not only to send the before-mentioned prisoners home, but also to send along with our people two or more sachems of each nation and of the Senecas to the far-away nations to bring their prisoners home, and also to bring two of their chiefs along here to Corlaer's house where his Excellency will be present and will then bury the hatchet and

[1] These Piscataway, or Conoy Indians from Maryland, first presented themselves to the Governor and Council in New York City on August 1. *Cal. N. Y. Coun. Min.*, 43.
[2] Translated from the Dutch.

Hiawatha determined to go to the Mohawk village. Five skillful scouts were chosen to guide and protect him on his journey.

make a durable peace and covenant between them and the brethren. With that Corlaer's wish will be fulfilled and the brethren will show themselves to be obedient children. Those of the far-away Indians who will be united with us in our agreement will also be protected by the branches of the great tree of welfare and there will then be an opening for the new brethren to come here and to renew yearly their covenant as the brethren do now.

Answer of the Senecas

We came on Corlaer's orders and have been to New York and come here now on Corlaer's demand and understand that your proposal is also to return the prisoners. As if it was an unimportant matter to us! No, to us it is a very important matter. Four years ago they killed one of our best sachems. But we answer here as in New York and nothing else: that we trust that all will be well, but the matter will have to be decided upon by the sachems in the country.

I should let you know also that I have a sister's child among those distant Indians called the Dionnondadoes and, therefore, you should also take care that she comes away with you, for you are all Corlaer's people. Just call my name, then she will hear it, and then the prisoners will know. My name is Adonderarseesha.

Present
David Schuyler Esqr.
Johannes wendel Esqr.
gert^{t}. Banker Esqr.
Marte gerritse Esqr.
kilian van Renselaer Esqr.
Magistrates of albany
Interpreted by
arnout Cornelise Viele

Propositions made by the hon^{ble}. Col^{l}. William Byrd, one of ye Councill and agent from his maj^{s}. Dominion of Virginia, assisted by Edmund Jennings Esqr. his maj^{s}. atturney Gen^{ll}. being authorized by his Excellency, Francis Lord howard of Effingham, his maj^{s}. Lieft^{t}. and govern^{r} gen^{ll}. and ye Councill of State off Virginia, to ye Maquase, oneydes, Onnondages, Cayouges, and sinnekes, in ye Toune hall of albany on y^{e}. 15th day of Septemb^{r} 1685

It is Somewhat more than a Twelvemonth Since the Lord howard of Effingham his Maj^{s} Govern^{r}. Gen^{ll}. off Virginia (being justly Provoaked by the Repeated injuries, both Virginia and Maryland had Received from you) came to New York to your Govern^{r} gen^{l}. to desyre him, (as being all one kings Subjects) to assist in warring against you, to Revenge ye blood you had Shed, and force you to have made Satisfaction, for ye Injuries you had done us, But by the medeacon of your govern^{r} (to whom you have always been Verry much obliged) my Lord howard was Perswaded to come to Albanie, and Renew the Covenant chain, you had so frequently broaken, both with the English and Indians of Virginia & maryLand, Upon which when my Lord howard in Company wt your noble governr came hither, he made you severall Propositions, for keeping ye Covenant chain of Peace, more firm & bright, both with Virginia and MaryLand, and all ye Indians of both Countryes below ye mountains; to which you readily Submitted, & caused hatchets to be buried, yt all injuries might be for ever forgotten and Buried in ye Pitt of oblivion.

You also did then Promise, not to come nearer our Plantacons, then the foot of ye mountains, all ye Land between; belonging to our frinde Indians, & not to you, being Left for them to hunt on, by the said articles; NotwithStanding which, Some Parties of your Indians have fallen downe, into ye foresaid Lands, belonging to our Indians, and have killed some of ym, Particularly one Nottaway on ye South Side of James River, and carryed away one Nanziatico from Toppahannock River,

Also this Last Spring a great Party of your Indians (quite Contrary to ye Covenant chain, you have so lately Renewed) fell on ye Sapone Indians, & fyred Severall gunns, wounded Some of ye men, & took one Prisoner which said Indians are (as all the Rest below ye mountains) our kings Subjects, & our governr. will Protect them.

Farther I have this to Tax you with, a Small Party of your Indians came about Two months Since, to an English mans house near Appamatock River falls, & there seized, and Carried away one Indian girle (Servant to ye Said Englishman) as she was washing of Linning at ye Door, & att ye Same Place, when your Indians Last year fell on ye appamatocks, you carried away three Indian Boys, Servants to ye said English family, whom I hear are now att oneyde.

All which being so Contrary to ye Covenant chain you Promised to keep So Bright, might justly Provoke us to make warr on you, Butt wee are not willing to beleive, that any of your great men, that Lately made ye Covenant were knowing of itt; we Rather

Twenty-three suns had passed since Hiawatha left his own village at Onondaga, when, after a five days journey, they reached the Flint Country. Hiawatha and his party built a fire outside the village, that their smoke might tell of their approach.

think, some of your young fellows have done this Contrary to your Consent or orders.

I therefore demand, that you shall Deliver up all Christian, Indian, or negro Servants, or Slaves, that are amongst you, & have fled or bein Caried away, from any of yr English masters, being Inhabitants of Virginia or MaryLand: and that you forthwith (if you have any men either in Virginia or maryland send to Recall them, and hence fordward take Care, that none ever approach nearer then ye mountains, according to your articles, with my Lord howard; which if you will Strickly observe, I am now Sent with this gentleman to Ratify and Confirm: & in order thereunto according to yr. aggreement made Last year by my Lord howard I have brought with me, some of our Indian Sachims, who in ye name of all our Indians are come to make a firm & Strong Covenant chain with you that may be Everlasting.

The Distance of ye. way being so great & ye Inconvenience of Passage by sea is ye Reason why so few of our Indians are come, but here is the cheif of ym., who in ye. name of all our Indians will Ratify & Confirm ye Peace, for all ye Indians both of virginia & maryLand are our kings Subjects, & if you will warr on ym. the great king of England will take it Verry ill, & all ye. English of virginia and maryLand will joyn against you, & you must not Expect any assistance from any of his majs. Subjects in america.

But now you again Confirming your Covenant chain, and Planting ye tree of Peace, I hope you will be more Carefull, to keep itt bright and clear, fresh and green, always united, always florishing, and if any of your young fellows doe Contrare to these articles, come within ye. mountains, and doe any Injury, to any English or Indian of Virginia or maryLand, You must certainly Expect that our People will kill and Destroy them, and therefore doe warne you from comeing there for ye future, upon any Pretence whatever.

Was given to each of ye 5 nations
15 yds. of Duffells
40 gilders wampum
1 fatt of Rom
60 Twist of Tobacco
40 Loaves of Bread
& a bullock divided amongst them

/S/ Wm: Byrd.

Present:
David Schuyler, Esq.
Johannes Wendell, Esq.
Gerrit Banker, Esq.
Marte Gerritse, Esq.
Kilian Van Rensselaer, Esq.
Magistrates of Albany
Translated by
Arnout Cornel. Viele

Answer of the Maquase, Oneidas, Onondagas, Cayugas, and Senecas on the proposals made by the Honorable Colonel William Byrd of the Council and Agent of His Majesty's Dominion of Virginia, assisted by Edward Jennings, Esq., his Majesty's Receiver General, authorized by his Excellency, Francis Lord Howard, His Majesty's Leftenant and Governor General and the Council of the Colony of Virginia; in the townhall of Albany on this 15th day of September 1685.[1]

The Onnondages answer through their Speaker Carachkondie

Brethren of Virginia

We agree to observe that which you told us, and not only we, the old men, but our young warriors will obey us by following this punctually and not coming within the mountains. Give hereon four beavers.

Concerning the heathen girl who it was supposed was taken from an Englishman's house when she was washing linen in front of the door, we do not know about this. It could have happened, but our troops have not come home as yet. Concerning the other three heathen boys who were taken the last year, we confess that they are in our country, but last year has been discussed and decided when Milord Howard was here—that the evil the troops who were then out might commit would not be held against them as they did not know then about the peace which was then made. And as they have been already accepted among the Indians as friends, it will be difficult to get them back. But if the girl will be brought back by our people who are now out, we will give her back.

The Sachem of the Senecas speaks:

Brethren: we have steadily kept the agreement made with the Governor of the Virginias as Corlaer commanded and have not gone to the English plantations, but have passed around the mountains.

[1] Translated from the Dutch.

A Mohawk messenger invited the party into the village. Deganawidah greeted Hiawatha. He saw that Hiawatha was suffering from some deep grief which caused him to wander far from his own people. Then Hiawatha told Deganawidah his sorrow.

If any evil has been committed, the four nations who sit here must have done it. We say so right in their faces (which the four nations did not deny), and we will keep to your orders steadfastly. We are glad to see that the tree of peace and friendship, which we will always keep green and flowering, will be planted again. Give three beavers.

The Cayugas speak and asked Taggojerhos, an Oneida, to be their interpreter:

You spoke of the three boys who are in our country. It is true, there are two in the Oneida and one in the Maquase Country, and we have understood what has been said on this matter and will keep it in mind, but we do not know a thing as yet about the girl. Give two beavers.

The Oneidas speak for themselves and say:

Brethren: we speak to you three: to Corlaer, the Governor of Virginia, and the Indians of Virginia. We will come in the spring and repay what has been charged to us now. In the meantime, we will make a place for the boys, this being in the way of a preparation to handing them back. You should know that a great deal of trouble is connected with this, to free them from those houses to which they have been given. Give two fathoms of wampum.

The Maquase speaker called Canondondawe began as follows:

That which we have been commanded by Corlaer and the Governor of Virginia we have followed. We declare for ourselves that we have had no part in what happened to the Virginians. But you, Cayugas, and Oneidas, I have to tell you and punish you, for you are slow in hearing, and therefore I will sing to you, to admonish you to follow your duty better. You Cayugas, you think that you cleared yourselves thoroughly by laying down the beavers, but we have to say to you, you did not do your duty.

Oh Brethren, Corlaer and Governor of the Virginia, where will I look for the peace covenant, where else will I find it but on our path, and but where will this path lead to but to this house, which is a house of peace and welfare, and started a song and sang completely the covenant song, and admonished first his own Indians and then the Indians of the Virginias to keep the covenant and charged his Indians not to exceed it as they have done until now.

Let us observe and keep to what has been commanded so sharply to us. Let me drive it into you with a song. Open now your ears, and he sang a song of admonishment, and gave one belt of wampum to the Governor and one belt to the Governor of Virginia, concluding all the proposals with a song and said that they were done for this time.

Collected by me, R[obert] L[ivingston]

*Govr Dongans Prop: to ye Indians westw^d^*
alby 15 Sepr 1685

purport of what the Governor desires to be communicated to the Indians

Brethren

I am sorry to find that our Brethren are headstrong people; & will do things that are not for their Interest, & not follow ye advice of those who have kindness for them.

The ffrench declard warr agt you, & by the Governrs means they wer afterwards willing to be at peac with you; you made peac with them without acquainting the Governor who would have made better conditions for you, then you your selfs have been able. The ffrench dar not meddle wth the King of England's subjects, & as such we esteem the Brethren, for he who was proprietor of this place, formerly his Rll. Highness, is at present or King, & able to protect them.

last year the great man of Virginia came hither with a resolution to have satisfaction from the Brethren for all the Injuries they have done to Virginia, but the Governor prevailed so far with him as to meet the Brethren at Albany, the peace was then made, the Ax buried, but the Brethern have not performed their parts, as they may see by the complaints of the Gentlemen who are com hither with som Indians of Virginia; according to the Agreement made last year wth you it is therefore the Governors desire that none of you Everafter go nearer to Virginia than the ffoot of the mountains, according to an Article agreed on the last sumer with you; if you do the great King of England will take it very ill, &

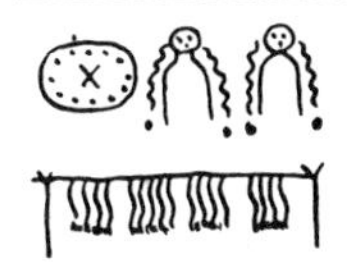

At the Mohawk council, Deganawidah told of Hiawatha's sorrow and mourned with him. He strung eight more strands of wampum. These he handed to Hiawatha, one after each part of his address.

the Governor not be able to assist you. Whatsoever is agreed upon now, let the Covenant be kept, & your words not broken, & be sure that the servants taken from the English in Virginia be restored.
For Mr peter Schuyler.

Present:
David Schuyler, Esq.
Johannes Wendel, Esq.
Gerrit Banker, Esq.
Marte Gerritse, Esq.
Kilian Van Rensselaer, Esq.
Magistrates of Albany
Translated by Arnout Corn. Viele

The Maquase, Oneidas, Onondages, Cayugas, and Senecas answer to the proposals made to them in the name of the Governor General, Colonel Thomas Dongan, in the townhall of Albany, this 15th of September 1685[1]

Carachkondie, speaker of the Onondaga, says:

Brother Corlaer
We understand that you are dissatisfied that we have been disobedient because of the peace making with the French without letting the Governor General know, of which we are ashamed and sad, but will observe his orders strictly from now on.
We understand also that the Governor of Canada is not so great a man as our King who lives across the great sea. Now we regret that we have given him so many beautiful belts when we made proposals with him. The evil that the young Indians of our nations have done in Virginia in violation of the covenant hurts us much and was done against our will and consent, but we will take good care from now on to keep them completely from those coasts and inculcate obedience in them. And we promise that no more harm will be done there again. Give one beaver.

The Cayugas speak and use Tageshérhos, an Oneida, as their speaker:

We have understood all the proposals, how everything has been repaired and again renewed, and agree to observe everything as it has been told to us as well by Corlaer as by the agents of the Governor of Virginia. Give one beaver.

The Maquase, after they had professed their innocence to the Indians of the Virginias and had renewed the peace with them, said through their spokesman, Canondondawe:

Oh Brother Corlaer and Governor of the Virginias, where will I look for the peace covenant, where else will I find it but on our

[1] Translated from the Dutch.

path, and where will this path lead but to this house, which is a house of peace and welfare, and began a song and sang the song of the covenant, and admonished first his own Indians and then the Indians of Virginia to keep the covenant and charged his Indians not to exceed it as they have done until now. Let us observe and keep to what has now been commanded so sharply to us. Let me drive it into you with a song. Open now your ears, and sang a song of admonishment, and gave one belt of wampum to the Governor and one belt to the Governor of Virginia, concluding all the proposals with a song, and said that they were done for this time.

The Oneidas said for themselves:

Brethren, we speak to you three, to Corlaer, the Governor of Virginia, and the Indians of Virginia and Maryland. We will come in the spring and repair what has been charged to us now. In the meantime we will clear a place for the boys, this being in the way of a preparation to handing them back. You should know that a great deal of trouble is connected with this, to free them from those houses to which they have been given. Give 2 fathoms of wampum.

The Maquas & Cayouges answer to arnout ye Interpreter, after he had Deliverd ye governour message to them [*Albany, October 14, 1685*]

Said

Wee thank Corlaer for his Care and Prudence, wee are nott Inclined to warr wt. any Christians, neither to ye. north nor to ye South neither are our Children ye oneydes, or our Brethren ye. onnondages that way Inclined; & wee shall take Care to Pacify ye Sinnekes & Putt yr mindes in quiet, nay yy must be att Peace, for ye Cayouges are most of ym. outt & Pairt of ye onnondages a fighting against a far nation of Indians, & ye. onneydes & ye Maquas are all out a Bevr hunting, ye maquause gave a Belt 12 deep.

The words that he spoke to Hiawatha were eight of the thirteen condolences. Deganawidah said that in future wampum strings should be held in the hand to remind the speaker of each part of his address; and, as each part is finished, a string should be given to the mourning chief on the opposite side of the fire, who will hand them back one by one.

The Sinnekes answer

That 24 days hence they will come wt ye 3 oyr nations to witt onneydes, onnondages & Cayouges and give there answer.

The maquase as soon as ye Interpreter had deliverd ye message, gave Presents to ye Sinnekes in arnouts Presence & Perswaded ye Sinnekes to obey ye govr. order & have no more Thoughts of warring wt ye french—, which ye Sinnekes Recd.

Memorandum of what ye Govr. of Canida Proposed to ye Sinnekes by ye Commandr of Cadarachqui at Cadarachqui

1. That they were att ye Liberty to warr wt what nation of Indians ye listed. gave 5 bleu Coats.

2. That they were not to beleive false Reports of any Indians. gave 5 bleu Coats

3. Recommended ym. to keep ye Covenant Chain, but withall acquainted ym. he was for what ye Pleased Peace or warr, doe give 5 bleu Coats.

This is ye Substance of ye Propos: which ye Generall of ye Sinnekes told arnout who was himself Present

Albany ye
14 of octobr
1685.

R. Livingston Cl.

Proposition made by anneride an Cayouger Sachim in ye behalf of ye Cayouges & oneydes in albany ye 28th day of octobr 1685.

I am sent by ye Cayouges & oneydes Sachim to acquaint ye governr that wee have Recd. ye Belts he Sent us by arnout ye Interpreter together wt ye message, & according to our Promise I am come to tell our answer wh. is yt. wee are no ways inclined to warr wth any Christians, our hearts being att Rest & quiet, for most all our Indians are out a Bever hunting, few being att home, we have Likewise Recommended ye Sinnekes to be att Peace, who have taken our advise & obeyd ye Govr. order, all being well & att quiet there, they together wt ye Onnondages, will come downe & bring there answer Verry Speedily: did give a faddom of wampum.

Present
Wm Teller
arnt Corn: Interpr.

Answer

You have done Verry well in bringing your answer according to Promise which wt ye first Conveniency Shall be Sent downe to ye Govr. genl. who will be well Pleased your men are all gone out a hunting;

We doe acquaint you from ye govr. that there are Some frenchmen gone up ye Susquehanne River to trade, which you are to Stopp, and all Christians that shall Come there to trade above ye falls of Susquehanna River, and to take all from ym. what they have, & to bring them here to Albany, & you shall be well Rewarded (Excepting Such as have a Pass under Corlaers hand & Seale) who will goe from hence & not ye oyr way; This you are to tell all ye nations as you goe home, was given 2 duffells Coats one for ye oneÿdes & ye oyr for ye Cayouges.

Rt. Livingston Cl.

Present
David Schuyler
Wm Teller
Sachims names
Annogogari
Sagodderastie

Propositions made by Two onnondages Sachims in ye Court house of albany ye 5th day of Novembr 1685

Wee have Recd. ye belt of wampum wh. arnout brought to our Country, by a Cayouger Indian, he not being able to bring itt any further by Reason of ye high water, as also ye Govrs message, wh. we have obeyd in Perswading ye Sinnekes to Peace, who have hearkned unto us; we are also off opinion yt. it is farr ye best to be in Peace, & not to warr wt any Christians, But Corlaer must likewise take Care that they be in Peace over ye Great water, yt Soe wee may all live in Peace & Tranquillity together, doe give a Belt of wampum.

Broyr Corlaer

Wee toe acquaint you yt. our young Souldiers shall goe no more towards Virginia or maryland, nor doe any harm there, butt in

After the eight ceremonial addresses had been made by Deganawidah, the mind of Hiawatha was made clear and the sun shone in his heart.

Pursuance to yr Commands keep ye Covenant chain wt ye Cornells of Virginia fast & Inviolable, doe give a Belt of wampum.

Present
David Schuyler
Wm. Teller

Propositions made by the Two Sinnekes Sachims calld Thoneregi & awanasse in ye Court house of albany ye 5th day of novemb 1685

Broyr Corlaer

Wee have Recd. your Belt of wampum, & understood your will & Pleasure, & have Consulted a long time about itt, finally we are Resolvd to make no warr upon ye french, nor any Christians, Since wee understand you would not be well Pleasd at itt, wee have throwne ye axe quite away in a deep water not in a Standing water, but where a great Current runns wh. Carries itt Immediatlly away. doe give a Belt off wampum 12 deep.

2. Wee doe now Renew ye Covenant not only wt Corlaer, but wt ye Govr. of Virginy & maryland, & shall keep ye Same Inviolable, wee wish yt wee may hear yt it is So likewise over ye great water, take Courage and Cause all ye Commotions there to cease, doe give 2 bevers.

3. Lett ye great king over ye great water know, yt we have So firm a Covenant on wt anoyr. both wth Corlaer, ym of Virginia & maryland, and oyr Christian Neigbours & therefore ye Christian Sachims yt live over ye great water, ought also to live in Peace wt on anoyr. yt ye Ships may come Safely, & ye goods bee good cheap, doe give 2 Bevr.

Answer to ye Sd. Indians

Wee shall forthwith Send doune yr. answer to ye govr. genl. who will be wel Pleased to hear yt. you are all in Peace & quietnesse; & yt you follow his advise nott to warr wt ye french wt out a Cause; & also yt you keep ye Covenant chain wt. ym. of virginia & maryLand, as for ye troubles over ye great water wh. you Speak off are all over, and all in Peace & quietnesse so yt yu need not fear but goods will Come as Plenty & cheap As Ever, & therefor you must Incourage your young Indians to goe out a hunting & bring yr Bevr. & Peltry no where but here wher you have always found Civil Entertainmt; neither are you to suffer any Christians yt Shall come to yr Country to trade wt you wtout ye Do have Corlaers Passe for we doe acquaint you from ye govr. yt yr are some french wt a Burch Canoe gonn up ye Susquehanne River to trade whom you are to Stop & all Christians thet shal Come there to trade above ye falls of said River & to take all from ym what they have, & to bring ym here to alby., & you Shal be wel Rewarded (Excepting Such as have a Pass undr ye govr hand & Seale) who are to go by ys toune; was given to each nation a Coat of duffells.

Robt: Livingston Cl.

Present
pr Shuyler
J. Janse Bleeker
Robt Sander
Livinus van Shayk
kiliaen Van Renselier
In this Propos: Sachquahan was Speaker

Propositions made by the Rever Indians that Live at Sckaghkook to ye magistrates of albanie in ye Court house the 21 day of Decembr 1685

Wee doe live fir ye Present in ye dark our Sachim is dead & wee come here to acquent you with it doe give six deer Skinns & 1 bvr Skinn.

2. Corlaer hath accepted us for his Children & ordained this house to be ye Place of Propositions wee are gladd yt it is still open. doe give four dear Skins.

3. All ye Indianes upon ye north River are dead & ye Indians yt Live upon this River are but few in number & therefore wee desyre yt Corlaer may keep a good watch over us yt we may live together without fear doe give 8 dear Skins

4. Wee are much greevd ye Sachim Wamsachko is almost dead & he Sends his Broyr now to Corlaers house in his Room who is to be Sachim after him & we are come to acquaint wt it. doe give 4 deer Skinns.

5. Broyr Corlaer his done much good & strenthend ye Covenant chain which wee have found. wee Pray that itt may Reman firm & Strong. doe give 3 deer Skinns & 2 Beer Skinns

6ly Wee have under stood what Corlaer said yt we Should nott be north Indians any longer butt all River Indians & therefore we will keep our Residence att Skachkook & endevor to Increase our number & behave our selfs like River indians & not depart. doe give 4 deer skins & one Beer Skinn.

Hiawatha and Deganawidah now composed the Peace Song. It had power, if sung without any error, to straighten the crooked mind of Adodarho.

7. It is now Ten years agoe Since Corlaer made a firm Covenant wt us wee doe lay hold of ye same & not throw it aside & desyre yt Corlaer may keep ye Same Inviolable doe give 5 deer Skins.
8. Wee doe thank ye Brethren for all kindeness we Receive. You know yt our Sachim WamSachko is Verry Sick which hath much occasiond our Stay at home & have hunted bett litle and therefore ye Present wee bring is but Small neverthelesse wee hope ye Brethren will accept of itt. doe give 5 deer Skins & 5 sides of Vonneson wt a head.

The 39 dear Skins being weighd in ye Presence of ye magistrates doe weigh 152 lb. Eng

Answer to ye Propositions

You doe well to come to this house whir fir yt Purpose ordaind by Corlaer to Renew ye Covenant have good Couradge & be Strong for the governr hath Received you as Children you need not fear but his fatherly care will Continue so long as you behave yourselfs as Children Concerning that your Sachim is dead wee are Sorry for itt but you know yt is a debt thatt all People must Pay therefore be Carefull and Deligent that you choose a good Sober Indian in his Room to witt for yt Sachim tht is dead as you have done for him yt is Still alive & yt your People may keep together att Skachkook where you have a good habitain & therefore you must Pursue your Bever hunting without any fear

is given then Back again 2 Runletts of Rom hold each 2 gal is wt ye Cask £ 1: 1
1 Runlet wine for ye sick Sachim 10: 6
20 lb Tobacco 7: 6
20 loaves 3
22

This is a true Copy
Translated ℘ me
Robt. Livingston Cl.

Wee the Grand Jurors for the Towne & County of Albany doe himbly represent to the Consideracon of thir honble these followeing inconveniencyes in order to their being redrest in such manner as to yor honrs. shall seeme equall & convenient

1. Wee doe finde that the greate liberty now taken on pretence

of hunteing Licenses & the like to trade with the Indians without ye town is the occasion of the greate decay of trade here & will if continued tend to the utter ruin of this place.

2. Wee doe find that altho' there are many acts & ordrs. against Such tradeing without the Towne, yett in regard of the dificulty of proveing it by Christian Evidence those acts come farr short of a Sufficient remedy—Therefor wee would humbly recomend it it to yor honrs care as a thing very convenient that some provision may bee made that for the future yt upon the testimony of an Indian in the afirmative the party accused so to have transgressed may bee oblidged to purge himselfe by an oath otherwise the accusacon taken *P* Confesso.

3. Wee doe finde that great Debauchery happens amongst the youth by goeing to trade with the Indians in their houses.

4. Wee doe finde very greate inconveniencyes not onely to our selves but strangers by the generall neglect there is of high wayes in some places quite Stopt up in others changed much to the disadvantage and allmost all wanteing repayre by cleareing or the like.

5. Wee doe likewise finde that the giveing of gifts to the Indians by particular persons thereby to oblige them to traffique with them is a great wrong not onely to the neighbour but to the publique also by occasioneing the Indians to Sett the greater vallue upon their Comodityes seing such contention who shall have them.

Corn van dyck voorm

The Cort Recomend the above Agreviances to his honor the Governors Consideracon *p* Cur: John Tuder D. Cl: [1686]

To the Right Honorbl Coll Tho: Dongan Lieutenant & Govr Generall under his Majty of N yorke & its dependencyes The Humble Petition of the Magistrates of Albany in behalf of them selves & ye rest of the Inhabitants of his Majestys Burgh of Albany [*c. 1686*]

Sheweth

That the scituation of this his Majty Town being on a barren soile and Confined to verry narou limitts the [(*torn*)] Collony[1] haveing Apropriatd all the adjacent Land to the town that is fitt for

The two men then told the Mohawk council of their plan for a Peace Confederation and the building of a Longhouse of brotherhood. The Mohawk speaker replied that his people would firmly grasp the Tree of Peace.

Improvemt & endeavor also to obstruct us in our trade So that The Inhabitants who have been at vast Charg & Exspence in Erecting & building this his Majtys towne, have no other way left for ther maintanance and Support of themselves & familyes but the Indian Trade wch of late years has very much decayed, to the great diminution of his Majtys revenue and detriment of yr Honors petitioners, and Cheifly by the Incroachmt the French have made both upon our Trade wth the Indians and the Confines of ys his Majtys province, under pretence of propogateing the Christian faith amongst ye Indians they debauch them away to Canada.[2] The Effectuall Cure that yr Honer hath allready taken Since yr Arryvale here for the removeing of those Evills doth Encourage us to adress in this Method, and presume to represent unto yor Honor, that ther Can be nothing more Conducive to his Mejtys Interest, and the wellfare of this his Majty Town, then that yor Honor would be Pleased to Grant and Confirm unto the Inhabitants of this his Majty town yr antient right & priviledge that non shall trade wth the Indians upon any pretense wtever but at ys town,[3] and also that yor Honor would be pleased to Interceed wth his Majty to send over some preists that might endeavor to propogat the Christian faith amongst the Indians, and regaine those Indians that are removed already to the french, and also that the french may be hindered from Comeing and Tradeing within his Majtys dominion on this Side of the Lakes all wch things will very much tend to the Increase of his Majtys Revenue and the Encouradgemt of Trade, and yr Petitioner Shall ever pray.

[1] The Manor of Rensselaerswyck.

[2] The desire of the people of Albany to replace the French Jesuits with English priests was the subject matter of another petition. O'Callaghan, 3: 418-419.

[3] This monopoly of the fur trade was granted by Governor Dongan in the Albany Charter of 1686. *N. Y. Col. Laws,* 1: 211.

Propositions made to ye Maquese, oneydes, onnondages, Cayouges & Sinnekes Sachims. by the Right honble. Col. Th Dongan, govr. genl. undr his majt: in ye Court house of albany ye 20th. of may 1686

Brethren

I had a great desyre to see you, & Am therefore come this Voyage to meet wt. you that wee may Continue the frindship between us, and to Redresse Some Inconveniences that may happen to our Brethren, wh. might be a kindenesse to us. I have yt. kindenesse for ye Brethren, that I slipp no opportunity to Testify ye Same, for I have Intelligence from al parts of ye world, & if ye Brethren wil be advised by me, They will finde att ye letter yt I am & will be ther Best frind. I am Sorry yt ye Brethren does not see, that yr number doth diminish & yt. wee are ye People that att Lenth must mentain yr wives and Children, and now & Then Protect ym. against all sorts of People yt will offer to disturb them as you have found by Experience, by ye last Trouble yt. ye. Sinnekes had wt. ye french when ye great Sachim of Engl: arms who is now king was Putt upon your Castles ye french would nott offer to goe any further in disturbing you & upon my Complaint to ye gr king of Engl: of ye Govr. of Canida's disturbing you, he was forthwith displeased. I hear there are a great mãy English dutch & french goes a hunting and Tradeing wt ye farr nations of Indians, without a Seale from me, I would not graunt itt; itt being a Prejudice to ye Brethren; They findeing once ye way to hunt & Trade as ye Brethren doe, will Contribute much to yr Losse

I hear Some french marry wt. yr. Squaes, if they doe I desyre you to take yt Care yt they goe not to Canida but that they shall live Close by your Castles or in yr Castles.

And I charge you neither to make warr nor Peace wt. any Christians without my approbacon; & yt you will Suffer no frenchman, nor oyr Christians to live or Build fort or house at onyaggero or

Scouts were sent to the People of the Upright Stone to see what they thought of the plan for everlasting peace.

any oyr Place that might hinder ye Brethrens Progress in yr Bevr. hunting.

And yt ye Brethren shall not Trade or Traffique, or Enter Into any Covenant chain wt any Christians french or English as to matters of Trade or Traffique wtout my Consent & approbation, butt you are to Continue to bring yr. Trade here to this toune according tto ancient Custome where you are Sure to have bread for yr wifes & Children when you want itt,

You are not to Suffer any to Trade or hunt, butt Such as have 3 litle Red Seals to show, a Patren whereof you Shall Take along wt. yu.

That you lett ye way be open & free through yr Country, for our Indians to come back from hunting, for our Indians wanting yt free Passage Come home by ye way of Canida & yr drink & Play away yr Bevr. & so yr wifes & Children are Reduced to great wants & we loose our debts.

I have anoyr Proposeal to make to ye Breth: Wh. is yt. they shal use all ye french fathers, verry Civilly, & not to Suffer yr young men to abuse them, after yr Drinking of Rom.

Proposal made by Rode, Sachem of the Maquase, to the Governor General in the name of the Maquase, Oneida, Onondaga, Cayuga, and Seneca. In Albany, May 21, 1686.[1]

1° We nations have come on the Governor's request. But before we begin to make propositions, we advise you that the Senecas have made 70 of the Dionondadees prisoner, of which five are set free: two whose father has come to bring them back to Canada, and three who have been sent back to announce the news to the others. Give 2 beavers.

2° Say that they hope all is peace in Europe between our King and the other Christian Kings, of which they are very glad.

3° That the treaty chain between the Governor and us is very old and steady and is kept unbreakable. And as my Lord Howard, Governor of Virginia, is also taken into the treaty chain, so let his hand and arm be bound, and even if he wanted to loosen the same, let his Honor, our Governor, keep it secure. Give 2 beavers.

[1] Translated from the Dutch.

After the Governor had made his proposals, they answered in the afternoon through a spokesman thus:

1° Brother Corlaer,

We have come very cheerfully on your request. We have heard you speak which has gladdened our hearts. We must thank his Honor for his liberal gifts, especially that his Honor has publicly informed us that provisions and ammunition have been sent [by the French] to Cadarachqui. Now we see that our Governor, who takes care of us and who keeps our welfare so clearly in mind, means well for us. Now we cannot contain our joy, but will shout that our eyes have seen and our ears have heard a person who tries for the welfare of the whole country and for ours in particular. Say further that they now see clearly what the inclination of the Governor of Canada is like, and what his nature is, and on the other hand they see the inclination of his Honor, which is not strange when we consider that we are Corlaer's subjects, in whose land we live. We are one head, one body, and one heart. We like to hear this which was not said just for the sake of talk, but because it is true. Give two beavers.

2° We understand that if the French attempt to build forts on this side of the lake, we will have to try to stop them. We will do this, and throw to the ground any such forts they might try to build. As to his Honor's orders that we should not be the first ones to take up the hatchet against the French, we will obey and not molest the French unless they attack us. But if they attack us, then his Honor will have to help us, for if we suffer then his Honor will also suffer, for if the body suffers then the head is not free from danger, for if one member suffers the whole body is in pain. On the other hand, Corlaer is obliged to help us for the Governor of Canada speaks very despisingly about his Honor and says that his help would not stay with us. But we trust that when it comes to that point, we will see something different. Give 5 beavers.

3° We have also understood that all covenants and agreements made with Christians will have to be made here. We accept this and will follow it. Not only we sachems, but all our young Indians

The Oneidas, after considering the plan in council for one year, reported that they would join the confederation.

are agreed never to listen to any proposals of any Christians unless they are made in this house.

Concerning his Honor's desire to be kept informed of everything happening with us, we will at all times, occurrences, and occasions send a messenger to keep his Honor informed of all transactions even if it was but with a "walhetook." Give two beavers.

We have been warned to be watchful. We will not sleep, but will be quick as foxes, and as soon as any disasters occur we will send in all haste a messenger from the Seneca country to Cayuga, and from there to Onondage, and from there to Oneida, and so to the Maquase country where there is a horse, and then here. We are very fast messengers, and even though we do not have any horses, we can walk so much better.

Proposal made by Oheda, an Oneida, for the Cayugas and them.

1° We have understood the proposals made by his Honor to us but addressed mainly to the Senecas who are the nation most distant, and repeated the whole proposal made by his Honor and agreed to follow the same. Give 2 beavers.

2° The Senecas have said that they will watch out carefully for all disasters, but we trust that we will also have young Indians who will not sleep, but who will use all their abilities by night as well as by day to discover everything and to make it known. And say that his Honor may continue to do as he has done, and to let them know all good news like a candle that gives light everywhere. Give 5 beavers and 1 belt wampum.

Proposal made by Rhode for the Maquase

We have heard his Honor's proposals with great attention, and we will also follow it in all obedience as we have been ordered. And our people will not fail to be on their watch and to give advice as soon as the situation warrants it. Give 9 beaver and 2 belts of wampum.

The Senecas and Onondages have given his Honor this belt to keep a light like a candle and to keep them informed. We give a belt to announce to his Honor that we have a horse in our country with which we will soon inform his Honor of everything.[1]

[1] On the next day Dongan wrote to the Governor of Canada that "our Indyans are aprehensive of warr." O'Callaghan, 3: 455.

Proposal of the 3 Maquase Sachems [*July 1686*][1]

The Governor has proposed to us that in case something begins to happen with the French we will let you know here and in the meantime we would keep quiet in order not to take up the hatchet before we are forced to do so. The Governor let us know also that in case the French intended to settle at our place or make fortifications, we should not agree and should prevent them from doing so. The sachems of all nations have been assembled to discuss this and ask that the Governor will keep his word and will come here as we urgently want to speak to him. We give hereon one belt wampum in the name of all five nations to ask the Governor to please come here, and we will then, when the Governor arrives, tell him what we wish to say.

Answer:

We would like to know what you have to tell the Governor. Then we will let him know it at the first opportunity, and he will then come himself or else will send someone else with what he wants said and done. In the meantime you can be sure that the Governor will do as he promised.

Return answer:

All the nations for seven days have been assembled in Onondage and have kept council. And the priest asks us what we kept council about, which we did not want to tell at first. But he promised to tell us something also. Thus we said that the Governor had ordered us to keep quiet and not to take up the hatchet. Then he told us that when the corn would be nearly ripe the French would come to kill us. The French intend also to send for you and if you go there you will be dead people.

[*note on side*]

We would also like to know if and when there is any danger as we do not know whether we will be dead or alive.

[1] Translated from the Dutch. The date is supplied from a parenthetical note made by Robert Livingston.

Two messengers were sent toward the setting sun. They carried wampum strings and an invitation to join the confederation. Arrived in the country of the People of the Muckland (also called the Great Pipe People), they built a fire and recited their message.

Present: *Maj. Baxter* *P. Schuyler, Mayor* *D. Wessels* *J. Bleeker*	*Albany, August 5, 1686* *Report by Onnachragewaes, alias Jannetje, a Maquase, of his message he has given to the Christian Indians in Canada.*[1]

Says:

That he has been sent by the Maquase sachems to the Christian Indians in Canada with 3 belts of wampum and has made known to them the conversation our Governor has had with those sachems concerning the country of Sarachtoge that for three years has been sold to the Christians. That the Governor, as an encouragement to the Christian Indians who were in Canada to make their homes here, wanted to give them as much land as they needed in Sarachtoge and would also have a priest there to instruct them in religion. And therefore it was the wish of the Governor as well as of the sachems that they should return again to their country and should take Sarachtoge as their residence.

To which the Christian Indians in Canada replied that they would be very willing to come to live at Sarachtoge and that the Governor of Canada says also that he does not want to prevent their coming here, but says first he wants to see a letter from Corlaer and then will let them go freely. Therefore those Christian Indians are very anxious that Corlaer will please write a letter to the Governor of Canada so they can be fully assured of his ready inclination to let them come here in this government.

Present: *D. Meyer* *Dirck Wessels* *Adrian [ ]* *Daniel Schrae*	*Proposal made by the Skachkook Indians August 7, 1686*[2]

Brethren, we are very sad, for some time ago we came to Skachkook as designated by Corlaer and have lit our fires there. And it was not yet burning before our greatest sachem died. Thus we as well as you have reason to be sad. But we have now chosen three others in his stead, and thus we send you Anachenne and Katoessaeck and Sehertarie, and are now ready to go to the Maquase's country and there to light our fires and do it so that it may grow into a big fire so that you and they, meaning the Maquase, may

[1] Translated from the Dutch.
[2] Translated from the Dutch. Brackets indicate unintelligible name.

PETER SCHUYLER (1657-1724), FIRST MAYOR OF ALBANY.
Courtesy J. A. Glenn, Albany, N. Y.

be able to and will freely smoke tobacco there. Do give a belt of wampum 12 deep.

KNOW ALL MEN by these *p*sents yt wee abraham Provoost & Elias Provoost are held and firmly bounde unto the Mayor Aldermen and Commonality of ye City of albany in ye Somme of fifty Pounds Courant money of this Province to be paid unto ye Said Mayor aldermen and Commonalty of ye City of albany and there Successors, to ye wh. Payment well & truly to be made, wee oblige ourSelfs and Each of us our and each of our heirs, Executors and administrators, for ye whole & in ye whole firmly by these Presents, Sealed wt. our Sealls, dated ye tenth day of Septembr. anno Dom 1686 annoq Regn. Regs Jaci: Secdi: angl &a Secdo. WHEREAS the abovebound abraham Provoost & Elias Provoost by and with the Consent of ye Sd Mayor, aldermen and Commonality of ye City of albany have obtained his Excell: ye Governors Passe to trade travell & hunt amongst ye Indians, of waganasse & ottowawasse under ye Command of Capt. Johannes Rooseboom,[1] as in and by ye Said Lycence, beareing date ye 21st day of august Last Past, Relacon thereunto being had, may more fully & att Large appear, NOW THE CONDICON OF THIS OBLIGATION is Such, that if ye abovebound abraham Provoost & Elias Provoost doe not Trade or Traffique, wt any of ye five Nations of Indians Commonly called, the Maquase, oneydes, onnondages, Cayouges, and Sinnekes for any Bevers or Peltry or any oyr. Indian Commodities (Provisions only Excepted) then this Present obligation to be void Else to be and Remain in full force and Virtue[2]
Sealed and Deliverd
in ye Presence of

Richd. Pretty	/s/ Abraham Provoost [seal]
Robt. Livingston Cl.	/s/ Eliase Provoost [seal]

ATT a Council held att ffortt James in New Yorke Sept. ye 30: 1686

PRESENT

His Excellency &c.

ORDERED that Johannes Roseboom, and those in his Company

[1] This relates to the Roseboom expedition to divert the trade of the western Indians from Canada to Albany. See the order-in-council which follows.

[2] Identical indentures were executed by: Johannes Dyckman and Jacob Bosboom; Cornelis Slingerlant and Hendrick Gerritse; Frans Winne and

Who have had Lycence to travell & trade Amongst the Indians, Do stay and Remaine in the Sineques Country, or in Some Convenient place near unto itt, untill those of Esopus and Albany, who have had passes from his Excellency the Governor: be joyned to them, and that they all use their Uttmost Endeavour to Perswade as Many of the five Nations of the Indians and the River Indians, as Possibly they Can to go in Company with them And if it Shall so happen that Any of them Proceed further on their Journey and Voyage then into the Sineques Country they are hereby Ordered to leave in Writeing Certaine Advice to What Place they are gon and also Abide there untill the Rest Come and be joyned to them, And Every Person Concerned is hereby Ordered to show all Civility and kind usage to the Indians att Ottowaas, and to use the best Ways and Methods to Influence them to trade and Correspond with the Inhabitants of the Citty of Albany; and (wch. may bee Very Acceptable and Obligeing) to Convey Safely to the Ottowaas, all Such of their Country as have been made Prisoners by the Sinequas Indians; And to the End that good Discipline May bee Observed, and all Disorders Prevented, the Severall Persons Concerned in the Aforesaid journey and voyage to the Ottawaas are hereby ordered to Make an alliance to Defend one another in case of Opposition, and Chuse fitt and Discreet Persons to be their Officers and one Commandr. in Cheife to whom all Others Are hereby Strictly required to yeild all due obedience, as they Will Answer the Contrary at their perills; And that they Continually keep A Strict Watch as Well by day as by Night and Proceed on their Intended Journy And Voyage Nothwithstanding Any Rumor that May happen, of Disturbance from the ffrench; and they are not in Any wise to meddle wth. or Disturb Any ffrench Indians or Any others Whatsoever Except Such as be Traders from Pensilvania, East and West Jerseys, whom they Are hereby Empowred to Apprehend and bring to his Maties City of New Yorke.

Hendrick Hanse; Dirk Alberte Bradt and Matthys Nack; Johannes Claese and Cornelis Jacobse. These are all found in the Livingston Indian Papers.

The Cayugas, after considering the plan for a year, sent back word to the Mohawk council that they would hold fast to the Tree of Peace.

And it is further ordered that Johannes Rooseboom Immediatly After the receipt of these Orders, Cause them to be read to all those who go I'n his Company and that he Send by the first Opportunity fouer Indians in a Canoe to the Ottowaas to give them Notice of their Comeing.

By order in Council
J. Spragge Secr.

Names of the Wawyachtenokse sachems:
Wanamanheet
Pinawee
Pachkanass

Memorandum of what the Wawyachtenokse Indians have said to Robert Livingston, Proprietor of Tachkanik, in the presence of Johannes Wendel and Hendrick Cuyler, Aldermen, in Albany, the 24th of January 1686/7. The speaker was Peter d Wilt accompanied by the Indians of Tachkanik, Roeloff Jansens Kill, Kinderhook, and other River Indians.[1]

1° First, as an introduction, said that they were brethren with the Indians of Tachkanik, Roeloff Jansens Kill, and other River Indians. Give 1 deer skin.

2° Say that if the Indians of Wawyachtenock would come to plant on Tachkanik, the other Indians who live further down will be afraid and could be easily destroyed for they have a very small heart. Give 4 deer skins.

3° Say that they are definitely decided to stay on Wawyachtenok as the other Indians who live further down among the English with whom they are related would be afraid. Give 3 deer skins.

4° Would like to be considered as brethren and to be in a covenant since Tachkanik lays near to them. Give 4 deer skins, and 2 wildcats, and 1 fox.

Translated by Dirck Wessels, Recorder

Answer on the foregoing by Robert Livingston

I understood that some of the Indians of Wawyachtenok would like to come and plant on Tachkanik and to come under this government. Therefore I have made that known to his Excellency who said that the path is open for all good Indians to come here in this government where they will be welcome and well treated if they behave themselves well. As you are decided to stay on Wawyachtenok, that is all right, but if you would like to come and live at Tachkanik or anywhere else in this government, you

[1] Translated from the Dutch.

will be given a tract. Has been returned: 1 half barrel of beer, 1 small barrel of rum, and 1 roll tobacco.

Proposals made by the Maquase sachems to the Magistrates of Albany, the 18th of February 1686/7[1]

Present:
D. Wessells
Levinus Van Schaick
Hendrick Cuyler
Adr. Gerritse

Translated by Arnout Cornelise

Brethren:

We come here to speak with the brethren on behalf of all the tribes of the Maquase, and to clean Corlaer's house that we may freely come to speak of important matters. Give one belt of wampum of 10 high.

2° We are sad when Arnout was sent with some messages to the Indians to the West that he passed by the first and second castles and talks with the sachems at Tionondoge. Do not pass by our door, for we are one people. Give one belt 12 high: thus they count them all so high.

3° We make known that the Governor of Canada and eight or nine sachems of the Dionondadees have asked us through a proposal of the Jesuit who lives at Onondage that we should come to Cadarachqui in the spring when the bark is being peeled from the trees to talk with him and the sachems of the Dionondadees. But the Maquase and the Senecas have rejected this and do not want to go, but the Oneidas, Onondages, and Cayugas have promised to go there, and we come to make our resolution known to the brethren. Give one belt wampum 10 high.

4° Pray that they may not be exiled but can be given hospitality by their friends when they come to make proposals, and to sleep over at those Indians' places.

Answer to the Maquase

We are glad to see the brethren here in Corlaer's house where you know that you can come freely to make any important matters

[1] Translated from the Dutch.

A runner was sent to the People of the Great Mountain, who lived far toward the setting sun. The Senecas were divided in opinion. One large band living west of the Genesee River were friends of the Erie, who were against the League. The band who lived near the Great Mountain, near Canandaigua Lake, were for the League.

known. You will always be welcome. As we see that the brethren are jealous because our messenger goes to the third castle, we never have differentiated between the three families of Maquases, but if it pleases the brethren most, we will come to the first castle of theirs since that is so much the nearer and makes no difference to us. Concerning what you say that the French have ordered you and the other four nations to Cadarachqui, you know well that the Governor General has advised you not to listen to the Governor of Canada when he orders you to come unless you are his subjects and have taken back your land from the great King of England. You and the Senecas have obeyed and, in contrast, in case they listen to the Governor of Canada without Corlaer's permission, the other three nations are very unwise. Therefore you will do well to remind them of their duty that they should not do this. In the meantime we will make your proposal known to the Governor, and when the sachems come here in the wintertime to make their proposals, they will be permitted over at their friends', in the homes of Christians, if they only let them know in time. Give 25 guilders zewant and 1 small barrel of rum

KNOW ALL MEN by these *p*sents yt. wee John harris are held and firmly bounde unto ye Mayor aldermen and Commonality of ye Citty off Albany, in ye Somme of fifty Pounds Courant money of this Province, to be paid unto ye Said Mayor aldermen & Commonality of ye Citty of albany and there Successors, to ye wh Payment, well and truly to be made, wee oblige our Selfs, and each of us, our and Each of our heirs Executors and Administrators, for ye whole and in ye whole firmly by these *p*sents Sealed wth. our Sealls dated ye first day of april anno dom: 1687 Annoq Regn: Regs Jacobi Secdi. Angl. &a

WHEREAS ye abovebound John harris by and with Consent of ye sd Mayor, aldermen and Commonality of ye Citty of albany have obtained his Excel: ye gov: Passe to Trade, Travell and hunt, amongst ye Indians of ottowawa, as by ye Sd Lycence of Capt. Jacob Lokermans beareing date ye 21 day of Sepr. 1686 doth appear who are all to be under ye Command and Conduct of Majr Patrik Magregory,[1] there unto Authorized and Impoured by his

[1] Patrick Magregory came from Scotland to Maryland in 1684. Becoming interested in the fur trade, he moved to New York, and was placed in com-

Excel: Thomas Dongan Capt genl. & governour in Cheeffe, as ꝑ his Commission beareing date ye 4 day of decr. 1686 may more fully and att large Appeare, now ye Condition of ye obligation is Such yt if ye abovebound John harris doe not Trade or Traffique wth any of ye five nations of Indians Commonly Called ye Maquase, oneydes, onnondages, Cayouges, and Sinnekes, for any Bevers, Peltry or any oyr Indian Commodities, Provisions only Excepted Then this ꝑsent obligation to be Void, Else to be and Remain in full force and Vertue

his
John *H* harris [seal][1]
mark

Sealed & deliverd
in ye ꝑsence of
/s/ Albert Rykman
/s/ L. V. Schayk

alby 25 apl 1687
Gov: Dongans Propos: by Akis to the oneydes onnindages & Cayouges.

To ye. oneydes onnondages & Cayouges

Brethern

I have had propositions from the Maquase and Sinicas att my house att Albany but have heard nothing from you—I am Sorry the Brethren Should Stand So much in their owne Light.

I heare that Contrary to their promise the Brethren intend to goe and Speak with the Governor. of Canida att Cadaracqui.

I hope it is not true, if it bee you doe ill, wee have given you bread when you wanted it—besides you have putt your selves and yor Land under the great King of England who is able to defend

mand of this expedition in 1686. He was captured by the French, taken to Montreal, and freed in 1687. During the Leisler Rebellion in New York he met his death in March, 1691. O'Callaghan, 3: 395fn. His commission as commander of this party is given, *ibid.*, 9: 318.

[1] Identical indentures were entered into by Patrick Magregory, Abraham Schuyler, and Dirk van der Heyden; Arnout Cornelise Viele and Cornelius Vanderhoeve; Jacob Lokermans, Anthony Brat, and Johannes Brat; Cornelis Gysbertse, Harpert Jacobse, and Gerrit Viele; Cornelis Claese and Andries Carstense; Peter Coeymans and Frederick Claes; Bent Robertson and Hendrik Willems; Solomon Frederikse and Johannes Onderdonk; Jurian Van Hoosen, Willem Hollie, and Symon Schermerhoorn. These are all found in the Livingston Indian Papers.

Messengers invited both bands to join the Confederacy. Both councils listened. After a year they sent messengers to the Mohawk council to say that they would grasp the Tree of Peace.

you from all Enimies—I Should be Sorry you Should make him angry whith the Bretheren for their breaking their promise.
He is Sending you Priests—I desire the Bretheren would not goe to heare the govr. of Canida you. need not fear him. hee will not meddle with any of the Bretheren that live within the great King of Englands Territoryes—hee will protect you in peace where you may Eate Sleepe and hunt in Safety.
I heare the Bretheren are about to joyne with the Maquase and Sinicas against the Twichtwicks—I wish the Bretheren were alikewise in other things—therefore I send the Bretheren a present of powder and Lead—Lett mee desire of you to bee advised by the Maquase and Sinicaes—
I am Sorry that Some of the Bretheren Contrary to their Condicon have been in virginia lett itt bee so no more Lest Such Inconveniencyes happen as may not bee easily Remedyed.
I take it Verry ill that those Indians that ye Brethren hes given leave to live upon ye Skuylkill and ye Susquehanne should Bring Bever and Peltry to Philadelphia, which is Contrary to ye aggreement the Brethren has made with us, I Desyre of ye Brethren not to Suffer any Indians to live there Longer but on Condition not To trade any where but at albany.
And also that ye Brethren would take Such french and English they Shal fynde goeing up those Rivers without my Lycence, or Pass, and bring them tyed to albany, and there Deliver ym. to ye Magistrates for wh. ye Brethren shall have all ye goods they fynde belonging to Such Persones to themselfs. I am likewise Informed that those that live there are about to Sell ye Land I' hope ye Brethren will not Suffer that, being already given by the Brethren to ys. government.

alby 25 apl 1687
gov: Dongans Propos: by akus to ye Maquase & Sinnekes

To ye Maquase and Sinnekes
Brethren I have Seen the Propositions you have made in my house att Albany and am glad the Brethren have overcome their Enimyes.
and I hope they will also prosper in all their undertakeings—I am sorry the Brethren are goeing to warr for fear Some of the Best of our Brethren Should bee lost.

Peace hunting eateing and Drinkeing well being to bee preferred before warr.
but since the Brethren must goe to Revenge themselves upon the farr Indians that kill Som: of the Brethren in their hunting I have sent the Senicas a barrell of powder and some Lead—and halfe a barrell to the Maquase and Lead also.
Brethren it is a great trouble to mee that the onendages Cajugaes and Oneides contrary to their promise will goe to Cadarachqui to the Govr. of Canida. Lett the Brethren advise them not to goe—
I take it very ill that those Indians that the Bretheren has given leave to live upon the Schoolkill and the Susquehanna Should bring Bever and peltry to Philadelphia which is Contrary to the agreement the Brethren has made with us. I desire of the Bretheren not to suffer any Indians to live there longer but on Condition not to trade any where but att Albany.
And also that the Bretheren would take Such French and English they shall finde going up those Rivers without my Lycence or pass and bring them tyed to Albany, and there deliver them to the Magistrates—for which the Bretheren shall have all the goods they finde belonging to Such persons to themselves.
I am likewise Informed that those that live there are about to sell the Land I hope the Bretheren will not suffer that being already given by the Brethren to this governmt.
[(*in another handwriting*)] I am Sorry that some of ye Brethren of the Maquase Contrary to ye Condition, have been in Virginia, lett it be so no more lest Such Inconveniences happen as may not be easily Remedyed.

Answer of ye Maquase & ye Rest of ye Indians westward to the Propositions of his Excell: Thomas Dongan Capt. genl. & govr. in Cheiff & Vice admirall of n: Yorke and ye Territories Depending thereon, Proposed to them in there Castles by Akus Cornelise who went from albany thither on ye. 25th. day of april & arrived here again ye 23th day of mey 1687.

The Maquase answer as follows.

Wee are Rejoyced to see ye Messenger of our Broy Corlaer here

Before this time the Onondaga nation had been approached. The people wanted to join the Confederacy, but they hesitated to say so openly because they feared Adodarho. When, however, Deganawidah's messenger approached them they agreed to grasp the Tree of Peace.

in our Castles, wee thank Corlaer for his good Councills, and shall Endevor to follow ye Same, Butt wee are Engaged wth. ye Sinnekes to warr wth. our Enemies ye Twick Twicks, which wee intend to Pursue wth. all vigor, & to molest no oyr Enemies, but ye Sd. Twicktwichs utterly to Destroy, by which means all Inconveniencies that might happen to be done in Virginia will be Remedyed, Since our Passage thither is now quite anoyr. Course. Wee thank Corlaer for his Present of Pouder & lead, which wee will not fetch wth. out due Respect & thankfull acknowlegements to ye Donor.

As for ye govr. of Canidas Propositions who hath sent for us all to Cadarachqui, wee have Sent an Expresse to all ye Castells westwaerdts to tell them not to goe by any means to Cadarachqui, but on ye Contrare if they had any thing to Say or to Consult, that they should come to Corlaer house in albany instead of hearkning to ye govr of Canida and to goe to Cadarachqui.

Wee have no People liveing att ye Skuylkill or Susquehanne, neither will we admitt of any of our folks goeing to live there, for it is Transported to Corlaer; we have help to winn itt, & if any will sell yt Land itt shal be void & of no Effect, itt being already Conveyed to this Government, and if we finde any french or oyr goeing up those Rivers to trade without Corlaers Pass, We shall bring them tyed to albany, & deliver them to ye Magistrates.

The Oneydes answer

That Corlaer will not take itt ill, that they have not been att his house att albany, they being from home when ye Sinnekes came by; wee thank Corlaer for his Present of Pouder and Lead, & when wee come to albany to fetch ye Same shall shew our Thankfulness

Concerning our Journey to Cadarachqui, wee were intended to goe there to Speak to ye Indians off ottowawa of Peace, But we will hearken to Corlaer's Councill & wholly hearken to ye maquasse our Brethren, & doe what they shall think fitt.

There is a generall meeting of ye Sachims of ye five Nations att a Place called Caninda near to onnondage about ye beginning of June, there we will meet & doe nothing without ye Maquase Vote.

Wee are glad yt. ye govr. will Send us Priests, since wee have been Long without a father.

Wee are unanimously ReSolved to make warr upon ye Twich-

twichs, & shall no more goe yt way towards Virginy, but only Pursue our Enemyes the Twichtwichs, & hope yt this shall be ye Last time yt ever any mischeeff shall be done in Virginia.
As for ye Land of Susquehanne wee have no People yt live there, & none is ye owner of ye same butt Corlaer being given for ye Behooffe of this government, & if wee see any People yt comes upon those Rivers without Corlaers Pass, wee shall bring them to albany according to ye. govrs. order.

The onnondages answer.

Broyr Corlaer
Wee have understood your Propositions made to us by akus, & are sorry that ye Sinnekes went So Silent by our Castles when we were abroad, by which means we were frustrate of yt good opportunity to come to Corlaers house, But when ye Sinnekes come doune wee goe long wth. them to fetch our Powder and Lead which Corlaer hath given us, for which wee shall be thankfull.
As for our Intended voyage to Cadarachqui, to Speak to ye govr. of Canida and the Sachims of ottowawa, wee can give no Positive answer before our general meeting of all the Nations be over which will be about ye beginning of June next EnSueing within four Dutch miles of our Castles, when we shall Discourse about itt.
Wee doubt not but ye great king of England is Powerfull Eneugh to Protect us, that we may Live in Peace, & wee doe Beleive yt. our king & ye french king know onanother Verry well for they are both of one Skinn meaning they are both white Skinnd, & not brown as they Indians are; wee would Rather live in Peace, butt itt Seems our Indian Enemies doe grutch our Breth: ye Sinnekes liveing in Peace, & we being united wth them are unanimously ReSolved to Ruine the Twichtwichs if it be Possible.
Wee Confirm that which we have done about ye Susquehanne, & shall never Tollerate any thing to be done against itt, wee have no People liveing there, & if any English or french come upon

At the Great Council of the Mohawks, when all the people were present, Deganawidah and Hiawatha reported that five nations, the Mohawk, Oneida, Onondaga, Cayuga, and Seneca, had agreed to bury their differences and establish a great peace league which was eventually to take in all the tribes and do away with war.

those Coasts without a Pass, wee shall bring them to albany according to Corlaer's order.
Wee shall Be glad to see a Priest here of our Broyr Corlaer

The Cayouges answer

Brother Corlaer
Wee thank you for your good Inclination & Council & for your Present of Powder & lead; we shall come Speedily to Corlaers house at albany and Speake of all matters.
Wee must acknowlege wee were Resolved to goe to Cadarachqui, to Speak wth ye Sachims of ottowawa about Treaty of Peace, ye Rather because we hear that they of ottowawa are intended to Deliver up some oneyde Prisoners; Butt wee Stand not to yt Resolution, but Submitt ourSelfs wholly to ye Issue of a Certain general meeting of all ye 5 nations which shall be held 4 D. mile from onnondage att a Place called Caninda about ye first of June 1687, & what will be Concluded there wee know not only this yt ye onnondages & wee have Solely given over our Votes to ye Sinnekes to doe therein as they Shall see meet, & ye oneydes have given over yr Votes to ye Maquase.
The Land of Susquehanne wee have wonn by ye Sword and as owners of ye Same wee have Transported itt to this government, & that which we have done therein is Irrevocable, & if any Person Should have any Design to buy that land, wee deSyre yt Corlaer may write to them, yt they have no such Thoughts Since itt is annexed to this government under ye great king of England whose Subjects we are, and those few yt dwell there to witt 10 or 12 white minke antient Inhabitants of Susquehanne butt belonging to our Castle whom we have in former times Conquered, amongst whom is one born Cayouger, shall use our Endevor to Send for them home to live in our Castle, & if we finde any Persones upon ye sd. River to hunt or Trade without Corlaers Pass, wee shall bring them to albany according to Corlaers order.
The Cayouges Said further yt ye ottowawas Indians had deSyred ye govr. of Canida to be a mediator between them and ye Sinnekes, & yt he would see to gett ye Indians together to Cadarachqui. Wee are Verry glad yt Corlaer will Send us a Priest whom we shall Treat Civilly, & shall have his Choyes to live where he Pleases; wee must acknowlege yt Corlaer shows himSelf like a Broyr in every Respect, Especially since he gives us Powder &

lead to fight our Enemyes, nu wee look upon itt as iff he fought with us himself.

Concerning ye Sinnekes

Akus hath Spoke to one of ye Sachims in ye Castle of onnondage, and made ye Proposition of his Excel to him, who Replyed that hee would Communicate ye Same to his Brethren & yt akus might Rest Satisfyed, because he could not come to Sinnondowanne by Reason of ye high water, & ye Lakes yt. were So full, wh. akus did fynde So accordingly; for being gone 12 mile from Cayouge towards ye Sinnekes was necessitate to turn back to Cayouge by Reason of ye high water & great Rain.

This is a true Copy Transl:
p me
Robt: Livingston
Cl.

N: Yorke 16 June 1687

Sr

The Inclosed is come to me out of England. I am Resolvd to observe ye Least title of itt, & I doe not doubt but you will doe ye Same, I have been Informed yt you have Sent for ye Indians yt live on this Side of ye Lake to Speake wth ym. att Cadarachqui, which I could not beleeve till father LamberVille writt Soe to me from onnondage assureing me of ye Truth of itt; which I admire att verry much, they being the king of England's Subjects, & lett me assure you this is not ye way to keep a Right Understanding between us; for if you have any ill Design against any of ye five nations on this Side of ye Lake, ye verry same you must have against me; I hear also yt your Christian Indians of Canida come on this Side of ye Lake to Debauch our Indians away to Canida; I Shal desyre of yu. not to Suffer yt any more for if yu. doe & if I can cach any of them I will Punish them Verry Severely; I am Expecting dayly Priests from England to Putt amongst ye five nations, and as Long as yr Priest Stays att

Deganawidah then said they must find out where the fire of Adodarho burned, for it was he who caused most trouble between the nations of men. "We must seek him out and cure his wicked mind."

onnondage, lett him not Intermedle himself wth any thing but his function and as for ye further Indians it is as free for us to trade yr as is for yu. untill ye meets & bounds be made between our kings. Sr. I am

Your assured friend and humble Servant
T[homas] D[ongan][1]

To ye Governr. of
Canida

NB This Copy was not Sent to ye Indians

Proposal made by 3 Maquase sachems and 4 sachems of Oneida, June 17, 1687[2]

1° We come here for the powder and lead which the Governor has promised to us as we hear daily rumors from the Governor of Canada and it seems that the hatchet hangs above our heads like the sun. Otherwise we would have waited till the Senecas and the others would have come with us. But because of the evil rumors which are confirmed, we will now take advantage of the opportunity to take it along with us. Give 1 fathom wampum.

2° We also come to renew the covenant, and that the chain may be kept clean and may all in the chain join hands. This will be very pleasing to us. Give 1 fathom wampum.

3° We see that the heart of the Governor of Canada is evil, and thank his Honor for the gift of powder and lead. Give 1 belt wampum 16 high.

4° Last night we heard from one of our people coming from Canada further bad news from there. Our hearts have been so upset over that that we could not sleep last night. In the meantime we keep our eyes on the Governor in order to find out what we should do now. But if some one comes to molest us, we will defend ourselves. Give one belt 16 high.

By the Oneida

5° We have understood everything concerning the proposals made for the Governor by Ackes concerning the war of the Wagannaes and the Twightwees. We and the Maquase were not yet completely of one mind then, but now we are of one mind which we

[1] Corrected draft in Robert Livingston's writing. There is a more polished version which was sent by Dongan to the Governor of Canada in O'Callaghan, 3: 465.

[2] Translated from the Dutch.

declare now to you in your presence in the house of Corlaer. Further, we thank his Honor for the powder and lead which is all very fine, but what will we put it in? We cannot just throw it with our hands like a stone. Give 3 beavers.
6° Brother Corlaer, the Governor of Canada calls us children which we now know is not so. Therefore may the tree of peace remain planted here steady and straight and may it not grow sideways so that we can really trust it, and there will not be any evil found in this house. And as I spoke of the tree of peace growing in goodness, thus we ask also that the heart of the Governor may be good and honest, and that it may not be altered by the exchange of letters with the Governor of Canada, but that we will always be supplied with ammunition in case of war so that we can defend ourselves. Give 3 beavers.

Answer on the proposals of the sachems of the Oneidas and Maquase

Brethren, we have heard your proposals concerning the great fear you have of the French which keeps you from sleeping at night, and also that you have heard these bad rumors confirmed daily. We are astonished to see that the brethren are so small of heart and so upset by such running rumors for which we can find no basis. If the Governor of Canada attacks you, you are after all men and not children, you certainly should defend yourselves and keep on the alert. You renew the covenant with Corlaer and ask that the covenant chain be kept smooth and clean. That is very good. And as Corlaer up to this day has never failed to work for your benefit and to take care of you like a father, thus he will always assist you with his fatherly mercy as long as you will behave well and follow his orders which will always turn out to be best for you. We will forward your proposal at the first opportunity.

To the Oneidas:

We are very glad to hear that you and the Maquase are united, and you must try especially to be united in carrying out what he [Corlaer] commands which is always for your good as you have

Deganawidah asked for two scouts to seek out the smoke of Adodarho.

discovered now by experience. He is the one who now gives you so much powder and lead, and because you lack firelocks to put the powder in, Corlaer gives you now 6 firelocks, 3 for each nation. You can really see now that he is a good father and not a stepfather, that you can trust him and therefore be sure not to anger such a merciful father and then the tree of peace will grow straight. For all that the Governor writes to the Governor of Canada is for your good, and if the Governor had not done this the French Governor would have made war on the brethren a long time ago. Therefore be courageous and not weakhearted and you will not lack anything as long as you obey Corlaer. We will send your proposal to the Governor at the first opportunity.[1]

Present
D. Wessells
h: Cuyler
albt. Rykman
Liv: Van Shaik
Joh: wendel

Propositions made by the Cayouges Sachims to ye Magistrates of albany ye 27th. day of June 1687.

1. Wee hear dayly Bad Rumours which Disturbs our heart, Insomuch yt our heart quakes in our body, & there is litle union among our nations, are therefore come here in Corlaers house for

[1] This proposition was considered by the Governor and Council on June 24, 1687. *Cal. N. Y. Col. MSS.*, 2: 166. Two days later a proposition was prepared which was to be delivered to the Iroquois by Akus Cornelise. According to the Duane Report, 1780, it was included in the Livingston Indian Papers but is not found there now. Duane's abstract of that proposition is given here:

> June 26, 1687—Proposition to the Western Indians sent to them from His Excellency the governor general by Akus Cosaliso [*sic*] (Express)—
> Corlaer is informed that the french and Indians are assembled at Cataracqui to war against the Senecas and other nations—they must not be afraid but on their guard; and [(*blank*)] the things [(*blank*)] or their [(*blank*)] and by no means go to the governor of Canada but let him know they are the King of Englands Subjects who will protect them.
> 2. advises them how to Conduct themselves in case of an Attack, says he shall be in a Instant to assist them which he promises to do as soon as possible. That they send their Wives Children and old people to Albany where he promises to provide for them. That if the french should destroy their Corn they must not [(*blank*)] for he will assist them. That he does not Choose they should fight unless [(*blank*)] to great advantage &c. [(*blank*)] That the governor will give them all the assistance he can in case they should be attacked on this Side the Lakes and that withall possible speed &c &c—
> Corelunin—"with this [(*blank*)] four of the Kings [(*blank*)—Coat of Arms] in Case any of the Castles should be without them."

Councill what we shal doe in yt Case, doe give a faddom of wamp.
2. Wee are ashamed to come here in Corlaers house, being Informed that ye oneydes have Divulged that we Should have done ye misheiff Lately committed in Virginia, Butt wee are Innocent, for ye oneydes have done itt, doe give a Bevr.
3. Wee are threatned by ye govr. of Canida, & since yt. ye Land wh. wee Live in is Corlaers Land, & wee and all that live therein are ye king of Englands Subjects, therefore Recommend the whole Case to Corlaer, In whose Care & well mannagemt wee doe not in ye least doubt, doe give a Small Belt.
4. Wee Believe ye. govr. of Canida Endevors to Deceive us and Seing Corlaer & ye govr of Canida doe Exchange Diverse letters, Doe desyre yt Corlaer may Search into ye Bussinesse, yt we may not be cheated. doe give one Bevr.
5. If ye warr should goe on which wee doubt not in ye least, we desyre yt our wifes & Children who will be necessitate to make yr Escape may be Defended here, Recommending them to Corlaers Protexion, doe give a Bevr & a otter.
6. The govr. of Canida hath a Verry wicked Intent; & when he comes to fall upon us, we shal forthwith come here & acquaint Corlaer yr with; & Pray of his Excel: assistence. doe give 2 Bevr.
7. We are now att Present in warr wth ye farr nations, & therefore our Bever hunting unfree & dangerous, & when We be attaqued shall be necessitate to come & fetch Pouder, & if we have no Bevers, desyre wee may have itt for nothing, doe give 2 Bevr.
8. Wee are come according to ye govr. Proposalls made to us by akus in our Castles to fetch ye Pouder & lead, for which Return ye Govr our hearty thanks. doe give 2 faddom wampum.

The said Cayouge Sachims after they had done there Propositions were asked in ye Presence of that Sinneke Sachim yt was sent to fetch ye Pouder, whither any of yr People had been so Dissobedient to Corlaers Command & gone to Cadarachqui, ye Sd. Sachims Replyed no, yt none of there People were gone, but yt. yr. were 3 Sachims off onnondage called Carachkondie, annagogga,

---

Two men volunteered. The Head Man asked them if they had the cleverness of the animals and birds of the forest, for such they must have if they were to approach the terrible warrior without being caught. They said they would be as clever as herons and cranes.

& aquirachronge, & one Sachim of ye Sinnekes called Canerat, butt none of ye Cayouges, & ye Sd. Sinneke Sachim Received a Reprooff for telling Such Storyes, who made his Excuse yt ye Sd. 3 Cayouge Sachims went along wth him to onnondage wth an Intent to Proceed on ye Journey to Cadarachqui, Butt yn alterd yr Resolution & thought upon Corlaers Commands.
NB one of ye 7 Bevr was given to ye Interpreter ye oyr Six weighd 6½ lb which wth ye otter & wampum was Exchanged for Pouder & wampum & given back.

Answer to ye Cayouges Propositions in albany ye 28th day of June 1687.

1. Wee are Sorry to See ye Brethren Soe much Concerned about ye Evill Rumors of ye french, & ye more to hear yr is no unity amongst ye Brethren, wee doubt not but you will take Corlaers Councel to heart, & aggree unanimously to Obey his Commands, Since he aims att nothing more yn ye wellfare of ym that Putt themSelfs under his Protexion, as ye Brethren have done long agoe, & now again Repeated yt you are ye Subjects of ye greatt king of England; Therefore wee acquaint you of ye great Care yt Corlaer takes of you, Spareing no Trouble nor charge to Send akus again Expresse to all ye nations to lett them know not to be any wise afraid, butt to Stand always upon there guard which now is Recommended to ye Brethren, and that they putt up ye kings arms in yr Castles;
2. We must tell you yt we are glad to hear yt none of your People are gone to Cadarachqui, thogh we were Informed by this Sinneke Sachim yt they were, which wee writt to Corlaer & Probably hath Disturbd him to hear off so unexpected Dis-sobedience, & wee will hope, yt it also shal be found false yt any of ye onnondages or Sinnekes are gone there; & if ye govr of Canida should Send for you, Corlaer Commands you that you lett him know, yt you are ye king off Englands Subjects, who will Protect you.
3. And if it should happen yt ye french fall upon you, you must not Stay in your Castles, nor keep in great bodyes together, so to Receive great hurt till Corlaer be in a Condition to help you, which Shall be assoon as Possible, & Since you are troubled about yr wifes & Children, Send yr wifes Children & old men hier to albany, where Corlaer will Provide for ym., and as for yr Corn,

if ye french should Burne it or Cutt itt doune, be not Troubled, ye governr will Supply you, for he is So much Inclined for ye Brethrens wellfare yt. he will nott yt you should fight but upon great advantages, till Such time yt Corlaer comes up in Person to Speake with you and all ye Nations, which will be in 20 days time. In Short wee assure you in ye name of Corlaer, yt he will give you all ye assistence he can in case you are attaqued on ys Side of ye lake & yt. assoon as Possible; In ye mean time have a Care of YourSelves & lett some of your Sachims come here att ye time appointed to Speake wth. Corlaer, who hath always a wakeing Eye, & a Ready Penn to make Enquiry of all occurrences. for to day this messenger antho. Lespinard goes expresse wth. a Letter from Corlaer to ye Govr. of Canida, to make narrow Enquiry of all things, whom you must Lett Pass frely, he haveing a Red handcershiff upon his Canoe.

4. Corlaer will be glad to hear yt. ye Brethren have no hand in ye Evill done in Virginia, & Since ye. axes are buryed in his house ye Brethren must have a Care not to doe any mischeeffe there, yt. such Inconveniency doe nott happen that not EaSily might be Remedyed. Wee shal send doune yr. Propositions to ye govr genl. wth. ye first.

Was given them 4 Baggs Pouder
f. 60 gild: white wampm.

Albanye 29 of June 1687
After ye. answer was given to ye Souldiers or young men of onnondage, There cheeffe Capt. called Cannadakte, who hath been at Cadarachqui 20 days agoe, was asked what he had seen there, & how affairs Stood who gave this following Relation.

First yt he see a great many men busy amakeing ye walls of ye fort wth Stone, which is about 3 times as bigg as this fort in albany, & yt there was about 80 Paces of ye wall to be made before it was Compleat,

2. He being in ye fort See great Preparations made for Provision yr being Eight ovens which dayly was four Times heated & yt

After looking them over, the Head Man said that would not do, because the heron and crane would stop at the first river or lake to hunt for frogs and fish.

he see a horse mill within ye fort; & while he was there yr came 20 Canoes from Canida loaded wth. Provisions; & So dayly Continue.

3. That he See a Room full of Indian Shoos & great Store off ammunition of Pouder Lead & gunns.

4. That he see about a hundred men in ye fort, but no Indians belonging to ye french, butt māy troops Expected.

5. Ye Sd. Indian Capt. seeing all these Preparations for war askd ye Jesuit wh. formerly lived at oneyde & yn at Cadarachqui what ye meaneing of all this was. Ye father answerd yt ye govr. of Canida was Intended to goe to onjagaro 40 D: miles from ye Sinnekes by ye way all Cadarachqui & there Speake wth. ye. Indians of Dowaganha & oyr nations (& he beleeves yt yt ye govr. of Canida is there this day) who will Speake wth. ye Indians in ye Presence of a greatt many of his Souldiers, whereupon ye. Sd. Indiann Replyed yt that was not ye way to Speake to ye Indians in ye Presence of so many Souldiers. there must be anoyr Design, Said farther yt he see 3 Sloops Such as are here upon ye Road & 10 Boats about 18 foot long as he demonstrated, & were bussy about makeing of more.

And ye govr of Canida Says he is like ye Divel never quiet then in yt Place & then In anoyr.; & yt what he now Relates is ye truth & may be noted doune he haveing Seen it himself.

Albv. 29 Juny 1687

Account of Presents given by ye Onnondages which were weighd in ye Court house 23 whole Bevr. weig 26 lb.

15 halfs			10 lb.
Besides 3 otters			
Given them Back again 10 Baggs Pouder is	9 lb.	19¼	
100 lb. Lead	3		
80 loaves	1 ¼		
60 gild in Strung wampum	4		
a hogg	2		
Rest lb.		6 ¾	10 lb.

To
His Excellency Francis Lord Howard
His Majties: Leiut. and Governor Genll: of
Virga: [at Albany (?)]

July 2d: 1687

May it please yor: Excellency
On Fryday the 24th: of June came to my house George Smith the Interpretr and brought with him a Chickahominy Indian, who was aboute three yeares Since, carried away by the Seneca's, and now made his Escape from them, upon Examination he declared, that at the head of James River, was aboute three hundred Seneca's, and that they had taken a Resolution, to destroy all our Neighbouring Indyans, and had under debate, whether it were not Convenient, for them first to destroy all the out plantacons of the English, to facilitate theire destroying the Indyans, and had carried theire Women and Children, on the other side the Mountaynes and Intended to build a ffort on the head of James River.
My Lord upon this News, I Imediatly wrott to the Severall Comandrs, on the ffronteers, to give them Notice of the Intelligence, and Ordered them to give Notice to all the Inhabitants, to be Vigilant & Stand upon theire Guards.
On the 27th. June I reced an Express from Collo: Browne, Comandr of Surry County, which Informed me, that very morneing a *p*tie of the Seneca's came to the Waynoake Indyan Towne, and there tooke away Six Indyan Women & a boy, and made an Attempt on their Fort, and presently Came on the Northside the Blackwater, enterd into Severall Englishmens houses, & Robbed & plundered them of all that was good in the houses, & threw the ffeathers out of the bedds and Carried away the tickings, which hath put all our Fronteers into a great Consternation, upon which I wrote to the Councell, to meete, that wee might Consider of the best way and Method to Secure the Peace of this his Majties: Countrey, and *p*event the Rapines of the faithless Enemy.
Accordingly Collo. Cole, Collo. Page and Collo. Leare mett, & wee haveing Considered all the Circumstances, and the great Terrors, & Indeede Hazards the Fronteers are in, and the officrs of the Militia's of all the Counties, but Henrico & Charles City, al-

Again the Head Man asked for two scouts to seek out the smoke of Adodarho. Two men volunteered, saying they would be as clever as humming birds.

leadging that they had no Comissions, & that without, the People would not obey Comands, Thereupon It was by the Councell Concluded, that the best way for the Security of the Peace, of this his Majties: Country and the preservation of the Inhabitants, was to Issue Comissions, to the Severall Cheife Comanders, of all the Fronteer Counties, that had not Comissions, to Impower them to put the Militia of theire Respective Counties into a Posture of Defence, and to that End to Traine a good Troope of Horse in each County to be in a readiness, to defend them from the Violence of these Savage Monsters, the Commission to be in force untell yor: Excellency's returne.

The Councell have also ordered, that the Inhabitants, shall soe demeane themselves, that they doe Comitt noe Acts of Hostility on the Indyans, unless they first assault them, in theire Houses and properties, and if the Indyans doe that then as the late Act directs, to pursue and destroy them, otherwise the people would have been in a Sad distracted Condition to see theire Estates destroyed before theire faces.

My Lord I thought it my Duty to give yor; Lordshipp this accounte and hope yor. Excellency will approve of this procedure of the Councell, which is done to the best of our Judgments, for his Sacred Majties. Service, and the preservation of this his Country. This with my most humble Service to your. Excellency, with my Prayers for yor: Health & prosperitye. I' am

Yor: Excellency's most humble Servt

/s/ Nathaniell Bacon

The Gentlen: of the Councell with
me present theire most humble
Service to yor: Excelly.

To his Honor the Governor[1]

We received this night two ambassadors from the Maquase country, the one named Sesten and the other Javochu, who have received news from the Senecas' country from messengers who have travelled by foot from castle to castle that the Senecas' country is being besieged by the French and the Indians. They have been fighting one another for a whole day on the hillside and had to flee to the castle, fighting all the way from the lake up to

[1] Translated from the Dutch.

their castle where they are now besieged. The Maquase ask his Excellency to please give the order so that the Indians who have promised to help them should now come, for they say that it is now time. They have given wampum thereon to his Excellency so that this will be done quickly.

Scheanhegtade	Your humble servant
July 2, 1687	the commissary of Scheanhegtade
Urgent!	Ryer Jacobse

N: Yorke July the 4th: 1687
Propos made by his Excel Tho Dongan gov^r genl. to Sadogaree ye genl. of ye Sinnekes & Some of ye Cayouge called Dihonsarest or Ja Romeetho & onnondage Indians & Carrhadgigoe

I have Sent Akus Expresse to all ye nations westward to acquaint to Putt up ye kings arms upon all ye Castles, & withall to forbid any of your People, goeing to Cadarchqui or any where else where ye french shal send for you. & fyndeing you here I acquaint you wth ye Same & yt all ye 5 nations be united together; & obey Such orders & Instructions as you shall Receive from me from time to time; for you must not halt & be Sometime on one Side & Sometime upon anoyr: & if ye french should attaque you must Not Stay in your Castles nor in great Companyes together least you Should Suffer great hurt, but in Small Companies together & doe not fight least upon great advantages, till further orders from me; & Since I Am Informd yt yr are a great many nations of Indians yt are in warr wth you, be not Troubled at yt. You shal have al ye help of al our Indians Nations also & if yr Corn Should be Destroyd, I shal take care to Supply yu you shal not want Provisions nor ammunition when your Bevr & Peltry shal faile you or any thing else yt Shal be necessary for you.

I have given leave to mr. Gideon & Salvay & his Company being french that Run away from Canida[1] to goe up by ye way of

[1] Gideon Petit "is from Rochelle. . . . Since he has been here [Canada] his trade has been always with the English. . . . Another named Salvaye . . . has also disappeared. He is a man of activity whom M. de la Barre and M. de Frontenac employed as an envoy to the English. . . . a knave who pretends to be honest." Denonville to Seignelay, June 8, 1687. O'Callaghan, 9: 326.

After looking them over, the Head Man said that would not do, because the humming bird is always hungry and is always looking for flowers.

Susquehanne & trade amongst ye Indians They have my Passe & you must tell yr People to do them No harme being gone upon Discovery.
[& if any french comes with Bevr. to yr Countrey wth a Design to bring them here You must lett them Passe freely whither they have my Pass or not, for yt weakens ye Power of ye french, and ye more they come in yt frindly way wth Bevr. the Better]
[You must not Suffer ye french to make any fort or Castle att onnyagaro or any where on yt Side of ye Lake, but hinder them as much as you can][1] & keep a watchfull Eye be not Drunk nor Sleepie least you Should be Surprised unawars, & Send me word from time to time how all affares goes wth you yt I may take Sufficient orders accordingly.

Was given them by his Excel

3 gunns
3 fatts of Rom
6 lb. Pouder
3 Barrs lead
1 Roll Tobacco

Proposal made [to Dirck Wessels] in the [Maquase] castle of Caignowage 1687, the 4th of July by the sachems[2]

Brother Corlaer, this is to ask you to help us and to take us in your arms, we poor ones who are now proposing to you. We ask for help, much of it, and in a hurry. Give 1 fathom wampum. Brethren, we intend to stay here and to live and die here, for where can we run. There is a great crowd of Indians who would pursue us everywhere anyway. Therefore, please be certain to heed us and to especially aid us in making our proposal.

Message to the Maquse sachems at Cachanuage from his Excellency, Thomas Dongan, Governor, sent the 7th of July 1687[3]

The Governor General has received your message with the fathom wampum sent by Sett and another Indian and has sent to the Indians of Schacktekook to come and help you.
His Excellency desires to speak with 2 of your sachems in Albany

[1] Material in brackets was cancelled in the original document.
[2] Translated from the Dutch. Material in brackets supplied from Robert Livingston's comment on reverse side of document.
[3] Translated from the Dutch.

and therefore I have been sent to come bring you in all urgency. Give 1 belt wampum.

By order of his Excellency
Robert Livingston

Proposition Sent by his Excellentie Tho: Dongan gov: genl. to ye Maquase by heeman alby. ye 8 of July 1687

Brethren
I am come here upon ye Rumor of this Bussinesse of ye french, but could never Believe, yt they would have come on this Side of ye Lake, to warr wth our Brethren ye Sinnekes, on Sight off this you are to Send Post from Castle to Castle, that ye oneydes, onnondages and Cayouges, march up wth. all Speed to assist the Sinnekes, and tell them not to Stay in yr Castles, and you are wth. al your Strenth likewise to march up, to assist them likewise. The north Indians & River Indians I shall gett together assoon as I can
I intend to be at Shinnectady my Self wth. all Speed, to hear from you, from time to Time, & if you should Be prest hard doe not Stay in any Castles, But Retire this way, and if you See any Danger, Send doune your old men women and Children & lett al ye Rest of ye Brethren doe ye Same and they shall be Provided for, Send by ye Posts one of these Belts of wampum to Each nation. I will make all Preparations I can to assist you as much as ye Shortnesse of ye Time will ꝑmitt me if need be.

Albany, July 8, 1687
Report of P. Olinder concerning the French and the Senecas[1]

To the Commissaries of Schenectady
Hethori with his 3 Maquase who have been in a battle bring the news here that the Seneca have already been in battle and that the Senecas have lost 70 men and 200 of the Frenchmen have

[1] Translated from the Dutch.

Again the Head Man asked for two scouts who would seek out the smoke of Adodarho. Two men volunteered, saying they would be as clever as the white crane.

been killed and 100 of the French Indians are dead. Those Seneca have brought the news to Cayuga. The Cayuga ask for help from the house of Maquase and Onondage, and now we Maquas ask our brother what to do about it. Because they have sent me a belt of wampum, I will send this belt back to Cayuga. We have no news from Akus. Thus we are daily anxious.

Pieter Van Olinder.

Propositions to ye Indians of Skachtekook by his Excell: Tho Dongan Capt. genl. & govr in Cheeffe albany ye 9 of July 1687.

Brethren, I am glad to See you here.

Upon a Report yt ye french are DeSigned to warr with our Brethren ye Sinnekes & ye oyr 4 nations on this Side of ye Lake, which I hardly can Beleeve, itt being Contrare to ye Covenant Chain Between ye king of England & ye king of france, and Lately Concluded; The Maquase have Sent to me & I hear they have likewise Sent to you DeSyreing off you to help them make up there Castle. Butt I desyre you to goe as farr as Shinnechtady and make hutts for yr. Selfs there as I Shal appoint you for a short time, where you shall stay till you have further orders from me, but if any of yr People are Inclined to goe to ye Maquase you may. I intend to be yr my Self monday next—& I Shal take care yt. you shall want for nothing [This assistance which I now Desyre you to doe to ye Maquase will Strenthen the Covenant chain Between you & them & Satisfy them yt your heart is good, Being willing to assist them Thogh I Value verry litle all these Rumors yett I Intend to Stay here and at Shinnechtady to see what will become of itt, in ye mean time yt ye Brethren look out & be upon ye guard].[1]

was given them 10 gunns
3 Bags Powder
40 Barrs lead
Some Biskett about 30 lb.

They made answer they were willing to Obey his Excel Commands & would march forthwith.

[1] The bracketed material was cancelled in the original, but has been retained here as an indication of Dongan's initial reaction to the idea of a threat of a French attack upon the Iroquois. It was, of course, an attitude that could not be conveyed to the Indians without harmful effects.

Proposittions made by his Excell. Tho Dongan Capt Genl. & govr &a to ye Maquase oneyde onnondages Cayonges & Sinnekes & Sent to ym. by Akus & Daniel Janse Shinnectady ye 14 of July 1687.

Brethren

I am Sorry of a Report yt. I have heard since my comeing to Shinnectady yt I should keep a Correspondence wth. ye governr. of Canida to yr. Prejudice; Brethren you doe me wrong in thinking soe for when he warrs wt. you he warrs wth. me. The Contents of ye Sd. Letter yt I sent to him by antho ye Baker[1] was all most on your Behalfs; Therefore lett me Desyre of you not to be Suspicious, but Beleeve Such messages as I have Sent to yu from Time to Time, & further I' assure you if yu. want any ammunition or arms for yr Selfs or your wifes or Children's maintenance I shall furnish ym. & I am come wth yt I'ntent as farr as this Place: I have sent up as many north Indians as are att home & I have Sent up for all ye River Indians & ye minnesinks to march up for yr. assistance; I am in Pain & in a great deal of Trouble to hear how ye Brethren doe, Therefor I command & Desyre of yu. not to keep yr Castles nor Engage many att a Time, for fear of being Lost; Be not Scrupulous if yu. be forced Send downe yr wifes & Children here & yr Selfs likewise may come in time of need where yu Shall be welkom & Supplyed with what you want. Send me word from time to Time how things goes, & if any Proposalls of a Peace be, Doe not Conclude upon any thing butt make a Cessation of arms & Send me word; Referr it to me I will make a Better Peace for yu. then you can make yr Selfs—I know ye french Better then you; and In ye time of ye Parle & Speakeing wth them, doe not Trust them, keep yr Eys open, for they are People yt. take all advantages, as you See now, by yr Invading of you on ye king of Englands Territoryes, Contrary to ye Covenant chain newly made by both kings, & Sent by me to ye govr. of Canida. I am Sendeing one home to ye king of England to give him an acct. of ye french govr. Proceedings & I beleeve itt will

[1] Anthony Lespinard.

After looking them over, the Head Man said they would not do, because the white crane is very wild and easily frightened, and that they would fly in terror when the clouds moved, forgetting their mission.

Cost him his head. Lett me know by ye first Post whether the Breth of ye 5 nations are of opinion that I should send to ye french to see if they be inclined for Peace or nott, if you be of yt. opinion & ye french advance as farr as onnondage Send me a Post & I will Send 2 or 3 messengers to ye french to know why they Invade ye Brethren in ye king of Englands Territories, and if ye french be willing I shal make a Better Peace for yu then you can doe yr Selfs.

[*Copy of a Translation*]

May it Please your Excell:

Just now Some Maquase Indians arrivd here, who tell us that a Certain north Indian called Sickheda Capt. of ye. Sckachtekook Indians, hath brought the news to Cachanuage ye first Castle of ye Maquase yt ye french & ye Indians have had a Batle again, & yt ye french are Put to ye flight, & have ye worst of it; But ye Said Sickheda being come here likewise & Examined by Jaques Cornelise, doth Say yt. ye. Indians have fought against three Companies of ye Christians & yt all ye officers are Still alive, Notwithstanding they often fyred upon them, and yt ye french are Pursued by three hundred Indians, as also 200 french kild & 200 Christian Indians, & of ye Sinnekes and Cayouges 20, Butt can give us no Certain account where ye Batle was fought, he doth likewise Report yt ye onnondages will Pursue ye french with there Canoes.

Wee are Informed by Dirk Wessells yt heeman hath Related Such news to your Excell:, & that without our knowledge; his Excel: may be assured yt wee shal not be wanting to give yr. Excel: an account of any certain news yt. wee shall Receive; no more for ye Present leaveing yr Excel: to ye Protexion of ye almighty god, we Remain

Your Excell: affectionat Frinds
ye Justice & Commis: of Shinnectady

Shinnechtady
ye 17 July 1687

Sander glen Justice
Ryer Jacobse

The Superscription was
To his Excell: Tho Dongan
govr genl. of n Yorke
@ albany.

His Excellency, Governor General Thomas Dongan [at Albany][1]

Because this Indian thinks he will be going to Albany, take this opportunity to let his Excellency know the information we have gotten until now in Cachnawage (mainly from Jannetie the Indian) concerning the battle which has taken place between the French and the Indians. What we had been told about this on our departure from Albany has been found to be untrue. Not everything about this first battle was as the Indian from the North told us. There has been here a Maquase who was himself in the first battle, but he had already left for Onondage where all the nations will now hold a general council day, for which the sachems of the first castle had already departed Saturday before we arrived in the castle Sunday night. As far as the first battle is concerned, what is being told here agrees with the report given in Albany with the difference that only 16 of the Senecas were killed. The Governor of Canada now stays with his army at Jagaro[2] and has many wounded and a lack of provisions. His Indians are suffering so much that others would have run away from the French after the first battle. At the moment I cannot hear of any more parties because one is very uncertain about the reports of the Indians. But we are on the point of leaving for Onondage and so hope to get some accurate information there about everything and all affairs that have happened there or are intended. Otherwise, I cannot discover anything else here among the Indians, though possibly it will come to [ ][3] and we are all with many greetings your Excellency's servant upon all occasions in these affairs. Cachnawage, July 18, 1687

Urgent! Dirck Wessels.

Propositions to ye five nations westward Sent by his Excell Tho Dongan Capt genl. & gov &a by akus to Dirk wessells & Robert Sanders now att onnondage; to Propose unto them now all mett there, albany ye 19 of July 1687

Brethren.

I am Sorry to See ye. Brethren are not more united amongst them-

[1] Translated from the Dutch.
[2] Niagara.
[3] Unintelligible word.

Two others said they would be like crows. The Head Man said they would not do, because crows talk loudly, boast, and are full of mischief. Adodarho would hear them long before they found his fire.

Selfs to assist on another in ther Extremity for if you doe not keep ye Covenant chain clean amongst yr Selfs how can we Christians Expect yt you can keep it to us; here I have sent to all ye Indians of this River to assist the Brethren, & have Sent Some of ye north Indians up To joyn wth ye Maquase to goe & assist ye Sinnekes, But they were not gone 2 days but there Capt. comes bak & brings a flyeing Report, that yey needed not to goe further for ye french were Beaten, & all gone & Retreited to yr Canoes upon which I sent a message doune to N: Yorke to Stop all ye men yt were Sent for up, to assist the Brethren if need were.

It is verry True yt ye french have invaded ye king of Englands Territories; But yt is under Cullor to warr wth ye Sinnekes wth a Promise not to medle wth ye Rest in case they doe not joyn wth them, wh. I am affraid some of ye Brethr: hath observed for we have another way to be Revenged of them, by our king at home who is a man that the french knows & fears, & can be Revenged of ym when he wil if he sends butt his orders to his Subjects here, & doe not doubt but it will Cost ye govr. of Canida his head for offering to Invade ye king of Englands Territories without acquainting me first. Butt he had such malice to ye Brethns ye Sinnekes yt he thought to Supprize them & cutt them all off in there Castles which Put me to a great deal of Trouble and Charges —In Provideing Such things as I thought were necessary to assist ye Brethns in Case ye warr should goe one, & ye Shortnesse of ye Time could allou me, & I am come my Self So farr, as alby & Shinnechtady to Stay here Purposely to heare from ye Brethren whatsoever thing might happen notwithstanding ye great Concerns yt I have to doe in other Places, & to give them Instructions what to doe, & my Self to take Such measures as may be for ye Brethren's Security; Butt I hear So many Various Reports, & Some Contradicting on another yt I doe not know what measures to Take, & if some be True I should be very Sorry for itt. yt is yt I hear ye Brethren is goeing to hearken to some Proposals off agreement wth ye french without my Consent, which is a verry ill thing done, they being the king of Englands Subjects; for in warring wth them is warring with us; & I know it is a thing the Brethren ought not to doe, nor a thing Convenient for them to doe for I can make a more advantagious Peace for them then they can themselffs. I know ye Brethren ye Sinnekes will not doe itt, Since I have Always found them true to there Promise; But I fear yr are some members amongst the Rest of ye Brethren yt are more for ye french advantage then for ye Brethren; Therefore I would have ye Rest not to hearken to them, but to joyn heart & hand togethere & follow my advise; wh. yu will finde ye same advantage to yu as to ye Rest of ye Brethren here ye king of Englands Subjects, yt are 100 to one of ye french; Therefore heareing of ye genl. meeting at onnondage; I have sent akus to those 2 gentleman to declare to yu my Intentions, to lett you know my Thoughts not to make any aggreemt. wth ye french, which is a Thing you ought not to doe without Passing throu my hands, which if yu doe I will not trouble my Self any longer wth ye Brethren but goe doune to N:Yorke, for wee can live without ye Brethren but can Scarcely beleive they can live without us; haveing Everything thrice as cheep here as Elsewhere. Therefore I Expect As I desyred before yt one off ye Captns & of ye Sachims of each nation, come doune to me wth. al Speed, that we may Conclude upon a means or method whereby Things may goe one wth. more unity & more advantage for ye Brethren.[1]

Memorand:

That about ye: latter end of March last some of ye English Inhabitants of Virginia were out a Deer hunting wth. some of yr: Apomatock Indians att ye. head of James River where a Party of ye Seneca Indians to ye Numb: of sixty or more (But of what Nation of ye. Seneca's tis not certainly known) in ye very Dawning of ye: Morning Assaulted them as they were asleep, and fireing all their Armes att them killed three English, and ye Appomatock King wth. divers of the Indians. & wounded many more before the English Could recover their Armes, upon wch: after they had overcome the Surprise the English put themselves in a posture of Defence, & the Seneca Indians comeing up wth. their Second assault fired at ye. English as formerly but wthout any mischeife, upon wch: ye: English made ye. same return, and killed ye.

[1] This proposed conference was held in Albany on August 5, 1687. O'Callaghan, 3: 438-444.

Finally two skilled warriors stepped forward. They said they were strong as the deer and the bear and possessed the powers of those animals. They were chosen, and set out through the forest on their mission.

Seneca's as said five or six, upon wch: ye: English Inforted themselves as well as ye. tyme & place would allow off, they Emediately sent home to their ffreinds for a supply of men & Armes, upon wch: ye Seneca's desired a Conference, & said they were sorry they had done ye: English any hurt, & yt they tooke them to bee Indians and offered satisfaccon. The English answered yt there Could be no Satisfaccon for Mens lives, & so they Continued by ye: English yt: Day wthout any farther Disturbance, but the Messinger wch: was sent from ye: English to give Notice to the Inhabitants & to bring a Supply of Amunition they intercepted in his return, & killed & Cut him in peeces, so prsently Marched away wch: had they not they would have paid deare for their frollick for then came a Party of neer two hundred men undr: ye Command of Coll: William Bird to ye. assistance of their English ffreinds wthin four houres after ye Seneca's departed, & had vowed seveire revenge for ye death of those they had slaine, This is a true Relation according to the Account has been given of those proceedings Dated the 21st: July 1687.

Present: *September 7, 1687*
Ryer Jacobs *Maquas discourse in Schenectady*
Myndert Wemp *Given: 1 Frenchman*[1]

Cornelius Viele says that the Maquas sachems state: that the Governor of Canada, as we all know, has started an unjust war against all the nations. The Maquase doe not yet have any prisoners, but that Governor has taken a hundred prisoners from all the nations to the West—Oneida, Onondaga, Cayuga, Sinnondowane. The stories of further battles and similar hostilities indicates still more on top of that. What is more, they [French] take our brother, the Dutchman, accompanied by some Mahikanders on a trip to the Ottawawa, prisoner also, from which they cannot but conclude that his heart is still obstinate, and that no one comes freely from Canada but refugees and those who have escaped. Therefore the nations have desired to revenge the unjust attacks of the French Governor and will do such exploits as the brethren [ ].[2] And this they will not stop.

And that a certain Arnout has rendered many services to this country and is also imprisoned about which they are very sad.

[1] Translated from the Dutch.
[2] Unintelligible phrase.

And to quiet the high-running feelings, to offset the sadness, and to wash away the tears in the house of Arnout and his family, they hand over this Frenchman, hoping that in our way he will be pleasing to you. And then request two wagons and Cornelius Viele as interpreter. As this place is at the same time a seat of this government and also subjected to all dangers, we do not want to pass you by, but report everything again and make everything known to the house of Corlaer.

Province of New Yorke
Governor & Councill *ffryday the 9th. Sept. 1687*

WHEREAS this Board has ben Certainly Informed that the ffrench of Canada have made Ready A great Many Snow Shews to the number of one thousand five hundred Paire and are Still Preparing More with Designe as is beleeved to renew the Warr Agt. the Sinakes in the winter It is thereupon thought fitt & this Day Accordingly Ordered by his Excelly the Governor & Councill that the Mayor & Aldermen of the Citty of Albany Doe forthwith Send an Expresse to the five Nacons of the Indians on this Side the Lake Ordering them that before the Winter Setts in they bring Downe from their Castles all their Wives Children & Old Men And Settle them att Livingstons land Kattskill & Along the River where they Can find best Conveniency that they may bee neare to have Assistance In Case they Should Want And that they bring Along wth. them all the Indian Corne & Provisions that Cann bee Spared by the Young Men who are to Stay in theer Castles
By Comand of his Excy John Knight D. Secry
Do. the Mayor & Aldermen
of the Citty of Albany.

Propositions made by his Excellcy: the Governor. of Virginia to the Representatives of the five Nations of the Indians in the Fort att New Yorke—Septemr ye 16th 1687

Brethren
Finding you have broaken ye chaine of Freindship wch: was made

---

Then Deganawidah spoke to the Mohawk Council: "I and my younger brother, Hiawatha, stand before you. We place before you the laws by which to frame the Great Peace."

between us of Virginia, and you in ye: Towne hall of Albany by the desire of yor. Great Governor: three yeares since, and Contrary to that agreemt. fall upon our Indians ye last spring when they were out a hunting, and killed diverse of them, and diverse Christians, and that you have since come wth:in our Plantations. And taken away diverse of the Indians Prisonrs: and plundred diverse of our English. I came to New Yorke on purpose to his Excellcy yor Governor: wee being all one Kings subjects to desire Satisfaccon for yt: Injury Or yt he would help me to make Warr on you. But he being So much yor: Freind hath once more prevaled wth: me to try you againe, he promiseing you shall make satisfaccon for yt. Injury, wch upon his desire I am willing to doe, and ye more because I see you have returned me againe those Prisonrs you then tooke,[1] but this I must tell you Brethren That since I cannot Know wch of yor Nations is guilty of this assault, I will for ye future if ever there bee ye like done againe desire yor. Governor. to make Enquiry wch of yor Nations doth it & those of that Nation wch are Guilty to bee delivered to me, That I may deale with them as they have done wth: us. Or that ye hatchetts wch: were buried in ye prsence of our Governor may [be] delivered me againe That I may use them in revenge on you for such Injuryes. You must now tell yor Sachims yt: they must thanke his Excellcy That hee hath prvaled wth me to passe by this, But yett you must tell them that when the Warr wth ye French is over, I expect satisfaccon, And yt I now expect ye return of that Boy wch is yett Prisonr wth them, And yt they remember to keep yt article of peace not to come againe wthin our Plantations, but make their paths to the Northward of us, And then tell them ye Chaine of Freindship shall bee still Continued, And as an assurance yt it shall on my part, if they desire it, I will send some of our Virginia Indians to help them against the French. Doe give to ye severall Nations a hundred gilders of Wampum.

The Answers of the Representatives of the Five Nations to his Excellcy:

They say: That it is very well my Lord will bee soe good to passe

[1] According to the Duane Report, 1780, the Livingston Indian Papers contained a transaction of September 3, now missing, in which the "Oneydas by Command of the governor deliver up the Prisoners whom they had taken in Virginia; are Severely reprimanded and threatned for the Infraction of their Treaty with that government."

by this Injury And that they thanke Curlair their Governor for getting my Lord to doe it. and that none of their Young men for the future shall come to the English Plantations, but will make their path to the Northward of Virginia:
And that they are very glad that if there should be any mischeife done att any tyme by their Unruly Young men to the English or Indians of Virginia: That my Lord will onely blame & have those suffer who doth it and not Lay the fault upon all the Nations And that they will be sure to tell their Sachims all that my Lord hath said & will give his ꝑsent of Wampum to the severall Nations And so wish his Lordship a good Journey to Virginia.
Vera Copia

Exam ꝑ
Jno: Johnson.

Present:
Capt. Stillwell
Capt. Sander Glen
Reyer Jacobs
Translated by Jaques Cornelise

Information[1] obtained from the Maquase[2] who have returned from Canada. The 8th of November 1687

Say that they have lost two men in front of the fortress Chambly where they ran after the French until they were under its walls, but had taken prisoner under the walls of the fortress one Frenchman and one woman and killed several, but they did not have time to scalp them. Also they were shot at a great deal, and the French slammed the doors shut so that they could not enter into the fortress. Say also that of those ten Indians which they first took as prisoners, seven of them had gone off to fight, but the French and their children and wives are now sent on this way. They left up there men to keep a watchful eye and also four parties to do all harm.
Stwanagy has remained there with a troop

[1] Translated from the Dutch.
[2] One authority states that this party consisted of Mahicans as well as Mohawks. Smith, 1: 75.

Deganawidah said: "The symbol of our League will be the Tree of Peace, the white pine. Under the Tree we must bury all weapons of war. The far-seeing eyes of the eagle will warn us of the approach of enemies. Men of the Five Nations must unite and act as one heart, one mind, one soul. They must forever spread goodwill and brotherhood among all nations."

Pagerawane with a troop
Aderatga with a troop
Pagniago with a troop
Say that they burned seven houses and killed 40 animals and many pigs and fowl. Say that the Governor coming next Friday should be at the end of Schenectady and that the Maquase chiefs will meet his Excellency there, and that on the orders of the chief of the troop.

Instructions for Arnout Cornelise and Akus Cornelise, interpreters, Albany, the 24th of November 1687[1]

When you have gone to the respective nations of Indians to the West as far as the Cayugas and Senecas, Arnout is to read the following proposals to Akus and he in turn to translate to the Indians of the several nations

Brethren

I have received your answer from Arnout and am glad that there are wise men of each nation coming to stay with me in the winter so we can keep council together as to what may be proper to be done in the matter of peace or war for the preservation and welfare of all of us.

Arnout tells me that the Governor of Canada has sent three of your prisoners as ambassadors to Onondaga and one to Oneida with belts of wampum, declaring that he did not intend to make war on anyone but only the Senecas and Cayugas, and the war with them, as he pretends, is because they interfered with his people. If that is so, then why did he take so many of the Onondagas and Oneidas as prisoners and bind them with iron chains and has sent some as prisoners to France, and sending news home to his King that he had taken them as prisoners of war. But to demonstrate clearly to the brethren that he is a liar, I have confronted him with the fact that if the Senecas had wronged him, he would get satisfaction. He says also that I am the cause of this war and that I incited the brethren to make war on him and he on the brethren, that I meant to bring about your ruination in this way. It is false, for he wanted to ruin the brethren because the brethren made war on the nations that bring their beavers to Canada, as the Governor of Canada himself said to Major Mac-

[1] Translated from the Dutch.

gregory. On the contrary, it is my duty to preserve the brethren who by their own will have submitted their lands and conquests to the great King of England.
But I understand very well what the Governor of Canada means. It is to bring about a misunderstanding between the brethren and me. But I am glad that the brethren know better and can see who means them well and who does not.
In the first place, the brethren know what trouble and toil I had to unify the five nations and also the northern Indians, for I saw what the Governor of Canada's intent was: first to ruin the Senecas, while the rest of the brethren would be neutral, and then to attack the brethren and ruin them also. Why should I want the ruination of the brethren. They have not done this government any harm, but on the contrary I love the brethren and want to do whatever I can to preserve them.
Come, brethren, to show you that he is a liar, demand of him what I have written in a letter by Major Macgregory. That is:
1° that he sends back those prisoners who have been sent to France and to free the ones he has there.
2° That he pulls down the two fortresses he has built on the path the brethren use to go and hunt.
3° And that he will engage himself not to assist any of the strange nations of Indians with whom the brethren are at war, and that only then will I hear of peace.
Send one or two of the prisoners back with his message in my name and then the brethren will see what tricks they have to create a misunderstanding between us. Brethren, do not be blind any longer. The Senecas made a peace with them two or three years ago, but to what effect. If he makes a peace with me the King of England will then keep him to it. I assure the brethren I will not do a thing without the brethren's advice. Therefore, I ask the brethren not to deal with him in anything, but only that which will take place in my house at Albany. And if he should do some harm to the brethren after such an agreement, then we are all engaged together in the affair. I know that he will be very

"The emblem of the leaders of the Confederacy," said Deganawidah, "shall be the antlers of the deer."

unwilling to make a peace here because he does not wish to recognize that the brethren are the King of England's subjects and thus to be in a choice position to make war on the brethren whenever he can find the least excuse as he has done with the Senecas. Therefore I request the brethren not to listen to a thing but only what will take place here, and to have some patience, for he has already asked me for peace and I do not want to hear of it but on such conditions as have been mentioned before. Therefore I have sent for the wise men of each nation to come to me.

I have sent him a very angry letter for his saying that I started the war. It is not strange to me that he tries to fool the brethren with that, for he tells me so and gives as a reason that it is because I did not want to let the brethren go to Cadarachqui when he sent for them, for I saw what he wanted to do with them if they did go. As another reason he gives that I gave the brethren (whom he calls his enemies) powder, lead, and guns, and has thus written home. But I have written him that it is certain that the brethren are subjects of the King of England, and that I have given them, and will give them again, ammunition and will assist them to the last.

This year has been a bad year for hunting. The old and young Indians will lose a lot. Therefore send 2 or 3 of each nation and I will send them something to drink the King of England's health. Let the sachems take care that everybody has a little and that certainly will not make them drunk. Let the sachems send messengers to the Minnesinks Indians to come and help them in the spring.

I just heard a report from two Maquase Indians called Johosaa and Oderachadiro who have come from a troop of their nation, which they have left behind at the Carrying Place, with two French prisoners, a man and a woman, and 2 scalps. They say that at the Carrying Place they caught up with 2 Christian Indians and 2 females who came here from Canada who declare that as soon as the Lakes are really frozen the French intend to come here and to make war on the Christians and Indians and are therefore very busily carrying many loaves of bread to Chambly. There are a hundred men who carry bread and they have thirty men to convoy them. Also that there is a house in Chambly where

the attic is filled up with snowshoes for the trip, to be used as soon as the weather permits. The names of the Christian Indians who reported this are Adirochronge and Rooskondawe.
Therefore I ask you to send over the number of Indians that I have advised you of before so as to be ready to collaborate with our people when the need arises.
You can hear from what the Indians say that if the French will do anything, it will be near this place, for they are very angry with us. Thus it will be very necessary that the brethren of the five nations send two or three hundred men here, having brought but few people now, until the spring, when I hope that more will be brought and will make a fortress on the Lake. If the enemy comes in your land as they did last year, I will be ready to come and work with you.
Brother Aquirachronge, the Governor of Canada has given you a cane[1] which, as I understand, has no face. Therefore I have sent you one which is not blind. I ask that you and all the five nations look through it and spy on the French and their Indians. I had forgotten that the Governor of Canada said that if the Senecas do not listen to him, he will kill them all. I assure you that if he could do that, he would not tell you so. When he does not kill you in his country, he will not do it in your country, or else he has to kill all of us too, together with the brethren, and he can not do that unless he takes us while sleeping.

Tho. Dongan

Symon Groot[2] Inhabitant of Skinnechtady in ye County of alby aged about 62 years born in a Village in north holland Called kellinwow Declares yt. he came into this Countrey in ye year 1638 being a boy & was in ye Service of ye west India Company when

[1] *Rotting.*
[2] According to the Duane Report, 1780, the Livingston Indian Papers contained drafts of three depositions—those of Groot and Labate which are given here, and another signed by Petrus Vinne and Barent Pulinds which is missing. They were prepared for the Governor and Council in order to prove the English claim of sovereignty over the Iroquois. *Cal. N. Y. Col. MSS.* 2: 171.

Deganawidah then recited all the laws of the Confederacy, recording each with a string of wampum. Hiawatha confirmed all that Deganawidah had said.

he came to n york wm kievet was governr & at albany Bastiaen Croll by whom ye Dept. lived 7 years in ye old fort (he being ye Commys or Commandr of ye west India Company) ye Sd. Croll had a great Trade wth ye. Sinnekes & ye oyr. Indians to ye westward, for in one year ye Deponent hath help to Trade & Pack up 37 thousand Bever yt were Sent to ye west India Company & ye [(*blot*)] ye Indians westward were always under ye Protection of this Place & brought Presents yearly & Renewed there Covenant chain in ye fort, and about 40 years agoe ye. Maquase being jealous ye french would make [war] upon them because ye Maquase were in warr wth ye french Indians Called Cahennajages for ye french would always assist those Indians, ye Deponent & anoyr called Solder Pieterse were upon ye Maquase Request Sent to ye Maquase Countrey wth horses to Ride Timber to make there Castle Strong against any attaque of ye french, & were att work 14 days, but then there were no Priests among ye Indians for this was ye 2 warr yt ye french & Maquase had, ye 3d. warr was in ye year 1666 when ye french came as far as Shinnechteady 20 mile from alby in Persute of ye Indians in ye midle of ye winter, & in ye Summer after into ye Countrey burnt there Castles Destroyd there Corn. Then a Peace was Concluded & hostages to be given on both Sides ye Jesuits were Sent to ye Indians, & Indians Sent some of there People to be hostages at Canida to Secure ye Peace fast & firm,

The Deponent Says further yt they have Endangerd them Selfs often in a warr wth ye Indians about Releaseing ye french Prisoners & Stealing them away in ye verry first warr about 40 year agoe there was a french Priest Stole from ye Indians about ye month of august who was wounded & kept in ye Commandrs house up in ye uppermost gart till march yt ye Sloops went doune to N yorke ye Deponent brought him Victualls 3 day all ye while ye french were Cruelly used by ye Indians then & ye Indians being askd why they torturd them they Sd they had learnd it of ye french.

This Deposition was taken before
me at albany ye 2d day of July 1688

Jean Labate born in Lorain in a village near Verdun called Bissonveau aged 74 years Declares yt in ye year 1637 he was brought in this Country by ye Renselaers, & brought up to ys Place then calld fort orange, but ye land Round about it was called ye Collony of Renselaerswyck—ye fort was then Erected by ye west India Company a Purpose for a Tradeing house wth ye Indians, for they had ye Sole Indian Trade all oyr Persons yt came out in ye Service of ye Renselaers being obligd to Swear that they were not to Trade wth ye Indians, Says further yt ye 5 nations Called Maquase oneydes onnondages, Cayouges, & Sinnekes, allways traded wth the west india Company & were in amity with them & yt diverse of Indians wth Straws throu there noses came & traded likewise. When ye Deponent came first to n: yorke ye govrs name was Wouter van Twiller But there was anoyr govr before him who was Called Peter Minnuit, & ye Commander of ye fort was called Marte gerritse, & ye Director of Renselaers Collony was Called Jacob Plank.

Says yt in ye year 1638 when Willem Kievet was govr of Manhatanes or n: yorke he went frequently to ye Sinnekes Countrey as far as Jagaro being Sent by ye west Indian Compy & putt up ye Companys mark upon 3 great blak oak trees on both Sides of ye River at Jagaro[1] and there being then a warr between ye french & our Indians was Sent by ye then governr. to Release diverse Poor french Prisoners among which there were 5 Priests wh they [bought] of ye Indians wth money one of wh was called Pere Prisalie the names of ye Rest he forgot & some they Stole from ye Indians in great danger of there lives, & being affraid to Return to Canida they were Sent in ye Companies Ships to holland & So to france; The french had warr then wth all ye 5 nations, and Afterwards a Peace being Concluded, There arose a Difference between ye Maquase & ye french inso much yt ye Govr of Canida called monsr Tressi Came in Person in ye Deep of winter in ye year 1666 to Shinnectady a village 20 mile into or Countrey wth 500 men, in Pursuite of ye Indians but ye Indians being upon there guard ye french were forced to Retreat & lost most of his men before he gott home as we were Informed but ye Summer fol-

[1] It has been stated that the first formal treaty between any of the Iroquois and the Europeans occurred about 1643. McIlwain, liii. This, if a valid recollection, would seem to place such an event as early as 1638.

When the scouts who sought the smoke of Adodarho's fire returned to the Mohawk Council,

lowing ye govr of Canada Called mr Costell when ye Maquase were out a hunting came wth 6 or 700 men into ye Maquase Countrey & Burnt there Castles & Destroyd ther Indian Corn, upon which ye Maquase came home & Pursued ye french as farr as Canida, but could not finde them, & So came home & Rebuilt there Castles where they are now to this day. long after ye french made a Peece wth ye Maquase & then & never before ye Priests came into there Castles Butt ye Indians would not Receive them till ye first English govr. yt came to n: yorke gave them leave.

att ye Same Time govr. nicolls was a Raiseing of men to assist ye Maquase & Sent up as far as ye Sinnekes Countrey & Jagaro to Put up ye king of Englands Coate of armes, in al those Places.

In ye year 1667 ye ottowawaes Dionendadees & Twichtwicks came & gave Presents to govr. nicolls Desyreing that ye 5 nations may open a Path for them to come & Trade wth ye English; which they did & diverse have been here from time to time of those farr nations of Indians.

He Declares yt he & one Brier Cornelise who had an Indian Squae to his wife were Sent by Cornel Nicols in ye Spring 1665 to take Possession off ye Sinnekes Countrey onjagaro & ye Rest of those nations as they were Deliverd to ye English by ye Dutch govr Petrus Stuyvesant

This Deposition was taken before me at Albany ye 2d day of July 1688.

Actum in Albany[1]

The Honorable Gentlemen, Magistrates, Mayor and Aldermen of Albany are requested that the Company to the Ottewawes should again enjoy its money stolen by the French since our creditors ask us for it daily which is unpleasant. Therefore we request that the Gentlemen please send an express-delivery to go and regain the same money to satisfy our creditors. It has been definitely promised to us time and time again that the matter would be dealt with for us and that it would be taken care of, but until now nothing has been done about it. And if the Gentlemen will now honor our request, we will be at their service. If not, we will be forced to go and regain the money in the same way it was stolen from us, with as large a force of the Indians and Christians as we can find for that purpose. For it is not only for our sake, but your interest

[1] Translated from the Dutch.

is also at stake, as well as our brethren's blood who have fought for us for the same and have not been able to fully prosecute their intentions. Therefore, we have all decided now to again command the same and to obtain our revenge. With this we are your humble servants.

The Ottewawese Company.[1]

Instructions for Arnout Cornelise
Interpreter

Since wee are Sent by ye Colonyes of Massashusetts Plymouth and Cannetticute to Treate with the Maquase and oyr nations westward, wee have Discoursd with ye Mayor Aldermen and Justices of ye Citty and County of Albany about ye Bussinesse who Concurr with us yt Somme Sachims and Cheeffe Captans be Sent for accordingly; Butt you are to take Especial Care yt this message doe not hinder or Divert there Pursute of there Victory against ye french which wee hear they Lately had, at which wee are much Rejoyced. But Rather tell them that wee give them all Incouragement Imagineable to Pursue the french Vigorously; Therefore itt would be Requisite thatt they fully Impower Two or three from each nation to come downe and Treat with us yt. wee may Renew our antient frindship, Since we stay here a Purpose for there Comeing where we shall Receive them with all kindenesse Imagineable; It will therefore be Verry acceptable to us yt you make what Speed yu can as farr as ye Sinnekes & acquaint them Herewith according to ye Inclosed order of ye Mayor.

We Remain

Your Loveing Frindes
/s/ John Pynchon
/s/ Thomas Savage[2]
/s/ Jonathan Bull
/s/ Andr Belcher

Albany ye 30 of august
A° 1689

[1] This is undoubtedly the Magregory company which had been captured by the French and taken prisoners to Canada.
[2] Colden gives this name as *John* Savage and omits Belcher's name. Colden, 1: 119.

. . . they reported that they had discovered the war-chief's fire at great peril to themselves. They said his hair resembled live snakes which hissed when he was angry.

PS: Wee are so farr from hindring
there Pursute against ye french
yt if 2 or 3 of there Sachims and
Captains cannot be Spared that they
send one from each nations so he be
fully Impoured to Treat with us. It
shall be Equally acceptable att the
Juncture wh. you may acquaint
ye. Indians accordingly & lett
them Come wth all Speed
Imagineable.

[Arnout Cornelise Alby 20 aug. 1689
Verry good frinde
These are to Convey ye. Inclosed Instructions & order of ye mayor, wh. we Desyre yt. yu may Effect & further wth. all Speed Imaginable Since we Stay Purposely for there Comeing, & Shall Satisfy yu for yr Trouble to Content; You may tell ye Indians by ye By that there are 2 men of warr to ye Eastward who have taken 10 french Ships who have Sent for men to Boston to man Sd Prizes. This is lately done So yt it is Supposed it is not very Safe for ye french at ye mouth of ye Canida River. This is all at ꝑsent. We
Remain yr Cordial frinds
John Pynchon
Th. Savage
and Belcher
Jonath Bull

We hear yt ye general Convention is now at onnondage So yt Probably youl finde all ye Sachims there which will Save yu much truble.][1]

Propositions made by Col. John Pynchon Majr Tho Savage Capt. andrew Belsher & Capt. Jonathan Bull agents for ye Collonyes of Massachusets Plymouth & Canetticute to ye River Indians as well Mahikanders as Skachkook indians in ye Citty hall of alby ye 12 day of Sepr 1689

Breth: We being Commissonated by the Severall Collonies in New

[1] There is both a signed, finished copy and a rough draft of this document. The former does not contain the bracketed material, while the latter does. The bracketed material was probably intended as a cover letter and therefore was not included in the finished document.

England viz Massethusets Plymo & Conecticote to renew the Anchant ffrindship and Leaug made by our predisors with the five Nations of Indians viz the Maquase; Oneydes; Onnondages Cayouges and Sinnecks,

We understanding that you are Subjects of this governt & by that means Wraped and Included in the Chaine or Covenant made with ye Nations we doe thinke mete to acquaint yu off ye grat Change or Revolution of Goverment in England and the Quarill now depending betwene Prodistants and Papists; Our great King haveing united the English and Dutch to be as One who are Resolved to Assist him with thire Lives and ffortaines against all that shall Opose;

understanding that the ffrench at Cannida with whose Nation we are Informd by the way of ye west Indies our grat King hath proclaimed warr is now at warr with you; who are in Amety and in Leaug with the Maques and the rest of the Nations and Soe Consiquently with us who are in the Same Chaine with them; We take this Opertunity to Let you know that the Easterne Indians being Instigated and Incoradged by the ffrench at Cannida who are yors and our mortall Enemies; have made Incurssion upon the Out borders of our grat Kings Goverment to the Eastward of Merimeck River & the places there adjasent.

All tho we are not Soe Emediatly Concerned it being out of our Collonies yet we hould our Selves Obledged in duty to Stand for the Defence of all or any of thire Majts Subjects; and we Doe Exspect that you will accompt it yor Duty Leikwise to doe yor utmost to kill and destroy all those of theire Majts Enemies and that you will not hould any Corispondance wh those of the Easterne Indians and will take all Opertunity of Advantag to destroy those of our great Kings and his Subjets Enemies.

All tho wee hear Proclamation of Warr wth ffrance be made in England yet we have not *p*ticular orders from our grat King Concerning that matter but Exspect them dayly which when we shall receive shall not be wanting to doe our utmost for the roting

They reported that his deformed body had seven crooks in it. He always held a war-club in his hands, which were like the claws of a wild animal.

out & Exsturpation of your & our Enemies ye french at Cannida which have byn Soe Trecherous to us both.

We have been Informed of a report you have receivd from the Easterne Indians of a designe the English had agt you and all other Indians to Mischife and Destroy them, & also yt we Should have Treacherously kild there Sachims; We doe now wash our hands of it and Declare it to be uterly false and that we never had any Such thought but on ye Contrary when there Sachims were Sent for were Civilly used & had Presents given them and Sent home in a Sloop Safely, but Soon after they Committed Severall murthers & Rapines, So yt wee can Esteme those falcities noe other than a Stratigem of the ffrench Jesuitts with whome they hould Correspondance to Sugest Such Notions to them on purpos to Sett us at variance: which If you adhere to will undoubtedly prove destructive to you & yor posterety ffor our parts we intend noe evil agt any Indians yt wil live peaceably wth us & to keep the Chaine betwixt us whole and doe Exspect the same from you; and doe hartily wish that those ffoure Easterne Indians of our Enemies which ware with you had been By you Secured as you were ordered by ye gent of alby in yr Castles which would have been very acceptable to our grate King & very gratfully acknowledgd by all thire Majts Subjets.

Propositions made by ye Honble. Col. John Pynchon Majr. Thomas Savage Capt. Andrew Belsher and Capt. Jonathan Bull Agents of ye Severall Governments of New England vizt Massachusetts Plymouth and Canetticut to ye. five nations or Cantons of Indians to witt ye. Maquase Oneydes onnondages Cayouges and Sinnekes in ye. Citty hall of Albany ye 23th day of Septemb: 1689

BRETHREN

WEE being authorised by ye Severall Collonies of N: England, Vizt Massashusetts Plymouth & Canetticute to Renew ye Covenant Chain of frindship which hath many Years agoe been made by our Progenitors with you ye Maquase Oneydes Onondages Cayouges & Sinnekes, have accordingly undergone ye Difficulties of a hard journey to come to this Prefixed Place, and have sent for some of your Sachims and Cheiffe Captains to Effect ye Same, whom wee are gladd to see safe come hither.

2. YOU have had notice of ye Late Revolutions in England where ye Late king James being a Papist and a great Frinde of ye French (who Putt a Stopp to your annoying and being Revenged of ye French Two years agoe) is Removed from the Throne and his Sonne in Law and Daughter who Ruled in holland and are Protestants and Professed Enemies to ye french Intrest are Sent for by the English to be king and queen in there Fathers Stead, by which means ye. English nation and ye Dutch are not only united in a firm Covenant Chaine but are able and unanimously ReSolved to Ruine ye French king, haveing the most Part of all the Christian Princes in Europe on there Side to joyne in that good worke, for as ye french of Canida have often Broke there Faith with you, Soe there king did at home with all his Allyes, Therefore So long as ye French king and ye. Jesuits have ye Command at Canida You can never Expect to live in Peace it being there only Studdy nott only to Dukkoy and Treacherously murther your People butt to Send evill Emissaries amongst you as they did Lately from ye Eastward, to Delude and Raise Jealousies against your Best Frindes who have kept there Covenant Chain Inviolable time out of minde.

3. WEE Cannot but take notice of your kinde answer to ye Interpreter Last march when he was Sent to your Castles to Inform you how Treacherously those Villans ye Kennebek or Eastern Indians had Murtherd diverse of there Majes Subjects without ye Least Provocation and were fled and therefore they there associates or Confederates to be looked upon and taken as Enemies;[1] when you did not only Show your greeffe for ye losse of Soe many of yr. Brethren ye Christians to ye Eastward but would endevour to Revenge there Blood by Destroying of those Perfidous Rogues who Broake there faith with you Some years agoe, and as you then did Verry well Remarke itt was by

[1] A war was then underway between the New Englanders and the Eastern Indians. The latter, however, maintained friendly relations with the Skachkook Indians in New York and, it was suspected, with the Mohawks. This was the reason for this conference. Smith, 1: 87-88.

"He is a cannibal," they said.

ye Instigacon of ye French Soe we finde by Experience yt that false Nation doth sett on ye Easterne Indians with whom they have a Correspondence to doe these Mischeeffs. But Since wee are Informd By ye way of ye. west Indies yt our great king and Queen hath Proclaimd warr against ye french as ye hollanders did Last fall, which if true wee doubt not in a Short time to have orders from them to Ruine ye french of Canida who are your and our avowed Enemies, & by yt means Procure you an everlasting Peace and Tranquillity.

4. WEE are glad to hear you had taken up ye ax to be Revenged of those Perfidous french who so basely Betrayed your People, and doe heartily Congratulate your Late great Succes in your Enterprise against them, not Doubting of your further Succes if Vigorously Pursued which wee doe Recommend unto you in an Especiall manner, and for your Encouragement wee can assure you yt ye English and Dutch have taken and Sunck many of the ffrench kings Best Schips of warr, and that Some Dutch Ships are now Cruseing about ye Mouth of Canida Rivere where they have taken tenn french Ships more.

5. WEE Cannot but admire yt ye Maquase who have had so many Proffs of ye Deceit of ye Eastern Indians should suffer themSelfs To be Deluded to hear any Proposealls whatsoever made by Such Villans Professed Enemyes to there Brethren ye Christians to ye Eastward; Especially Since they were So Strickly Charged by the Gentn of Albany not only to Stopp your Ears & not to accept of there false Presents but send them Prisoners here; for by there owne Proposealls you may Judge what Persones they are, they Plainly tell you they are in amity with ye french your Enemies who Supplyes them with amunition to Destroy ye English and will never be wanting to furnish them with what they shall ask to doe ye Same to you; Wee are further Informed how falsly they have InSinuated to you as if we had Sent for there Sachims and Destroyed them, and yt ye English had Combined to cutt off all ye Indians in ye Country, Such notorious falcityes are Invented by the French Priests to try your Stedfastnesse and to make you become like ye waves of ye great Lake. Butt wee can assure you that there Sachims when Sent for, were not only Civilly Treated with Presents and other Tokens of frindship but Safely Conducted home in a Sloop, who

for thanks fell upon the English & Murtherd them, neither did we ever intend any evill to any Indians that will live Peaceably with us, but on ye Contrare Doe Resolve to Keep firm and whole ye League or Chain of frindship which So long hath been maintained betwixt us, in ye Doeing of which you will be always safe, and since wee are Informed yt ye 3d. Castle of ye Maquase utterly Refused to have any thing to doe with these foure Easterne Indians but by all means would have Sent them as DeSyred, wch was ye occasion of there Parting from ye Rest, wee must acknowlege them to be Prudent People, who have a great Veneration for ye Chain of frindship and therefore wee Recommend you that have had this failure to follow there Example for ye future.

6. WEE Expect yt if any of ye Easterne Indians our Enemies come near any of the Brethren of ye 5 nations or within your Reach or knowledge, you will not only Deny them all manner of Succor or Releeffe, Butt will accompt it your Intrest to kill & DeStroy them, as well as ye french there Confederates, which will be very acceptable to our king, and wee his Subjects shall take it as a Signall mark of your fidelity.

7. WEE must further Lett you understand that there are Diverse of our ffrinde Indians, as those upon Canetticut River, Pequots, Moheegs, Natiks, and all Indians to ye Southward of them who are in actuall Service against ye Eastern Indians, and are Linked in ye Same Covenant Chain with us, That you doe them no harme when any of your People come neer our Parts Either in Pursute of our Enemies or to Visite your Brethren among us, for ye Prevention whereof it will be Requisite you have a Sign, which for ye first Six moons will be by holding upright ye Butt end of yr gunn and for Six moons after yt holding up of both your hands, and not above Two to appear till Such time they be Discoverd to be frindes, Least Some mischeeffe might befall ye Brethren, which wee Should be much greev'd att, & ye Same Signs we will give to our People both Christians & Indians, & when that time is

Deganawidah then walked back and forth before the Longhouse, singing the Peace Hymn and other sacred songs. Many people came and learned the Peace Hymn. With the power of the songs they were made strong. The Hymn of Peace had particular power.

Expired wee Shall Take care to send yu new ones as occasion shall Require.

/s/ John Pynchon
/s/ Thomas Savage
/s/ Andr: Belcher
/s/ Jonathan Bull.

Answer of the five Nations vizt Maquase Oneydes Onnondages Cayouges and Sinnekes to the honble Col. John Pynchon Majr Thomas Savage Capt. Andrew Belcher and Capt. Jonathan Bull Agents for ye three Collonies of N: England vizt Massashusetts Plymouth and Canneticut in ye Citty hall of Albany ye 23th day of Septembr: 1689[1]

Names of ye Sachims
Tahaiadoris of ye Maquas Speaker
Rode
Sinnonquirese
ToSoquathe
aquedakoro
SaggaddoochquiSaa
The oneydes
Takajerhos
Canjaquarie
Schaihohade
Dekonrado
The onnondages
Carachkondie
Culsagonno
The Cayouges
Tarondaketho
The Sinnekes
Adondareerha
onerjo

THE Speaker Tahaiadoris Cheefe Sachim of ye Maquase made a Long oration to ye 5 nations and Repeated ye Propositions made to them yesterday and DeSyred them as they were come wth a good heart hither to hear ye Brethren of ye 3 Collonies of n: England, they should be attentive to hear ye answer which was to be made to them. Then ye Speaker addressed his Discourse to ye gentn. of N: England and Said

BRETHREN

You are come here to this Prefixed Place which is by the Christians appointed to be ye house of Treatty for all Publique Bussinesse with us ye 5 nations, and doe Return you many thanks for your Renovacon of ye Covenant chain which is not of Yron now as it was formerly, but of Pure Silver, in which chain are Included all there Majes. Subjects from ye Sinnekes Countrey quite to ye Eastward as farr as any Christian Subjects of our great king lives

[1] A different version of these answers is given in Colden, 1: 120-125.

and from thence Southward all along N: Engld. quite to Virginia, doe give a Bevr.

2. WEE are Verry glad to hear of ye good Successe our great king hes had against ye. french by Sea in takeing and Sincking so many of his men of warr; you say wee are one People Pray let us goe hand & hand and joyn together here also and Ruine the French and all our Enemies, as yu. have Said in yr. Proposealls. doe give a Bevr.

3. WEE acknowlege that ye Covenant chain between us is Antient & of long Standing which wee have always kept Inviolate for when you had warrs Some years agoe with ye Indians; we were DeSyred to fall upon those yr Enemies which wee Readily did and Pursued them Closely which ꝑvented ye Effusion of much Christian Blood That was a Sign we loved yu with true and Unfeigned love from our hearts. did give a Belt off wampum.

4. YOU are Pleased to Recommend us to Pursue our Enemies the French Vigorously which wee will endevor to ye. Uttmost for they are your Enemies also, and we being but ill Provided of men in this Place if ye french our Enemies should Come and make an Attaque upon itt, we therefore DeSyre that our Brethren of ye 3 Collonies may Send us a hundred men for our assistance, there is Victualls Enough amongst ye Christians here for there Entertainment. doe give one Bever.

5. WEE acquaint ye Brethren yt we have taken up ye ax against ye french of Canida, we have bore much with them from year to year, The governr. of Canida thought we were affraid of him Butt he was Deceived; Wee acquaint you further that this warr with ye French is never to be laid aside, wee will never give ye French a Smile, nay wee will never be Reconsiled with them So long as there is a frenchman alive. Yea if all our People should be Ruined and Cutt in Peeces, wee will never make peace wth them, & hereupon ye Brethren of ye 3 Collonies may Depend. doe give a Bever.

6. YOW Spoke yesterday of ye onnagongues and Aurages meaning ye Eastern Indians, we never were So Proude to Beginn a

Deganawidah called together all the People of the Flint, and from among them chose one man who was to approach Adodarho and sing the Peace Hymn before his lodge. The Mohawks followed the singer.

warr without Cause, you tell us that they are Treacherous Rogues, we Beleeve it Verry well, you likewise Inform us that they will undoubtedly assist ye french if they should come wth an army, which if they doe or joyne with any of our Enemies ye french or there Indians we can assure you wee will kill and Destroy them as Enemies, doe give one Bever.

The Maquase Said for themSelfs

7. YOW told us Yesterday of ye 2 Signs which we approove of very well accepting of them, and thanke you for y^r Carefulnesse, and you being Sachims sent here and now bounde home Probably some of these Rogues ye onnagongues may Lye in waite upon ye Path to doe y^u. a mischeeffe wee Maquase does therefore Send 5 of our men with you to Convey you home as farr as ye English Plantacons, what ye other four nations will doe, we know nott, doe give a Belt of wampum.
8. WEE doe Return ye Brethren our hearty thanks for the Presents yesterday given, but Especially for ye Pouder and Lead, althogh our young men who are unsationable doe wonder y^t according to Custome in time of warr Some gunns are not also given, Because they are in much want of them. Doe give a Bev^r.

The 5 nations Say

9. WEE have now Spoke of ye warr, and are now Come to ye Covenant chain, which we Promise to keep Inviolate, and wish y^t ye Sunne of Peace with its Beams may Shine over us all in Peace y^t are in said Chain, doe give 2 Belts of wampum ye one for ye Sunn and ye oy^r for its Beams.
10. THEY doe Plant the Tree of Peace and Tranquillity here whose Roots are fast in ye grounde and Extend themselfs as farr as y^e. uttmost Bounds of y^r. Collonies, and if the french should Come to shake y^t Tree, wee shall feel it by the Roots which will moove, But we Trust y^t it will not be in his Power to shake that Tree which hath been Planted here So long among us, if he can Ruine y^t tree of Peace then he will be ye Devill. doe give 2 Bevers.

After the Speaker said he had done the Agents told ye Interpreters to acquaint ye 5 nations that they had not answerd upon ye 2 main Points of ye Propos:

First Concerning ye Entertaining of ye 4 Eastern Messengers

Enemies to ye English that are in ye Covenant with yu. 2ly. That they did not Declare whether they would look upon ye Eastern Indians as Enemies, & if they came neer any of the Brethren or within there Reach or knowlege they would not Accompt it there Intrest to kill and Destroy them.
Who answerd that they would willingly have Deliverd up ye Sd 4 messengers and helpe to bynde them, if ye Christians had Come to ye army to fetch them, & yt Jannetje the Messenger had no orders from ye Sachims to Engage the Delivery of sd 4 messengers at Shinnechtady to ye gentn. of albany.
2. That they cannot Positively Declare warr against the Eastern Indians, they haveing Committed no acts of hostility upon them, neverthelesse are Resolved to live and Dye with there Brethren of N England, But ye french and there associates wee are Resolved to warr upon, for in ye Spring when wee took up ye ax against ye french, it was not by Councill or advise of any Body, but our oune Inclination to be Revenged neither did any Soule know of our Intentions for when wee Came to alby to acquaint ye Magistrates with our Design, our men had been out 14 days against ye French.

After the Propositions were over the Sachims of ye 5 nations Sent the Two Interpreters to ye Gentlemen Commissionate from ye 3 Collonies of n: England and Prayd to have ye Favour to Speake with them in Private, Since they had Some what to Communicate which was not free to be Disclosed and being mett Together there Speaker said as follows.[1]

WEE were not willing to Speak this Last Proposition in ye Eye of all ye People for this Reason, least by Some falsehearted Per-

[1] Colden states that the reason for this private conference was that the Iroquois were divided on the matter, with some favoring the Eastern Indians. It would appear from this account that the Indians' desire for secrecy was motivated by fear that their plans would be disclosed. This may or may not conflict with his interpretation. Colden, 124. The conference was completely private, for not even Nicholas Bayard, a prominent government official then in Albany, knew of it, though he described the public conference. Extract of Bayard's letter, September 23, 1689. O'Callaghan, 3: 621.

As they marched through the territory of the People of the Upright Stone, the Oneidas joined them. The Mohawks and Oneidas, walking together through the forest, met the Great Pipe People and also the People of the Great Mountain. Together all four nations marched through the woods toward the Onondaga settlement.

sones our DeSigne should be carried to our Enemies before we have Effected our Bussinesse or Enterprise, Butt now Gentlemen we have Sent for you to Declare our mindes fully to yu. and what our Resolution is Vizt. to tell yu that wee Esteem your Enemies ours, & we are DeSignd and ReSolved to fall first on ye Aurages or Penekook Indians, & then to fall on ye onnagonques & so our Enemies ye french, And in Testimony of our fidelity and truth in what we have Said to you we have now Sent or order'd five of our men to guarde yu. home, & also to Distinguish between your frinde Indians & ye Eastern Indians your Enemies By observeing where they Live, & if they see cause to make Discovery where ye Aurages or Pennecoke Indians are, yt we may see our Path Plaine as our manner is to see and know ye way as clear as we can before we make any onSett, & in a word which is as much as can be said yt your warr is our warr & we will live and Dye with yu

Adondarerha ye Cheeffe Sachim of ye Sinnekes Rose up and Said Brethren of ye five Nations I Rejoyce in your Resolucon, & our Renewing ye League and Strenthening ye Chain and thanke ye Maquase that they have orderd five men to guarde our Brethren home. I would doe ye Same but yt I live So farr off however I will Send one of my best men for yt Service.

A True Copy
Examind By me
Robt. Livingston Cl.

Examination of three french Prisoners taken by ye. Maquase & brought to Shinnechtady, who were Examind by Pr. Schuyler Mayr of ye Citty of Albany Dome: Godevridus Dellius & Some other Gentn. that went from albany a Purpose; and Report as follows, on ye 3d. of march 1689/90.

1. That about ye. midle of Januarie they went from Mont Royall being about 300 men french and Indians to witt 160 french among which only 19 Souldiers taken out of diverse Companies ye Rest all them yt frequent ye woods Bosslopers[1] & Inhabitants & 140 Praying Indians and others, with Positive orders to murder and DeStroy all People they mett withall at Shinnechtady Except

[1] Bushlopers or *voyageurs.*

Such as beg'd for quarters;[1] as also to Burn ye Place and to take with them those that they could cary along; after said Compe. had marched Some days from Canida Some french & Indians yt. were Sick and Timerous Returnd So yt. ye Party were 250 yt did ye Exploit at Shinnechtady ye Commanders name was Monsr. St belina, by ye Indians calld ochquese.

2. After Enquiry of ye Particulars of ye Murder they Confessd yt 4 or 5 french had murderd ye Minister of sd. Village called Petrus Tessemaker, first shooting him throu ye leggs, & then hewd him wth. there Swords most barbarously, & being askd if they had Expresse Orders to deal so Cruelly Said That there order was to doe what was done.

3. Being Inquired concerning ye Prisoners they carried along with them, Said they were well Treated by ye way, and within 4 or 5 days journey of Canida Some of our Prisoners went with ye. Indians and ye Remainder With ye french, Butt yt. we need not doubt of there good Entertainment at Canida Since they will be deliverd to ye Jesuits, to be instructed in there Religeon

4. That they had eat about 20 or 30 of ye horses they Caried along with them, & intended to carry 7 with them to Canida.

5. That neverthelesse Provisions begann to grow Scarce in there army, & therefore 2 men were Dispatchd upon Skeats who goe 25 leagus in a day to cause Provisions be sent them from mont Royall.

6. That ye 10 Prisoners whereof these now Examind were 3 were taken by our Indians about 2 a Clok in ye. afternoon, being at ye Same fyre yt ye body of ye army went from in ye morning; attending some Sick Persones who could not march So fast as ye Rest.

7. That ye. manner of keeping there Skouts out a nights both in Comeing and goeing was 30 men who marched Constantly Round ye army al night about a musket Shott off, but neer Shinnechtady the number of sd. skouts was Doubled.

[1] This is a description of the famous Schenectady massacre of February 1689/90.

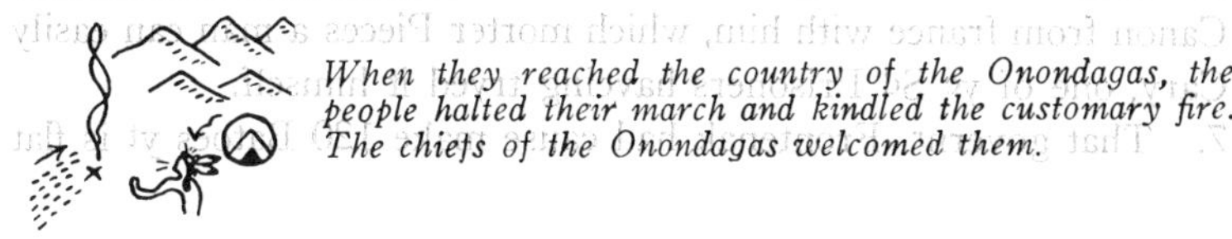

When they reached the country of the Onondagas, the people halted their march and kindled the customary fire. The chiefs of the Onondagas welcomed them.

8. That by ye Tract they trapand some Maquase Squaes neer Shinnechtady, whom they Compeld to give an accompt of ye Condition of ye Place, & kept Sd. Indian women till they had Committed ye. Massacre.
When they were within Some miles of Shinnechtady ye officers had a Consultation about falling upon albanie, one monsr. De Tallie who had been formerly here did Presse hard to Attaque it; Butt because there orders was Expressly for Shinnechtady ye DeSign on alby was put by.
9. That they had lost but one only frenchman at Shinnechtady, & one Sore wounded.

The Sd. Prisoners being Examined about ye affares of Canida doe Say

1. That Last Summer 8 or 9 ships arrived att Quebek whereof Two were men of warr, who brougt Store of amunition and Provisions, with wh. Shipps ye Earle of Frontenac came for govr: & monsr. Callier govr of mont Royall, & ye Indian Prisoners; but brougt no Souldiers & yt ye Marquis De Denonville late Governr. went away with Sd. Shipps.
2. That they Expect for certain yt. 12 men of warr will come this Summer with Two Thousand men & 2 years Provisions for Canida.
3. The governour Frontenak upon his Voyage to Canida met with a french ship loaden with Biskett bounde for ye north west Passage, caried ye Same along with him to Canida, and Sent her Loading with great store of Porke & meale come from france up to Mont Royall.
4. That Provisions were not dearer att Canida now then formerly, a Minot of meal being sold for a french Crowne, adding yt. ye Dammage done by ye Indians to there Corn in Canida was Inconsiderable.
5. Governour Frontenac came to Mont Royall about ye middle of Septembr: which Place he hath fortifyed with a Ditch 10 foot deep & 12 foot Broad Round about ye. Toune Except at ye River Side where he hath Built a Stone Redout, where ye guarde is kept.
6. That he had brought 12 Smal morter Peeces & Some Small Canon from france with him, which morter Pieces a man can easily Cary, one of ye Sd Prisoners haveing tryed it himself.
7. That governr. Frontenak had cause make 120 Batoes yt is flat

bottomd boats fitt to carry 8 or 9 men with Provisions & ammunition, as also 100 Burch Canoes at Mont Royall, ye first were all made & ye later ye greatest part Ready; & yt it was much discoursd among ye french of light Labers to Storm ye fort of Albany; all which together wth. ye Morter Pieces are makeing Ready to come Early in ye Spring with 1500 men to Attaque Albany by ye french calld fort d'orange.

8. That governour Frontenak went in ye month of Novemr to Quebek, & was designd to Return to Mont Royal in ye winter or at longest early in ye Spring, to accomplish there DeSign upon albanie.

9. That for that Purpose monsr. d'Lute was to goe assoon as Possible in ye Spring with 50 Souldiers to ottowawa to bring doune ye Indians to Mont Royall.

10. For ye PreSent there are 6 Companies of Souldiers at Mont Royall of 50 men each Besides 6 or 700 Burgers & Inhabitants

11. The kings Souldiers at Canida are Computed to be 15 or 1600 men, & ye sd. quantity of Burgers & Inhabitants who are fitt to carry arms BeSides there Indians -

12. That Sd. Souldiers are Divided in ye following Tounes & forts Vizt.

Quebek
Mont Royall
Chambly
Troy Riviere
Sorell
Chattague
Bout de lyle
La Prarie de Magdalene
La Prarie d St. Lambar
Longeul
Robang
La Chine
Culjerie
La Pont au Tremble
La Chyne
Boucharville
St. Surplis
Chanpleyn
Batiskan
St. Francois
Bekankour
Lyle Jesus
Le Pointe Levi
Bau Port
St. Jean
Laurette
La montaigne

Besides 2 more which they could not call to minde one whereof hard by Quebek in which about a hundred men are in garriSon

A great multitude marched to the fireside of Adodarho. The singer of the Peace Hymn led them: Mohawks, Oneidas, Onondagas, Cayugas, and Senecas.

13. Doe Say yt. it was divulged at mont Royall That 400 men were gone from Quebek under ye Command of Perneuffe & Courtemanche being all Bosslopers Inhabitants & Indians and no Souldiers, Towards kennebek River to take a Certain English Fort; & yt anoyr. Company but not So numerous under ye Conduct of monsr. artell were gone towards ye Province of n: Yorke to doe mischeeff there.

14. That ye french king was Pleased to give Cadarachqui to govr. Frontenak as a gift, Who was verry much Displeased at his arrivall when he heard yt it was Deserted, & yt govr De denonville had given orders to Demolish it. The garrison yt Lay there being 80 men were Come home whereof 8 were Drowned, most of the amunition being throwne in ye. water, and among ye Rest 4 or 500 Small arms, & have Sunk ye Canon about 20 Leagus from mont Royall.

A true Copy Examind
pr Robt: Livingston
Cl.

Propositions made by Pr Schuyler Mayr. of ye City of albany to the cheife Captns. & Leaders of a Company of 350 Indians of ye 5 nations now bounde upon an Expedition to Canida all Encampd at Skinnechtady & present at ye Proposicon this 12 day of august 1692[1]

Brethren

1. I am glad to see you so fordward In Complyeing wth: Corlaers Commands given you when he was Last here & yt. yu Prosecute ye war So Vigorously & with Such a Strenth I hope ye Brethren of ye upper nations will not faile to Send a Considerable Party doune Cadarachqui River to joyn with yu. & yt. may have good Successe in yr undertakeings.

2. The french Praying Indians have always hitherto done ye Brethren & us ye. most mischeeffe & are Capable if not quashd to Continue our allarms, neither is it Probable yt. ye french can doe any thing without there assistance who are there Spyes Skouts

[1] This was a prelude to an attack upon the French posts north of Lake Champlain, an extremely successful undertaking. Schuyler's design was "to animate the Indians and preserve their enmity against the French." Smith, 1: 106, who, following Colden, mistakenly dates this action as 1691. This report was read before the Council on August 23, 1692. *Cal. N. Y. Coun. Min.*, 75.

& guides to doe us harm, I doe therefore Recommend ye Brethren to lay there Principal Dissign against them In which you must be more wary & Cunning then formerly when ye Brethren were out wth Lawrence who lett them Escape after they were in there hands.

It is in Vain for yu to think to treat or Parley with them Since Experience hes often taught you yt ye Jesuits & they are to Cunning for yu. therefor yu must Dally no more with them but give them a Blow at once & DeStroy there Indian Corn & then come to talk with them, there necessity then & no hopes of Recovery will be ye best argument to cause the Residue to come along with yu. whom you may assure shall be well treated here and Lookt upon by this governmt. as ye Rest of ye Brethren they behaveing themSelfs as true Subjects to ye Crowne of England from whence they were Enticeing & debauched by ye deceitfull french who are nott able to Protect them from ye fury of this governmt. neither shall there Desertion be any more minded, & for there further Incouragemt you may assure ym that all care shall be taken by this government to Instruct them in ye true Christian Religeon as yu See is dayly done to ye Brethren here whose hearts are any wise Inclined to ye Christian faith neither shall they want food for there wifes and Children when they come, we haveing Plenty of Corn this not being so Barren a Countrey as Canida is where they must give a Bever for a Bushell of Indian Corn.

3. Assoon as yu. have accomplishd ye Design wth ye Praying Indians you are to Doe what dammage yu can to ye french & also Destroy there Corn it being ye time of there harvest which will Reduce them to yt mean Condition yt they will have no thougts of comeing abroad to annoy ye Brethren.

4. We must Enjoyn yu. to goe by ye way of ye Lake where yu. will meet such Small troops that come hither to doe mischeeffe to yr wifes & Children & by yt means Prevent there evil Dessigns

5. Since it grows late in ye year we must Recommend yu to make all ye Dispatch Imagineable & not linger so long at a Place whereby

The singer walked before the lodge of Adodarho, trying to cure his sick mind by the power of the Peace Hymn. But, if the Peace Hymn is to have any power, it must be sung without error. The singer hesitated and made a slip.

yr Dissign may be broke; for if any Prisoners should be taken in ye mean while the Enemy will have advertisemt & So yr Labor is lost

Lastly: I must with greeffe acquaint you of ye many Complaints I have had of ye Poor Inhabitants of this Place Since my arrivall, occasiond by yr young men killing there Catle horses & destroying there Corn & burning there fences which is unsufferable Since we have furnishd yu with what necessaries you wanted & graunted ye Request in every Respect. yr arms are all Repared at our Charge, we have given yu. Provisions of Beeffe Porke & Pease and here is now Pouder & Ball to annoy yr Enemyes therefore Proceed to doe mischeeffe to yr Enemyes & have a Care in yr march out and home to doe no more harm to yr frinds

Given them 15 bags Pouder
200 lb Lead
2 Barrels Pork & Beefe
12 Shepl of Peese
4 quarters of Beefe
400 flints
30 loaves

att which all ye whole Compe of 350 men made a great Shout & Returnd thanks & was also given them upon there Request a Dog a Pistol a Sword 7 ps of Silver money & 2 Sheets of Paper, ye Dog they killd & Sung Some of there warr Songs over him.

Rode ye Sachim of ye Maquase was Speaker

Answer of ye Cheefe Capts. of ye five nations of ye Maquase oneydes onnendages Cayouges & Sinnekes to ye Mayr. Pr. Schuyler Esqr. at Shinnechtady ye 14th day of august 1692

Broyr Pieter

Wee Returne yu. our hearty thanks for takeing upon yu. ye trouble to come hither to [(*torn*)] & Dispatch this Party to Canida, who are come upon Corlaers Request to Pursue ye warr against yr & our Enemies & to keep them in allarm in there Countrey; The Provisions & Ammunition you bring us is Verry Seasonable & acceptable Wee are now mett together of all ye 5 nations to acquaint yu. yt. we have Concluded to follow your advise Relateing ye Praying Indians & will follow yr advise in every Respect, to ye utmost of our Power, which we Esteem very good and wholesome, but what ye Issue will be is knowne only to ye god yt dwells in heaven, who must blesse our undertakeings; we can assure y^{u} of nothing but of our design & Inclination w^{h} is to Spoyle & annoy ye Enemy, & we will use all means Imagineable to Putt ye Praying Indians out of a Capacety of ever doeing you or us any more harm—we will Spare them no longer.

Broy^{r} Corlaer you Sett us on dayly to fight & destroy your Enemies, & bidd us goe on wth Courage, but wee See not y^{t} you doe any-thing to it yourSelfs, neither doe wee See any great Strenth you have to oppose them if they Enemy should breake out upon you; we hear of no great matter is like to be done at Sea, we hear nothing of itt; The warr must also be hottly Pursued on y^{r} Sides, what is it y^{t} our neighbours of n: England and ye Rest of ye English y^{t} are in Covenant with us doe, they all Stay att home & Sett us on to doe ye worke, & yett when ye least harm is done to y^{r} Cattle or Corn you chide us Severely for itt, you cannot Expeckt y^{t} this warr can be Carried on without Charge & Expence & dammage to w^{h}. must be born withall.

Formerly when any Pouder was given us we had gunns along with it, but y^{t} Seems to be forgotten, now we cannot hold out without all necessaries fitting for ye warr, we Remember y^{t} ye old Corlaer was So kinde to us & So Intimate y^{t} he would doe nothing of y^{t} Relateing to ye warr without ye advise of Some of our Sachims takeing Caniackke one of our head men into his Cabinet Councill, & he told us y^{r} Catle were our Catle we were all one People & there was no Difference, but we fynde it is not Soe now. are all those Papers & Transactions w^{h}. Passed between him & us burried with him, since we are So Sharpely Reproovd for killing of ye Catle & eateing ye Corn which cannot be helpd in these times. We deSyre y^{t} Such faults may be passed by

We doe acquaint you y^{t} there are 380 men gone downe Cadarachqui River whom we hope to meet at Canida, & doubt not but shall doe Some good Exploit before we come back, & so ended there answer given a Small Belt of wampum & 3 faddom

The May^{r}. Replyed

That they must not think much tto be Reproovd for doeing of ill, y^{t}. he was Sorry they had So bad memories to say y^{t}. Corlaer

Another singer was appointed, but he also made an error in the song.

told ym our Catle were there Catle, its a grand mistake for yr Bevers are none of ours & yu may verry wel Remember yt Sr Edmund Andross who was So Intimate wth Caniachko yr Sachim Causd yu to pay to Capt Sander 20 Bevers for a horse yu kild of his & 16 Bevr. to his Broyr for anoyr horse, here they both Stand who Recd. ym., therefore yu. must not think to destroy ye People yt live here at yt Rate: yu tell us we must mentain ys Post & not desert Shinnechtady but ye People cannot live here if yu destroy there Catle & Corn therefore lett me hear no more Complaints.
As for what our neighbours doe to ye warr we hear Sr Wm Phips is gone with Some Ships to ye Eastward to annoy ye french & yt he was Sending a great Party by Land to Destroy ye Indians Corn, & we Expect orders every day from our great king to cause ye Rest of our neighbours give there assistance towards ye Careing on of this warr.

Adogaounwa

The tall oneyder Capt Stood up & in ye behalfe of ye whole Compe of ye 5 nations Return there hearty thanks to Corlacr for his Present of Provision of amunition & hope they shall make good use of itt to our & there oun Satisfaction & DeSyre ye Mayor to Stay to day to heare there Result
The Mayor desyre them to Despatch Since he would willingly goe home this afternoon being Saturday

Copy the Mayr. Letter to Majr. Ingoldesby Comdr in Cheife &a.

albany 17 aug 1692

HONble Sr
I Send yr honr. inclosed ye Proposition I made to ye. Indians at Shinnechtady with there answers who goe away to morrow I hope they will be Successfull and attain there aim about ye Praying Indians; I have had Private Discourse wth ye Capt. Canochquonnie after ye Propositions were done none being present but R Livingst[on] & hillie who told me he had 2 Belts of wampum wh. he would give to ye Praying Indians, he is so earnest to accomplish ye Design, yt he will Ventor to goe into ye Castle & Speake with ye Indians not doubting but he had yt Influence upon them not only to bring them away but yt they would knock ye french in ye head yt are in ye Castle, & desyre 2 Belts of wampum of me to joyn with his, I disswaded him from yt fearing ye Jesuit

& ye Indians would be to many for him if they once gott him into there Clutches. then he ReSolvd to goe and Lye in ye. Plantacin of his father as he calls ye Indian yt was his master neer unto ye Castle & So discourse him there, & if he were dissapointed in this he would draw up ye whole Body about ye Castle & tell ym if they would come away they should be welcome Else they would fall upon them & if he founde any in ye woods he would Destroy ym if they would not Surrender; in fyne he could not tell what would occurr & to ye best of his understanding he would Cary on ye Matter. I have Strikly Enjoynd him to give ym. a blow if Possible & not to Trust to ym. nor ye french & to Incourage ye Remaindr. to come hither to whom I have Sent 2 belts one in ye behalfe of Corlaer & I for ye minister. I have withal assured ym. they shall have a minister & Land to Plant upon & Provisions for ye first year, & be lookt upon as ye Rest of our Brethren without any Distinction, neither shall they be forced to goe out to warr agst ye french butt live Peaceably & quietly in ye govermt the Place of there nativity, & diverse oyr arguments to Induce ym. to come, & doubt not but he & all ye Rest of ye Capts. who I have Discoursd Severally will Endevor to bring ym here, by one means or oyr ye way & method cannot be Exactly knowne till they be upon ye Spott, he hes also a DeSign assoon as ye upper Indians come downe to cause ym fall upon ye french & yn the Praying Indians will draw out for there assistance & So Surprize ym that way. I am in good hopes to hear good news of this Design, which being brought to passe is of great Import to this govermt. I have Promisd him a good Reward if he does ye bussinesse. I have left no Stone unturnd to Promote ye Design ye more because yr honr Seems So fordward & yt Sundrey Persones are willing to Contribute towards it, I send yr honr Inclosed ye acct of Charges amounting to £54:15:3 which we could not avoid in Dispatching his Considerable Party wherein yu wil fynde I have been as Sparing as Possible Therefore hope yr honr. will take care yt ye £54:15:3 money be pd. to Broyr [Stephanus van] Cortlandt who wil Send it up else I need not hereafter offer to Employ anybody

Then Deganawidah walked before Ododarho's lodge and sang the song without error. Adodarho heard the song, and his power was broken. The war-club dropped from his gnarled hands.

for ye Publike haveing Engaged my Particular Credt for ye Same. I Remain

Honble Sr. Your most humble Servt
Signd Pr Shuyler

Albany, September 6, 1692
Copy of the Mayor's [Peter Schuyler] Letter to the Council concerning Arent [Schuyler][1]

Gentlemen:

My brother, Arent Schuyler, has brought a commission here to make a trip to the Schowaenos.[2] As to the matter itself, to bring those Indians here, that is very good and cannot but bring the government great advantages. But I did not know that the circumstances of the present time could suffer such a hasty intention without having communicated this to our Indians. Gentlemen, it is Indians and not Christians with whom we are dealing, and we should concede something, especially in time of war. These Schowaenos are Indians in a public war with our Indians who show a great displeasure because the government makes peace with those Indians without their knowledge. For they would say about these negotiations as about the making of peace, which is true, that in our court house it has been decided that no one would speak of peace with the French or with the Indians who are our enemies and theirs but by common consent. They do not mind that those Indians come over here, but for that they first want to get the whole house together. Our five nations also murmur about the Minisink Indians that they did not go to war even though they asked them to do so. Neither are they satisfied with the River Indians because not one of them has gone to Canada except in order to trade. And as a means of showing that they are serious, they have especially sent to me from the army five Indians of each nation upon hearing the rumor of the coming of Schowaenos. They desire that as long as the army is still out,

[1] Translated from the Dutch.

[2] On August 18 Arent Schuyler appeared before the New York Council "with the far Indians called Showannios and Some Senecas. . . . Showannios want to make peace." The Council gave its reply and some presents on the following day. On August 22 they were provided with an escort home under Arent Schuyler's command. This letter of Peter Schuyler was read by the Council on September 8, and it was noted that the Five Nations were jealous "because of the intended peace with the Showannoes; soothing letters to be written." *Cal. N. Y. Coun. Min.*, 74-76.

they should not be allowed to pass through their territory. They also had heard that they came to speak with them. What is more, an important sachem of the Senecas who is here at the moment has openly declared to Hilletje who, on my request, gave him an oath on this matter that he cannot understand how the Christians can be so drunk in their minds as to negotiate a separate peace now without their knowledge with Indians who are their open enemies. They should remember that Corlaer requested them here in the court house to offer belts of peace to the northernmost Indians and should allow them passage through their territory and that they had already done this last year, not doubting but that their belts had made them come over here. So much so, that we say that they should not have done this without us. He added further that if the government had made peace with the Schowaenos, their enemies, without the Senecas' knowledge that then the Senecas could just as well make peace with the French, our enemies, without our knowledge. So that this matter is not without disadvantages. However, while your Honor and the Honorable Council have gone so far with this work that it will be continued, I would nevertheless advise with your Honor's permission that then at least 10 or 12 of the most important Schowaenos should come here to wait for the return of the warriors from Canada. Then I will do my best to persuade the five nations to send each one 5 or 6 of their most important men with belts to the Schowaenos with whom, with your Honor's permission, I will send then a similar number of Christians from here who know the language and can show that the meeting came from the whole house. They could then meet each other on the way or in the territory where brother Arent is going with his company so that everything may go well. Gentlemen, I myself think that this is the most certain way, for if our Indians are beaten in Canada it might bring us trouble here. Reminding you of this and leaving it all to your judgement, I am

Your humble servant.

When he had finished the song, Deganawidah walked toward Adodarho and rubbed his body to give it strength. By Deganawidah's power and the power of the Peace Hymn, the body of Adodarho was made straight and his mind was made healthy. His heart became as a pine tree, clean and good.

Springfield, June 21st, 1693[1]

May it please your Excellency

Having received from Major Wessels a memorial signed by several gentlemen by order of your Excellency, dated the 16th of this month, I am obliged to recognize with all humble gratefulness your concern for our affairs. I am very aware of the dangers if we should come to a break with our Indians, especially with the Maquase with whom we have lived in peace for such a long time following the agreements made which we will try to maintain, being so much more to his Majesty's interest in this conjuncture of time. Therefore I am very willing to accept the excuse you make for them, putting all the blame on the French Indians, because of the great difficulties and troubles Major Wessels has taken to make us understand it, and not only through writing. But while there were no French Indians around here at that time,[2] we do find the definite declarations and accusations of dying persons against two Indians to wit, a Maquase and a Skachkook, now under arrest, to be so positive and explicit that they, in my judgement, should be required to give a definite excuse or be brought to trial. I have sent your Excellency herewith the copies of the testimonials which have already been taken in this matter. Yours

[John] Pynchon.

Some Remarks upon ye Present State of affares at albany Relateing to ye Indians of ye 5 nations & Particularly of ye message sent to ym from ye Govr of Canida [July 1693][3]

1. That it is nu manifest to ye world yt ye Jesuit milett at oneyde doth keep a Constant Correspondence with ye Enimy of Canida haveing now Recd. a Packet of letters from ye Count of frontenak govr of yt Place wh. he Refuses to deliver fearing his Secret Intrigues might be Discoverd

2. That Sd. Packet of letters & Belt of wampum Sent by ye govr. of Canida doth amaze & bring ye 5 nations into Confusion obstructing there Intending DeSigns against ym by ye notion of a Peace.

[1] Translated from the Dutch.

[2] Several Mohawks were being held by the Massachusetts authorities on suspicion of committing several murders at Deerfield "although it is proved French Indians have done it." *Cal. N. Y. Coun. Min.*, 86.

[3] This incomplete draft by Robert Livingston was probably intended as a memorial to Governor Fletcher. The latter probably used it as the basis of his conference of July 3 and 4 with the Iroquois. O'Callaghan, 4: 41-44.

3. That it is Evident Such underhand Dealings wth. there Majes. Subjects of ye 5 nations hath great Influence upon them who are wearied wth. this long warr, & if not Prudently Prevented will lull them a Sleep till ye govr of Canida hes an opportuntiy to doe them or us a mischeeffe.

4. That it can be Esteemed nothing else but a Stratagem or fraude his So earnest Courting of our Indians to a Peace Since if he were Real ought to make his application to his Excel there Majes. Viceregent here & not to ye 5 nations Subjects of this Governmt.

5. That nothing can be more advantageous to ye french nor Destructive to there Majes. Subjects of these Parts yn. this way ye french govr takes Since first he gains ye Point of Saveing his People from all Incursions of Sd. Indians, & if a Cessation be Effected will Endevour to Debauch ye Sd. 5 nations from there allegeance to there Majes. & get them over to his side & by Consequence must turn our Enemyes Since Such Sort of People can never be neuters

6. That ye Sd. Jesuit Milet hath not only an absolute authority & Power over ye [(*torn*)] of oneyde where he Resides but a great Sway over all ye 5 nations by his Emmissaryes who he Constantly Imployes for ye french Intrest, a Sufficient Testimony hereof is ye 5 nations calling a genl meeting at onnondage upon this verry message from Canida wherto they Invite ye Christians of this Governmt. & ye River Indians.

7. That by such & oyr Evil Practices of ye sd Jesuit & french of Canida many of our Indians dayly Desert & Runn overto ye Enemy, Particularly 4 Mohogs whom People Put great Confidence in are upon Pretence to goe and fight ye Enemy Runn over to ye french being now seen at mont Royal by ye Jesuits messenger.

8. That ye Indians of oneyde are So farr from *p*forming there Promise in Delivering up ye Jesuit millet [(*torn*)] yt not to send ye Indian boy but in a jearing manner in yt understanding ye Scriptures.

Then Deganawidah spoke to the gathering of the nations and said: "In every nation there are wise and good men. These should be appointed chiefs. They will be the advisers of their people. They are to be selected by the clan mothers, but they must have the goodwill of all the clan."

9. That we have Reason to beleeve ye Jesuit milet hes Recd Particular Instructions from ye govr. of Canida Concerning ye mannageing of this Peace Since ye Sd. Jesuit doth So Passionatly Expresse himself a great frinde to ye English Even to be Sacrificed for their Service.

That these & ye like maladyes wh this Poor Province now groans undr may be Effectually cured we doubt not in ye least but yr Excel in yr great wisdom will Contrive Such Proper methods as will accomplish ye Same, & with all Submission & humility doe offer as our advise ye following

Albany 27:august 1695

May it Please yr. Excell

According your Excell order of ye 17th. this Instant wee sent Emediatly Gerrt. Luykasse & Itawacam one of our River Indians to acquaint the Sachims of ye five Nations that your Excell was to meet them here in albany the 10th. of Sepr. next Ensueing. but upon there arriveall in the Mohoggs Countrey meets some of the Mohoggs that had been up messengers to oneyde to Enquire about the news they had heard Concerning the governr. of Canida s goeing to Cadarachqui who brings the news that there hes been five french Indians upon ye Road between oneyde & onnondage

---

[Legend for the 1697 map]
alby 2 m[arch] 1696/7
Drafft of this Countrey

1. Albany
2. Sconectody [Schenectady]
3., 4., 5. Maqs. Castells [Mohawk Castles]
6. Anoyedess [Oneidas]
7. Anondagos Laek [Lake Oneida]
8. Anendagos [Onondagas]
9. Soscihanes River [Susquehanna]
10. Cayougos
11., 12. Senecass
13. the ffalls of Gagrae [Niagara]
14. Leake of Caderaquee [Lake Ontario]
15. Caderaquee [Fort Frontenac]
16. Laek Alettae [Fort LaGallette]
17. Montt Royall [Montreal]

a. Halfe Moone
b., c. sarach Togae [Saratoga]
d., e. Carying place
f. wodd Creek
g. Leak of sacrementt [Lake Saint Sacrement—Lake George]
h. Croune Poyntt
j. otter Kill
k. Rock Rogie
l. Lamott [Fort La Motte]
m. Sint Teares [Fort St. Theresa]
n. Shamlee [Chambly]
o. Sorell
p. Troreveare [Three Rivers]
q. Queebeck
r. Reliance
s. The Hed of Connecticutt River.

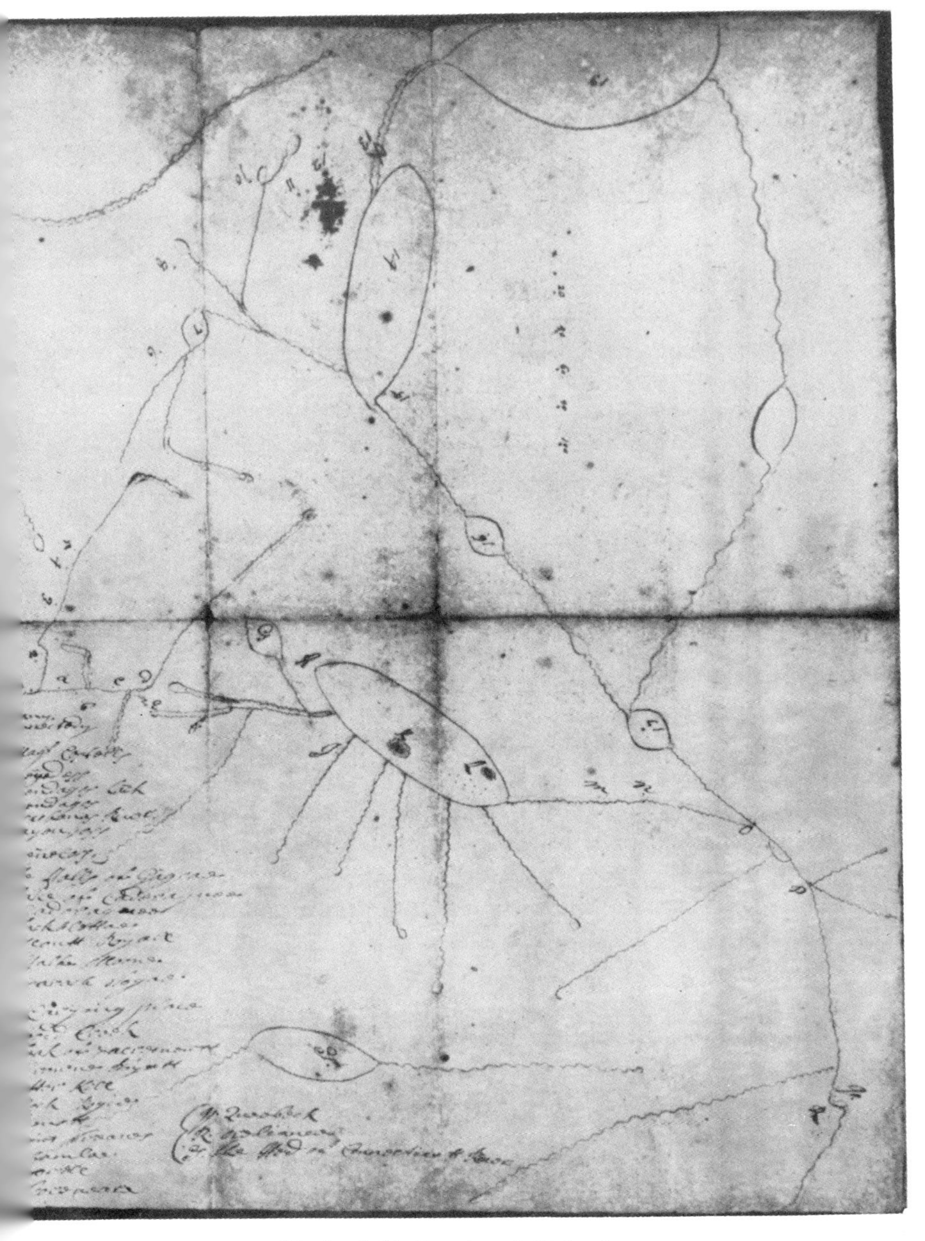

"Draft of this Country 1696/1697."

Courtesy Franklin D. Roosevelt Library

who meet with three of our Sinnekes [s]quaes kild one & took two Prisoner a litle after Comes three onnondages fyndes this Squae & followed the french Indians there tracts & overtook them & fyred at one anoyr. & lost one of there men & ye oyr two made there Escape to oneyde whereupon the oneydes persued the french Indians again took one Prisoner one wounded & anoyr. they kild. by the Examination of the Prisoner the oneydes understood the french had Cadarachqui in Possession & yt Severall Partyes was Sent out from thence to allarm ye Countrey whereupon the Indians avised Gerrt Luykase not to goe forward because it was very Dangerous upon the Road & yt his Excell could not Expect the Sachims to come doune being they had Receivd a Belt of wampum from onnondage & sent gerrt Luykas with a guarde of there young men back to albany & told him that they would follow the next day with the message from onnondage who we Expect Every hour upon ther arriveall we shall give yr Excell a full account thereof. ye 22th of this Instant was there a Party of french Indians at the flatts who took a Indian girle of ye River Indians.[1]

alby: ye 13 of aug 1697

To Col. Beekman

Since my arrival here I fynde by all Circumstances yt ye french of Canida have a deSign to Invade us; ye Scouts yt went out on munday are Returnd with great Consternation haveing Seen many traks of ye Enemy wh they Positively Conclude to be there Skouts, & durst not proceed further; we have Sent out 20 men Skouts today, and have Sent for all ye farmers in, & are putting our Selfs in as good a Posture as we Can with yt Smal handfull of People we have; I therefore desyre yt for ye better Strenthening & defending this part of his majes. Province to Send us ye assistance of one hundred men or fourscore at least for ye present without wh we will not be able to maintain this post, as it ought & I shall not faile to acquaint yu from time to time what advise I shall Receive of ye Enemies approach, I know it is very inconvenient for yr People at this juncture but of Two Evils ye Least must be Chose, if this Place should be lost ye Consequence would be much

[1] An unsigned draft with this note on the reverse side: "aug 1695 Majr. abeels Letter to his Excell B: fletcher Capt genl."

worse & therefore depend on sd. number now desyred I shall not ad butt Remain in haste

Sr

Yr humble Servt[1]

The Distance of onnondage from albany 270 miles viz[2]

From Albany to Shinnechtady by Land	20 miles
From Shinnechtady by water to Tionondoroge where ye Praying Maquase Indians have their Setlement	28
From thence to Orachkie ye first Castle of ye Maquase	4
From thence to a deserted Castle calld Iuchnawrede	16
From thence to Canajochere ye 2d Castle	4
From thence to Canaoge a Village	4
From thence till ye Place where ye great Castle Stood cald Tionondoge burnt by ye french	8
From thence to ye Litle Carying place	16
The Litle Carying place itSelf	1
From thence till where our River divides itself into 2 branches one Running north ye oyr west [to] wh. we keep	8
From thence to Youriskene a great Creek yt runs towd. oneyde	56
From thence to ye Island	8
From thence to ye great Carying Place	16
The Carying Place with ye Creek halfway	15
From where yu begin in ye oneyde River to the oneyde Lake	20
From ye East end of ye Lake to ye Creek yt goes up to onnondage fishing place on ye South Side of ye Lake	20

[1] Draft in Robert Livingston's writing.
[2] This description of the route to Onondaga was appended to Robert Livingston's observations on his trip there in April 1700. The published version of that document did not include this item. O'Callaghan, 4: 648-652.

The Clan Mothers of the People of the Flint brought forward nine chiefs and one war-chief; the Clan Mothers of the People of the Upright Stone, nine chiefs and one war-chief; of the People of the hills, fourteen chiefs and one war-chief; of the People of the Great Pipe, ten chiefs and one war-chief; of the People of the Great Mountain, eight chiefs and one war-chief.

from ye mouth of ye Creek calld Quechoo to ye fishing place 6
& from thence by Land to onnondage Castle 20

In all 270 miles.

Albany ye 11th. June 1700

Gentn[1]

Here inclosed is ye Copy of a Message arrived from onnondage Last Night—It is therefore thought Requisite by ye Rest of gent. that you be here to give your opinion in ye matter with all Speed being the Indians are in great hast. This is all at present.

from Gentn.
Your humble
Servant
/S/ Pieter van brugh

The Indians being askd what ye meeting is for doe answer that they know not but that there is Sayd. there is a great deal of news

Albany ye 11th. of June 1700
Propositions made by 3 onnaders who are Sent messengers by ye Sachims of onnondage

Present
Pr. van Brugh Mayr
Jan Janse Bleeker Recordr
Johannis Schuyler
David Schuyler
Johannis Roseboom
Evert Wendel
Albert Ryckman
Wessel ten Brooke

Brother Corlaer & Quider

Wee come to acquaint you that ye Sachims of ye Sinnekes are gone to Canida to Speake there give 7 hands wampum.

Brother Corlaer & Quider

Wee come also to acquaint you that there are 5 waganhaes from there Severall nations arrived in onnondage give one beaver Skin

Brother Corlaer & Quider

Wee desyre ye baggs with Pouder may be made [(*torn*)] may have been which will Incourage these Strange nations to come to

[1] Not addressed, but contains the following note on the reverse side: "The Mayers letter for me [Robert Livingston (?)] & Majr wessels to come to alby."

us pray give us ane answer thereof before wee goe home yu. often told us yu would make them larger gives 3 beavr Skins.

Answer made to ye 3 onnondage messengers in ye Presence of Aqueendero ye Cheiff Sachim of onnondage in alby ye 14 of June 1700

We doe thank ye Brethren for their kind message & are Sorry to hear ye Sinnekes have forget themSelvs So much as to goe to Canada without leave of Corlaer & against yt wh. was Concluded upon by all ye 5 nations.

We doe Send Lawrence Claese to onnondage with a belt to hear what ye Dowaganhaes Indians have to Say & bring us an acct of it & if Possible to bring two of ye Dowaganhaes here to See how cheap Pouder & lead is Sold.

We doe also Send him with anoyr Belt to Stop ye Sinneke Sachims going to Canada (if they be not already gone) till such time that Corlaer comes hither.

As for ye Pouder bags yu may tel ye Sachims they are as large as they can Reasonably desire. doe give a litle wampum.

The Sachim of ye Skachkook Indians who were desired by ye onnondages to Send a messenger thither to hear what ye Dawaganhaes had to Say doe make their apology

That they are Sorry they have no Indians at home to goe thither neither is there any of ym yt can Speak ye Language and desire to be Excused, we are Satisfyed we Shall hear all when Lawrence Returns, & if we hear any news in ye mean time we shal acquaint yu.

R: L: Secry for ye Ind affares.

Instructions for Lawrence Claese
Albany, June 14th, 1700[1]

1° You will immediately go to Onondage and tell the sachems that you have been sent from Albany to hear the proposals of the Dawaganhaes Indians.

[1] Translated from the Dutch.

Deganawidah then said to the chiefs: "I place upon your heads deer antlers as emblems of your power. Your old names are taken away and new names which have more power are given you. Remember that all your power comes from the Great Peace."

2° That they will receive them well and if they want to live with them they will consent gladly and if they propose something different which violates the covenant chain, they are not to be answered before they have spoken here with me.

3° That if the Senecas have not yet departed, you will go to their territory and hold them back with wampum until they have spoken with my Lord [Bellomont][1].

4° That you will extract all the news of the far Indians so as to inform us about everything as well as what happens in Canada.

5° If it is possible, bring some of the far nations of Diowaganhaes here and tell them that they will have powder and lead enough and show them how big the sacks will be, and if the Dawaganhaes will not come with you, the sachems should bring them here when my Lord is here on August 10th, and he will be here as it has been told to them.[2]

6° That the sachems do not detain the far Indians as they have always done, but urge the Dawaganhaes to come here and give to three of the five Dawaganhaes these three stroudwaters and tell them that you could not carry any more for them this time, otherwise you would have brought more. To the other two say that they should come with you and they will have enough powder and lead and clothes. If the Senecas have left, give both belts to the Onondagas, but if not, one belt to the Onondagas, the other to the Senecas.

Present
Col Pr Shuyler
Pr van Brugh
Interpreted p
Capt Joh: Bleeker

Propositions made by Joseph henry & gideon three Christian Maquase in albany ye. 19 of June 1700

We come to acquaint yu yt about 10 days ago ye onnondages have desired us to have a meeting at onnondage, & we did not understand that they deSigned to have any of our Brethren ye Christians their wh. we thought it our duty to acquaint yu. withall. gave 7 hands of wampum.

They were answerd yt ye onnondages had Sent Two Several mes-

[1] Claese was unable to prevent the Seneca from going to the French in Canada. Schuyler and Van Brugh to Nanfan, July 5, 1700. O'Callaghan, 4: 690.

[2] Claese was similarly unable to persuade the Far Nations to come to Albany. *Ibid.*

sages for us to be present at ye meeting, & we had sent Lawrence Claese to be there to give us an acct of all Proceedings.

John Baptist van Eps's Report
about ye Indians

On the 31th: of July 1700 I Arrivd in onnondage where I founde Monsr: Marricuer and the Jesuit Bruas with 12 other frenchmen from Canida who had made propositions to the five Nations of Indians Two Days before I came there, and Pressed them for an answer, but upon my arrival ye Sachims adjourned for three days, Then I Informed them what orders I had to tell them from Corlaer, that they were to make no Meeting with ye french nor to hearken to what they Sayd or to give any answer, and if ye french proposed any thing to them they were only to tell that they were goeing downe to the place appointed to Speake with Corlaer and if they had any thing to Say they might goe and Lay it Before him there.

Whereupon d. kanitsore asked me if it would be Convenient to send for ye french to hear what Corlaer Sayd, I' Replyed that what I was ordred to Say was only to them and that Neither they or I were to Speak with the french, notwithstanding they sent for ye french in our Meeting and Repited to them my Instructions, the Jesuit Bruas Spoke to them in these words, Children, what are you become Corlaers doggs or his Prisoners, that he sends you such Strick orders not to Speake with us or doth he Intend a warr again, I Desyre you only to Reguarde what wee have proposed to you and doe Soe, Which forcd me to tell ye Sachims—Brethren you are sencible that Mischeif comes not from Corlaer but from ye Northwards or Canida and that they have used you Like doggs and kild yu. and when Prisoners Burnd and Tormented you which you are Sure Corlaer hath Never done.

After that ye french went out, ye Sachims Layd doune 9 Beavers and Said Broyr. Corlaer wee have had a Meeting with ye french therefore take these to Ease and setle your minde, which I would

Then Deganawidah repeated all the laws that he and Hiawatha had made for the building of the Great Peace.

not Accept of but told them Brethren you cannot Serve two Masters I am only sent in the name of Corlaer to forbid your meeting with ye french, as I have told you at first but as I am Informed you have had a Meeting with them why doe not you tell me what they have proposed to you whereupon they Sayd the french had Spoke to them by five Belts of wampum and Desyred as follows

By ye first Belt Children it is now peace between the great kings over ye great Water, Lett it Likewise be peace Between you and us and ye Rondackses ye waganhaes Twightwees tionnondadees & all our other Nations of Indians

By ye 2d. & 3d Belt Children wee desyre that our prisoners here amongst you may be Releeced as wee doe hereby Releece yours that are among our Nations of Indians and that you will appoint one out of Each Nation to fetch them where wee shall Expect you nine Days hence.

By the 4th. Belt Children now I have turned up the Bottom of my kitle which Signifyes Peace

By the 5th. Belt, Children wee desyre that a Jesuit may be admitted to Lye in your Countrey as formerly to Instruct you.

After ye 3d. days were Expired (which the Indians took to Deliberate in) they cald a Meeting with the French and Gave ye following answer to there propositions by Dekanitsore Speaker and Sayd they could not allow of a Jesuit to Lay in there Countrey and upbraided them of there former Evill Practices how they had used them and told the french if wee want a Minister Corlaer will Supply us

Sayd Further you Desyre ye Peace come Lett us have peace and gave one Belt of wampum but for ye Covenant made with Corlaer it Shall Never be Broke by us they further allow that out of Each Nation an Indian Should goe to fetch there prisoners from Canida

Albany ye 5th
of august 1700. /S/ Jan Baptist van Epse

By his Excellency the Governour &ca[1]

Instructions to Coll Peter Schuyler Robt. Livingston Esqr: both of his majes. honble. Councill of this Province and to ye Mayor

[1] An abbreviated version of this, omitting the introductory paragraph and the first three clauses, is given in O'Callaghan, 4: 751-752.

aldermen and Recorder of ye Citty of albany, and Sheriffe of ye County & City of ye Same for ye time being, and to hendrik hansen Esqr. one of ye. Justices of ye Peace and to ye Commanding officer of ye fort and garrison within ye Said Citty of albany, which sd. Persons are appointed Commissionrs. for management of ye Indian affares.

1. You are to use your best Skill and Endeavour to ꝑserve ye Kings Peace within ye Citty of albany, and in order thereunto, tis necessary you should by your Example and admonitions discourage faction and parties as tending much to ye disturbance of ye peace and good Correspondence that ought to be between his majes good Subjects, which division of ye people, and distinction of parties have been kept on foot and fomented by ill men to Serve their own private ends, and gratifie their oun malice, without regard to ye honour and Interest of his Majestie, or ye wellfare of this province, wch. as a fronteer to ye french of Canada, has been, and will always in time of war be more exposed than any of his Majes. Provinces in america, and therefore requires yt its Inhabitants Should be entirely united, and of a peice, for their Common Security, and as bound by their allegiance to his majestie.

2. You are upon notice and Complaint of any of ye. Indians Subjects of his Maje. of any acts of hostility Committed on them by ye French or their Indians, to take and use ye. most effectuall & Speedy Course to releeve and assist ye Said Indians, and if you see cause you are to Send ye Commanding officer of this garrison for ye time being with Such a number of ye Souldiers as yu Shall think fitt to ye assistance of ye sd. Indians Subjects of his Majes: giveing such orders to ye said Commanding officer, as yu in yr best discretion shall think proper for his majes Service & ye Security of his Subjects, & all officers and Souldiers in his majes. Pay are hereby orderd to obey all such orders as they shall receive from you, from time to time, for ye ends & purposes aforesaid.

3. You are by all fair means to encourage and Cherish the Indians, Subjects of his Majesty, to ye end they may Continue

---

The fifty chiefs of the Five Nations each gave to Deganawidah a string of lake-shell wampum as a pledge of truth and loyalty to the laws of the Great Peace.

firm under ye. obedience of his maje. and for ye advantage of ye trade of this Province.

4. You are upon all Emergences yt. shall happen to give me notice thereof to New Yorke, or in my absence from this Province to ye Leiut governour & Councill, sending at ye same time your opinion & advice, what you think most proper to be done for ye remedying all mischieffs that shall any way be putt in practice against his Maje. and his people within this his Province, or against ye Indians, Subjects of his Majestie.

5. Upon any message from all or any of ye five nations of Indians, or from ye Nation of Skachkook or River Indians Mr Livingston aforesaid as being his Majes. Secretary for ye Indian affares in this Province is Immediatly upon ye arriveall of ye Indian messenger or messengers to Summon & Convene all ye above Comrs. or as many of ym as shall then be in Town, and them being So Convened shall ConSult upon ye Subject of ye message from ye Indians, he to make a minute (in a fair well bound book to be kept for yt Purpose) of ye ReSult and opinion of ye Sd. Commissrs. upon all Such messages, every minute to be Signed by ye Commisrs. then preSent, and by him ye Sd. Mr. Livingston as Secretary.

6. And for avoiding and preventing all Superfluos Charge[1] for or by reason of any messages from ye said Indians, ye said Commissioners are hereby directed to Signifie to all ye said nations, that they send hither no more then three Indians at most on any message whatsoever, & ye messenger or messengers So Sent are allowed to Stay here at ye kings Charge, no longer then three days at most to rest and refresh themSelves, and to be allowed three shillings *p* day each messenger and no more, for his or their Support dureing ye Said three days and proportionatly for a lesse time if he or they shall return home Sooner, wh. said three shillings *p* day is to be paid to ye Sd Messenger or messengers in ready money & yt by mr Livingston aforesaid who is hereby directed to make punctuall payment accordingly, from time to time,

[1] Bellomont was attempting to eliminate two malpractices, both of which he alleged were indulged in by Schuyler. One was the bringing in of excessive expense accounts for the entertainment of the Indians, and the other was Schuyler's personally entertaining the Iroquois sachems at the King's expense, by which means he "studies to make himself popular." Bellomont to Lords of Trade, October 17, 1700. O'Callaghan, 4: 716.

out of y[t] part of his Maj[es]. Revenue of Excyse which is under his y[e] said M[r]. Livingstones Collection, and I doe absolutely forbid that any provisions or money be given to any Indian or Indians at y[e] kings Charge from y[e] day of y[e] date hereof, otherwise than as is before Expressed, whereof M[r] Livingston is to take notice and to Conform himSelf to this my order accordingly, and my former Instructions to y[e] Commissioners for management of y[e] Indian affares, bearing date y[e] first day of august 1698, are hereby Revokd. given under my hand and Seal at arms at albany y[e] Third day of Septemb 1700 & in y[e] Twelfth year of his Maj[es]. Reign /S/ Bellomont.

Albany y[e] 1st of June 1701

Gent[n][1]
Inclosed is a Copy of a Message sent from onnondage whereupon y[e] Gent[n]. appointed to mannage y[e] Indian affairs have thought Requisite to Dispatch y[e] Gentleman with y[e] Inclosed Instruction and the Bearers hereof to acquaint the hon[ble] Leiutenant Governeur therewith, to whom y[e] Principale is Sent, y[e] Gent[n]. also desyred me to acquaint you that the Bearers hereof are not agreed for there Trouble, but Leave it to y[e] Consideration of y[e] hon[ble]. Govern[r] & Councill, and therefore Desyre you will be pleased to order that they may be Satisfyed before they come home. So Remain

your most humble Serv[t]
R[t]. Livingston Jun[r].

Albany y[e] 19th: of august 1701

Uncle Livingston
Here inclosed is a Message just now given by 2 Indians arrived from onnondage together with an answer thereto Given by y[e] Gent[n] appointed to mannage the Indian affairs. the Like thereof is also sent to his hon[r].

[1] Superscribed: "To Coll Peter Schuyler & M[r]. Robert Livingston Esq[rs] of his Maj[es]. Council for y[e] province of New Yorke &[a] att New Yorke."

Deganawidah made the Onondagas the Firekeepers of the Confederacy, with Onondaga the capital.

In case not is doune towards ye sending for Canida I would humbly Desyre you if ye Govr. and Councill think Convenient to Send any body up to onnondage that you would be pleased to put for David Schuyler and me wherein you will much oblidge

Sr
Your Dutifull
Coz: & Sevt: to Command.
/S/ Rt Livingston Junior

26 Sepr 1701

Mr Levingston
Pray transcribe the inclosed Journal[1] fair and stick it [together] handsomely to send home to the Ministers lett it be done by to morrow evening I am

Your humble servt.
/S/ John Nanfan

[*Robert Livingston's note*]
Leiut Govr ordrs to Translate ye Journall from onnondage

Present
Coll: Pr Schuyler
Mayr D: wessels

Proposition made by four Sachims of ye Mohogs ye 26 of Augst 1702

Broyr Corlaer
The Rest of our Sachims of ye five nations have appointed us to goe and Conclude ye Peace with ye Cristien Indians Caled onnagongue,[2] but the warr breaking out and as wee are Informd that Indians of yt nation are at Shachkook wee therefore think it not need full for us to goe on that Journey further yn Shaahkook where wee are goeing to See our Brethren there & to Recommend our message to those Indians of onnagongue if wee fynde them there
Brother Corlaer
The Late Govr. my lord Bellomont promised us to build a fort

[1] This was the journal of Bleeker and Schuyler on their trip to Onondaga and the Iroquois deed to the lands west to Detroit. Both are published in O'Callaghan, 4: 889-905, 908-911. These documents were sought for unsuccessfully in the Livingston Indian Papers by James Duane. Duane Report, 1780.

[2] The Mohawks, on August 9, had advised Governor Cornbury that they intended to go to New England to renew their covenant with the Abnaki, and he had asked them to stop in Albany on their way at which time he would give them some messages to carry with them. Conference between Cornbury and Mohawks, August 9, 1702. O'Callaghan, 4: 995.

in our Country and to Supply us with men & great guns therein, which wee have Desyred your Excel to perform but it seems the Interpreter hath not Informd your Excell what wee Desyred therefore pray assist us therein or Else wee must as able as wee can Depend upon our Selves in Defence to an approach of Enemys. Therefore may lett us have a Speedy answer of yr. Excell minde to our Desyre

Present
Johana. Schuyler
Hendk. hansen
Johs: Roseboom } *Aldm.*
Johs: Cuyler
David Schuyler
Hille ye Interprettesse

Proposition made by four Mohoggs who upon ye Desyre of ye governr. of Canida to there Sachims were by them appointed to goe and hear what he would say[1]
albany ye 27t. of octobr 1702 in ye Citty hall

BRETHREN

Wee your Brethren of ye Two Castles of ye Mohoggs Countrey are come home, wee know it is Lately Concluded by ye Brethren that wee should be quiet and give Ear to none but you.

BRETHREN

Wee have upon Desyre of ye governr of Canida been sent there and now come back, but when you heard yt wee designd to goe you Sent up to cajojockharie our Castle and Desyred us and ye french Indians that came for us, first to come here, but what you have proposed to said Indians was not made knowne to any of us.

BRETHREN

Before wee went to Canida wee came here as you Desyred but know not on what I'ntent for our Ears were Stopt so that wee should not hear your Discourse with ye sd. french Indians.

BRETHREN

As I told you before, wee went to Canida with our Ears stopt, and heard off nothing till wee came there where we heard your

[1] Cornbury had told the Five Nations not to heed the Governor of Canada's orders to meet him. The Onondaga and Seneca agreed not to go, but the Mohawks insisted on going. Conference of Cornbury and Iroquois, July 21-23, 1702. O'Callaghan, 4: 992-994.

Adodarho was made Firekeeper of the sacred fire burning at Onondago. He was made the chief speaker at the Confederate Council.

Proposals to ye sd Indians Repeated which so Shamd us that wee knew not what to think, as also heard them tell ye governr. of Canida that Since our Indians had been with him quider by a Belt of wampum to ye Sachims of Cagnawage Desyred them in albany in ye time of Twenty five days, whereupon ye governrs of Canida told them to take up ye Belt again and he would give them an answer ye next Morning.

Brethren

When wee came back from quebek wee went to ye Castle Cagnawage where ye Canida Indian Sachims ordred a meeting and told us they had Receivd an Answer from there father upon ye Belt of wampum to tell us, that Quider is not to Concern himselfe with his Indians who are one flesh and Blood with him there father, and hath ordred them to Stay and not goe whose Commands and orders they have Resolved to observe. gave a string of wampum

Brethren

When ye Govr of Canida Sent for us he Desyred wee should bring our Prisoners with us, wee took Two prisoners And gave them to him, and yn Desyred he should Return his Prisoners taken from us, whereupon he gave us ye Two English prisoners whom wee have Brought with us.

Brethren

While wee were with ye govr. of Canida he sayd but litle to us, and comeing in Cagnawage ye Sachims in there meeting asked us what wee had proposed to there Indians in ye propositions at albany; wee told them that wee knew nothing thereof, whereupon they cryed out that they were glad to hear that our Broyr Corlaer tooke so litle care of us, but Slighted and doth what he thinks fitt without us. Sayd further That ye Governr. of Canida Says when he sent for us he saw that Quider held us fast by ye arms And when he saw wee were goeing he went and gave his owne Indians a belt of wampum, but had it been given to us, he should not had hindred his Indians to come which Belt of wampum they Say hath been sent to Each Castle and none would accept thereof have therefore Sent it back to our Brother Corlaer.

Massage Sent from ye Sachims of onnondage by 3 Indians with 7 hands of wampum who arrived here in albany ye 17th. of march 1702/3

Brother Corlaer
Wee are sent Expresse from ye Sachims of onnondage to acquaint you that the Sachims of ye Sinnekes Countrey have appointed a generall meeting of ye five nations to be held in onnondage and therefore Desyre that Quider Meaning Coll: Peter Schuyler with one other Gentn: may appear in said Meeting to hear what shall be proposed therein.
That a Message is Sent from onnondage to Cadarachque to Desyre ye french there, to Send for Monsr. Maricur and Some Sachims of ye Praying Indians in Canida to appear in Said Meeting.
That on other message will be sent here to acquaint you on what day said Meeting will be held
That after they had Ended there Massage two of said Three Indians caled cachnagahoroton & Tigwachwagarocko, Privately in ye Evening Reported, off a great Division among the Sinnekes Relateing ye Sending home the Jesuit out of there Countrey Say That Since Last fall when Lawrence ye Interpreter was there when the Sachims Resolved that ye Jesuit Should be sent home to Canida, It seemeth by the Influence he had on Some Indian Squaes there, they have had a Private Meeting with Severall young Indians of said Countrey (Inclined for ye Jesuit) and Desyred ye said Indians to Remember the Compassion which ye governr. of Canida in the Late warr hath had with them In Sparing them all from being Ruined and therefore for ye quiet of there Countrey that they ought to Endeavor to keep the Jesuitt therein. gave a Bunch of Strung wampum which the Indians told ye Squaes to take up again. and by a Belt of wampum to ye Squaes did in manner assure them that ye Jesuit should not be sent home
which assureance was also privately Confirmd by Severall of ye old Indians Inclined to ye Jesuitt.
The Said Two Indians Say further that severall of ye Sachims Inclined for ys. Governmt. bidd them tell Quider not to be wanting in Comeing himselfe with one other Gentn. well Supplyed with

Deganawidah said: "A chief must always speak the truth. His tongue must be straight. He must have a big heart, be kind, considerate, generous.

Provisions wampum Belts and other Necessaryes So that monsr. Marricuer when he comes there with his Lyquor and other Presents may not have opportunity to Reflect on this Government as he lately hath Done.

The 23th of March 1702/3

A message sent from ye Sachims of ye Mohogs Countrey To Desyre that Coll: Schuyler doth not Delay. To be timely in ye Generall Meeting at onnondage to prevent Such Evill Designs as Monsr. marricur might Endeavor Impose on ye five nations.

Proposition Made to the Schakook Indians Meet at Shinnechtady on there Journey and Convoyed By severall Mohogs to settle In ye Mohogs Countrey this 6th. of July 1703.

Present
Coll: Pr. Schuyler
Majr Dirk Wessels
Mayr Albert Rykman
Recordr Johs. Abeell
Capt. Evert Banker
Capt. Johs. Schuyler
Capt. James Weems Commandr
Jacob Turck Esqr high Sherriffe
and severall oyr gentn. from Albany & Shinnechtady
John Baptist van Eps } *Interpreters*
Lawrence Claese }

Children

I was Surprized when yesterday first Informd That you were Minded to Desert your habitations Which so many years by your fathers hath Been Setled and hitherto By you kept in possession which Caused me Send by Leiut Jacob Schoonhoven to Know who Was the occasion of yt Design by Whom you Returned Me noe Answer but I Recevd from Hendk ye Indian who Is None of your Nation seven hands of Wampum Whereby he sends Me Word to Make Noe further Enquire In yt Matter which I took Noe Notice of but was ye more surprized to hear that You & Your familyes were on Journey to Setle with the Mohogs In there Countrey whereupon I Tought Needfull To send Majr Dirk Wessells Capt Johs. & Capt Myndert Shuyler To advice you to Return Bak to Shaakook & Remain there Untill his Excellency Your fathers arrival from New York who Is Dayly Expected and to Consult with him which sd. Three Persones Brought Answer that you were Resolved to Goe on sd. Journey Contrary to your fathers advice on Which wee In our Duty to Her Majes. & The Good will wee Bear to You Who Doe Professe To be Her Majes. Subjects have Resolved To Meet you here and further advice you to Return to your said Habitations gave on Bunch Strung wampum.

Answer made By The Schakook Indians To ye above Proposition ye 7th of July 1703

Present
Coll Pr Shuyler
Majr Dirk Wessels
Mayr Albert Rykman
Recorder Johs Abeel
Capt John Schuyler
Capt Evert Banker
Capt. Myndert Schuyler
Capt James Weems Commandr
Jacob Turck Esqr high Sherriffe
& severall oyr Gentn of albany & Shinnechtady
John Baptist van Eps } *Interpreters*
Lawrence Clause }

Awanie Sachims of ye Mohogs [sic] *Speaker*

Father

Wee Must tell you that wee were ye first setlers of this Countrey and that When you Came (meaning ye first settlement of Christians here) You Entrd into a Covenant with us whereby you Cannot Pretend To have any Command over Us; You Remember In ye Late Warr You gave us ye Hatchet In hand to strive for your Countrey And wee were always obedient To all Your advises and Directions Whereby wee are Become a Small Nation the flesh taken from our Bodyes and doe observe that what Governor of Canida In ye sd. warr hath Left Us You Design to take from us If You hinder our Journy therefore Be Not against our Setling with ye Mohogs our freinds In There Countrey Where wee may Bee Strenthend again it Is The Place where our Nation formerly Dwelt and kept there fyre Burning there so Now wee are Goeing Up to Setle & Kindle our fyres there again.

Whereupon they were Answerd That wee Never heard that they had had a setlement With ye Mohogs & Told them when they were Last Removed by Sr Edmund Andros it was from The Lake Towards Canida and Planted at Schaakook and Therefore Recommded them to Return again from Whence They Came Untill His Excellencys arriveall to Which They would Not hearken But Rose

"A chief must always be ready to help those who are in want. His aid must be given willingly, and he must receive no pay or reward for his services.

Up in a Passion & Went on There Journey up To ye Mohogs Countrey.
The Copy hereof sent doune
To his Excell: my Lord Cornbury.

Present
Albert Ryckman, Mayr.
John abeel Recordr
Capt Evert Banker
Capt Myndt Schuyler

Message from ye Sachims of onnondage brought here by Tarrigjories and an other Indian from ye Mohogs Country the 21th: of august 1703.

Say that two dayes agoe two Messengers from onnondage came to ye Mohogs Countrey and desyred ye Sachims there to forward the News That a frenchman from Canida is Lately arrived in the Sinnekes Countrey, who saith that he is sent from ye Governr. of Canida Since it Seemeth that Corlaer hath Evill designs against ye five nations is therefore come to tarry there 40 days to watch the motion of Such Designes and on occasion to Live and die with them
Saith further that ye Governr of Canida orderd him to Inform ye five nations that he had an army of 500 Indians and 10 Christian officers Ready and were goeing out to fight against ye Eastern parts of new England since Corlaer dayly Disturbe him by Sending Vessells to Cruce in ye Mouth of ye Canida River therefore was fully Resolved not to Return untill they had made Some attack along ye Sea Costs of new England.
Brother Corlaer
The governr. of Canida threatens to Goe towards New England. wee would advise you to be watch full on your gaurde Send out Spyes for he is a false harted man ye Divill cannot know his minde he talks of new England but ye Design may be against you.
as for us wee doe not trust him altho ye Jesuits are in our Countrey wee doe not pray with them from our hearts.
Brother Corlaer
Wee also acquaint yu. that ye Sachims of ye five nations are comeing to albany who Desyre you will be pleased to meet them there, to give Consult of matters for ye good of ye Countrey. Give 7 hands of wampum
Wee doe also acquaint yu. that Eight of ye Sinnekes Cayouges onnondages & oneydes whereof DCanitsore is one are goeing to ye Praying Indians at Canida to Consult about matters for ye good of ye Countrey who after there Return will give an account thereof.

Propositions made by The Schaahkooks Indians the 24th of Sepr 1703

Father
Wee must acquaint you that last Spring it Seemd verry dark unto us, but now since our father came here our Eys are opened & Shows Light,

Father
It is now Eighty five years since ye first Christian came here in this Countrey then wee tyed them with a Roap but now they are fastned with an Iron Chain to ye tree of welfair so that wee hitherto have stood firm to ye Covenant Chain with our father.

Father
Wee are much Rejoyced to hear that our father hath been so carefull as to Recommend those of ys our Castle who are gone to Setle among the Mohogs to Return to there habitations by us, which wee hope they will observe and doe as our fathers Directs them.

Copy of Coll: Shuylers letr to my Lord Cornbury

May it please your Excellency
Since my Last to your Excellency by Leift C: Congreve I have Receivd by 2 Indian messengers from Col: Partridge of hatfeild ye Inclosed Letter Relateing ye Late Distruction by ye Enemy at Dearfeild in new England and by Johannis Luycasse from Lawrence Claese ye Interpreter in onnondage ye Inclosed Information, ye Commissioners appointed for ye manageing ye Indian affairs have Resolved that 2 Trusty Indians be Sent out to Canida by whom wee may have some I'ntelligence of there designs, which Indians I think to procure in few days and to despatch them away for that purpose.

May it please yor Lordship
The time appointed for ye Countrey detachment here posted for ye Security of her Majes fronteers being so near Expired I have payd them untill ye first of aprill 1704 and Syned ye Sloop of John van ness by whom I design to Send doune undr Command of Mr. george Ingoldesby Leut. as many as willing to goe Severalls

"A chief must never forget the Creator of mankind, never forget to ask Him for help. The chiefs must work in unity, lest their nation become divided. Any great move must have the consent of all the Five Nations.

of them doe Stay here. This with Submission to yr Excell: is what offers at present from Albany ye 28 march 1704

May 1704 Copy of Col. Pr Shuylers Letter to his Excellency [*Cornbury*].

May it please your Excellency
Inclosed is a Translation of ye letter come from ye Interpreter at onnondage whereby your Excell may perceive what Intrest ye governr. of Canida makes to gain our Indians by given such Rich presents not only to those Indians to them affected but also to ye Indians affected to this governmt.

may it please your Excel. I have thought it would been Requisite for me to goe up with all Speed takeing Twelve or thirteen men with me but not being Suplyed by ye Colr. as your Excel & Councill directed to pay me out of ye Excise at albany for my Journey thither £30: for my oune acct. out of ye money Raised for ye building of batteries at ye narrows £156: which if I had Recd. should have disbursed thereof for ye necessary occasion of ye sd. Journey, which now I cannot doe. doe therefore tarry for your Excellency further orders & Directions therein and doe pray ye favor of your Excellency if ye Colr. hath not yet payd ye Said money that your Excel will be pleased to give an order to him that ye Same may [be] payd and that your Excel & Council wil be pleased to order in Store house Smal presents for ye Indians which wee have verry great [need] off dayly, this with submission to your Excel is what humbly offers at present from

your

Citty of Albany May the 19th. 1704

Present { *Johannis Schuyler Mayor*, *Jacobus Turk*, *Capt. James Weems* } *Esqrs.*

This day arived here from Onidat Conoquine of Waddowsechta & Oyemdunas two Sachamakes wth. severall other Indians of yt Nation who say that they have been out afighting against the Wagonnas, and in the fight they have lost five Men one of wch. was a Sachiem, and that they and ye. Coeugas stand true to ye Covenant Chain, not forgetting their Brd. Corlar & Queder & that they are resolv'd to admitt no Priest or ffrench Man among them, they are likewise resolvd, (when they have here provided themselves wth. powder and Lead) to go againe against their Enimy whereupon they layd down two Beavers.

2. They say yt. Bror. Corlor may See that he has always kept his Indians togather, not haveing any confidence in the ffrench Indians, wch makes the ffrench, look upon him wth. a great deale of Distrust and Envey, and yt ye reason why he has brought So little peltry, is the keeping his men So Close togather in their Castle not goeing out often to hunt He comes likewise as he says as an arrow out of a Bow to dispatch imediately, that he may returne to his Castle not trusting the ffrench, and Says his men will be coming to this place space of tenn days to this Citty to buy Gunns powder and Ball, that he designs but once more to go amongst his Enemys to revenge ye Injury they have recd, and to returne to his Castle imediately, in ordr to keep a strict Eye upon the Enimy, He complains very much of the scarcity of Arms & Amunition, and desires that his people may be furnished at a Cheaper rate, considering ye. dificultys they lye under.

The Comrs. Answer

1st. we are very glad to see such good friends as you here, but are sory for the prsent occasion of yor. comeing. We hope you may have good success upon yor. desyn of revenging the loss You have susteynd, We are very well assured of yrs. and the Coyeguas fidelity to the Covenant Chain & you may be Satisfyd or. Bror. Corlar & Quider will have a perticular Esteem for you, when they shall be acquainted wth. yr. Resolutions, of not admitting Priest or ffrench Man among you.

2. We are well satisfyd wth. yor care and Conduct over yr Indians in the keeping them togather, not trusting the french, who have no reguard to their word and tho it may have been a hinderance to yr trade, yet it has been a Security to yor. Indians, the lives and Security of whom, is always in the thoughts & care of yor Bror. Corlar, and preferrable to trade

---

"A chief must be wise and very patient. He must never let his temper get the best of him, lest he be unable to cast good judgment. His skin must be seven thumbs thick, so that he will not feel the darts of his enemies. Always remember that the Great Confederacy was organized for peace. Peace and friendship among all nations was the aim of the Great Law.

3. The speedy journy you have made hither, and yr. Intentions to make the same hast back againe Shews in you a Vigorous resolution to revenge ye loss of our five Brors. and since you Say you resolve to go but once more amongst yr. Enimy we dont question but you'l take yr. leave of ym. So handsomely, that their posterity may repent the provocation they have given you, We Wish you all ye good luck imaginable, We shall lett you have the best powder and at the Cheapest rate, and you may be sure we shall lett you have good powder, to fight against such treacherous Enimys, We hop to see you here again, and to hear of yr. Victory over yrs. & our Enimys. In the meane time we prsent you with a Small quantity of good pouder enough for one onsett, and we hope it may be Successfull.

Onnondage the 20th: of may 1704

Gentn:

Just now comes here ye Brother of Monsr: maricuer decd. with a priest and three and Twenty men from canida, they have yet made no proposition say that they have no news & are come only to condole ye death of ye Said Marricuer and one Sachim who died here the Last winter, the Priest told me that he had Letters from ye English Minister taken at Deerfeild to Coll: Peter Shuyler, and that they would be sent to albany by an Indian of onnondage french affected knowne by ye name of Ohoengewaene, the Sachims here Desyre that ye Gentlemen of ye Indian affairs will be pleased to Show kindness to ye Said Indian and have but Litle Discourse with him. The presents which ye french give to ye Indians on both sides affected are admirable. The Priest tells me also that three Indians were gone out from Canida to New England the Sachims affected to this government Desyres the Brethren to be on there guards least there might be considerably more Indians out, wee have yet no answer from ye Sachims Relateing a passage for ye farr Nations, The Indian that brings ye said ministers Letters is to goe from hence in a day or two to albany. this is what humbly offers at present from

gentn
Your humble Servt.
/S/ Laurence Claese

Copy of Col Shuylers Letter to Mr. Whiting
Albany ye 22th. of May 1704

d Sr
Yours by ye Bearer John Phillips I have Recd and am Sorry to hear off so much Losse of people about your Parts, as you Desyre I have Made an Enquire whereabout ye french and Indians should have lately made a Setlement, and as I am informed if any Setlement be made, it must be upon a River caled quaasick which Runns towards New England. assoon as I Receive more certain Intelligence shall not be wanting to give you notice thereof. Three days agoe wee have Receivd news from our Interpreter in onnondage that off ye five nations of Indians as they were on hunting towards ye farr nations were kild about nine but no certainty whether by ye farr nations or french committed, I' am by his Excellency our governr Required to goe up to ye Sinnekes Countrey to which I think to march about Seven weeks before I can Return in ye mean time if any thing comes to Ear here worth giving you notice of I Shall Leave orders with my Broyr. John to acquaint you thereof.
These with my Respects to Govr wintrop & mr Richd. Leut do
Remain

May 1704: 24th *Copy of Col Shuyler Lettr to his Excellency* [*Cornbury*]

May it please your Lordship
On Saturday Last ye. 20th. Instant may I came to albany where I found ye Inclosed Letters from new England in one thereof your Excell may see that ye Bearer a person Belonging to albany was Engaged or hath made promise to goe with one or more Indians this way to Spy the french fort Late Built, which in my opinion is not well done of him to Engage to goe this. an New England would been anoyr mattr he being [one] who not live [(*blot*)] to goe have thought Requisite to Referr ye same untill your Excellency

"The eagle on top will watch over all people who wish to rest under the Tree of Peace. He will warn if danger approaches. Send messengers to the four corners of the world, to the North (bear), West (panther), East (moose), and South (fawn), inviting all nations to join us."

further orders, here is also Inclosed Letters from ye Interpreter at onnondage whereby your Excellency may see what is Relateing to ye Indians wee are & have been in Continual trouble with these Dayly messages from the Indians and under Deficulty for want of Stores to Suply the necessary Expences so that with Submission to your Excel it will be very needfull to Send up some Poud^{r}. Lead Linnen & provisions since none will give creditt here.

This is what humbly offers at present.

from

Present
Coll: P^{r}: Schuyler
Maj^{r}. Dirk Wessels
Maj^{r}. John Schuyler

Propositions made by three Mohogs and Some River Indians and Waganhaer Come from Tiogsagrondie
Albany the 20th of June 1704

Brother Corlaer

When wee were here two years agoe tradeing with you you spoke to us and gave us toakens whereby you Disyred the Rest of our Brethren at Tiogsagrondie to Come Likewise and trade At Albany Now wee Come again and desyre that you Will Not be dissatisfyed altho ye Rest of our Brethren Are Not Come with Us wee Come to see what Price your goods are at which wee hope are Cheep for wee Esteem a good Market above any other thing.

Brother Corlaer

I't is our Cheeffe Sachim Caled Tyhadagrio and ye Setler of Tiogsagrondie who sends us to you and desyres That You will Bee well Suplyed with goods for That he certainly will Come with ye Rest of our Brethren ye next Spring whereof you may be Assured and Expect him Accordingly and you Brethren ye Sinnekis Coyouges and onnondages wee desyre youl permitt us a free passage trough your Countrey.

Brother Corlaer

Wee have already told you that our Brethren will Certainly come doune ye next spring Whereof you may Bee Assured for they are Resolved That no thing shall stopt them Lett it be peace or warr for They are Realy inclind to trade and Bee Come a People with you and doe desyre to Bee Remembred To their Brother Corlaer and quider give one Beaver Coat and two Black Beavers

Answer given to ye above Proposition ye 20th. of June 1704

Brethren
Wee are glad to see you here again And Under That token off Effection and Inclination To trade with us off which wee shall Not Bee wanting to Acquaint your Brother Corlaer off, wee Expected you here The Last year when you would have meet with a Cheeper Market of goods then there is now wee are Sorry that ye Goods at This Present are so Schaers the Like hath not been Knowne There these Many years is occasioned By thee hard warrs in Europe but now perceiving Thee good Inclinations of ye Brethren and hearing your Promises to Come thee next With a great Number So wee Shall depend Thereon and Endeavor to Bee Plentifully Suplyed with goods Suteable to your minds against your arrivealls
Brethren
Wee are also glad to hear you So well Minded and Resolved that Lett it be peace or Warr it shall Not hinder your Comeing but wee Most Reccommend you as Knowing that thee french are a Jealous and Deceitfull People Not to hearken to them But stand by your said Resolution on which wee depend and assure you that goods then shall not Bee wanting gave 12 Kegs of Rom one gunn & tenn Pounds of Powder one half vat Strong Beer Whereof one Kegg the gunn and five Pounds Powder was given for their Sachim Tiohadagrio.

Albany ye 21 June 1704

This day Comes a Messuage from onnondage gives acct of ye farr Nations and ye Indians at Tiogsagrondie have had an Engagement and Killd on Both sides and yt ye Indians of said Tiogsagrondie have Been to desyre assistance from ye five Nations whereupon a meeting is Resolved and desyre that quider will make all hast to bee there forthwith.

Message Sent from ye Sachims of onnondage by ye way of ye oneyde and Mohogs Countrey hither, arrived ye. 2d of Septembr 1704

Inform that ye Said Sachims by Seven hands of wampum have

Thus was formed the Great Confederacy of the Five Nations, in the days before the arrival of the white invader from across the Big Salt Water in the east.

acquainted ye Sachims of ye oneyde and Mohogs Countrey as they doe acquaint there Brother Corlaer how that one Sachim of onnondage caled ohoengewaene with his Companie few days agoe by Consent of ye other Sachims was goeing to Canida to Condole ye deaths of monsr. marrecuer & to take ye hatchet agst New England out of ye Governr of Canidas hand & comeing between ye onnondage River & Cadarochqui ye said Sachim ordred two of his Companie out hunting who Staying out Longer then he Expected he went with the Rest of his Companie to Look for them tho found them not, but as he observed the tracts of there Strugeling with others, and the course they were gone he Suspected them to be taken by ye waganhaes who are Subject to ye governour of Canida & then Returnd home to onnondage to acquaint the Sachims of ye five nations and there Brother Corlaer thereof in order that they might be on there guard against ye french & there Indians that Indians of the five nations had made a Setlemt. near Cadarachqui and Since the waganhaes have also Setled there about (who now consist in much greater number yn those of ye five nations) they are Resetling back to ye five nations again

Answer by 7 hands of wampum Sent by the said Messenger to ye Sachims of onnondage ye. 2d. of Septembr 1704

Brethren

Wee have understood & Considerd the tydings you Send us and are Sorry for ye Losse of two of our Brethren which (as you have Informd us) wee will acquaint your Brother Corlaer off, and what he shall propose in that matter shall give you an account of as soon as it comes to our hands in ye mean time wee must Recommend the Brethren to be on your guards and warily watch ye motion of ye french and there Indians Especially if there tydings prove truth be carefull and make sure of such french as are among you who under pretence of friendship are your greatest Enemys and therefore Strick those who Strick you.

Hatfeild 2d Aprill 1707

Colo Shuyler

Sr we have Recd the Captive Boy ꝑ mr Shelding and Return you many thanks for yor kindeness therein & have Sent you ꝑ this

Bearer the post Seventeene pounds Nine shillings to make & Compleate the dues for his Redemption the money is as ffollows

In bitts & double bitts	11: 5:0
In half pieces	1: 7:0
In shillings	4:10:0
I'n shillings Groats & pennys	0: 7:0
Pd by Mr Shelding at	6:12:0
	24: 1:0

which I hope & desire it may be to yor & the other Gentlemens good Satisfaction & content please to do what you can at all tymes to obtaine mr Williams his daughter or any other Captives you may hear of within your Reach & [(*torn*)] Now Sending mr Shelding with some Others to Canada with or Governrs Letters prevent [(*torn*)] hazzard as much as you can inciteing yor Indians accordingly mr Shelding prsents his Service to yorself & the Gentlemen with thanks for all yor kindenesses to him wn last with you. & Sr yor propossalls of a Signe for yor Freinde I'ndians wn Out in case of meeting with or Out Scouts the tyme of the former being Nere Expired, Wee shall have some ptis of men in a Litle while up Upon or River & the ajacent woods Westward it may be as high as Coccoassett its best Yor Indians be not in those ptts without advise to us Except in case of their discovery (of any forces of the Enemy & their intentions) to us or or men Out as aforesd wch faithfully done will be well accepted & rewarded Especially if they take a due care & payns therein, or Wonted desire of yor Enformation of the Motions & designes of the Enemy will always be verry Gratefull to his Excellency or Governr & to us all with wch I take Leave & Subscribe my Self yor much oblidged ffreinde & verry Humble Servt.

/*S*/ Samll Partridge

Present my Service to yor Bror
& the rest of the Gentlemen
deliver the Enclosed as directed

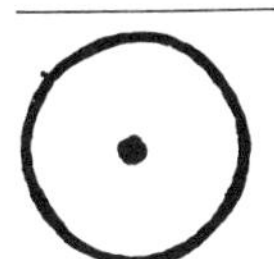

This is the sign of the League: the never-ending circle with the Onondaga Council Fire in the center.

Albany the 13th. of may 1707

May it Please your Excellency

Since my last to your Excell of ye 7th. Instant Hend: ye Indian haveing been out with others a hunting on the Coast of new England on the 9th. Return'd heather with Severall others from thence in a great Surprize giveing us an acct. yt. ye. Inhabitants of that Country had put them in Danger of their lifes which they were oblig'd to Secure by flight takeing no notice of the Sign directed the Indians, rely wholy on your Excell: to put a Stopp to these troubles and press us very hard to urge it to your Excell:, I inclosed Send your Excell: there Proposition, hopeing this may find you in good health and Safety return'd from the fateague, of your Journey which is ye hopes from

my Ld yor: Excys: most dutifl. and
most obedient Servt.
P[eter] S[chuyler]

Just now by a letter from Lawrence ye Interpreter wee are informed yt 17 of our Indians have brought into Coeyoega Six and thirty men besides woomen & Children from ye farr nations of Indians who since their Captivity he Says are Resolved to Settle in Coeyoega amongst our Indians.

[*c. May 28, 1707*]

May it Please yr. Excellency

My Last to your Excellency was the 13th of this Instant, Since that time came here Seaven oneydes with this Inclosed acct wee could wish to have the happeness to See your Excellency here Wee have no news from canada, but hear of two or three Partys which are Sett out against new England with five or Six in a troope, wee have likewise an acct. of Deacon Shilding his arrivall at montriall who is Sent from the Govermt. of boston, to ye Govr. of Canada what his bussiness is wee doe not know hopeing this may find you in health & Safely Returned from the fateague of your Journey wh. is the hope of

my Ld. yr: Excellency
most Dutifull and most
obedient Servt:
P[eter] S[chuyler]

att a Meeting of the Comms^r *of the Indian affairs in albany the 28th of May 1707*

Present
David Schuyler Esqr *may*^r
Capt. myndt Schuyler
Capt. Pr. van Brugh
Mr. John Cuyler
Mr. John abeel

This day came here odistanond and Tohotsjoge with five more onneydes who doe acquint ye Gentleman yt they are Sent by there Sachims of oneyde Castle yt ye Chiefe Sachims of the five nations of Indians are are comeing down to albany & in their way to condole the death of onnagranooum the Mohog Sachim Late decd., and to come here to Renew the covenant Chain with my Lord Cornbury & the Commissioners here, & yt. the Said Sachims & other Indians of the five nations may be here Expected in tenn days next Ensueing, to which they give Seaven hand of wampum as a toaken.

Phil: Livingston D. Secry
for ye Indian affairs.

att a Meeting of the Commissrs of the Indian affairs in albany this 6th day of June 1707

Present
Collo. Pr. Schuyler
David Schuyler
Johs. Schuyler
Henry Renselaer
Evert Banker
Pr van Brugh
Killian van Renselaer
Henry Holland

Onnogharichson Sachim of Canada Desires a belt of wampum to goe under the ground from hence, to there Sachims, yt they Should Shute up the Path of n: England, yt there Indians Should not goe & Skulk there anymore, & yt ye govr of canada Should not know thereof, wh. belt is given to him accordingly, & Says yt. he Shall bring an answer himself in a Short time if his undertakeing has Success or not. Likewise there is given To ye Sd. Sachim three small belts of wampum to Releace mr. williams ye minister of dear feild his Doughter from ye Indians if She be possible to be gotten, for money or Els to give an Indian girle for ye Same, wh: he promised to doe if it was in his Power

Ph: Livingston D: Secretry
for ye Indian affairs

At a Councille held at ffort Anne in New York this 6th day of May 1709

Prsent *Coll Schuyler President*
Coll Heathcote *Mr Barberie*
Mr Van Dam *Mr Philipse*
Coll Wenham *Coll Peartree*
Mr Renselaer *Capt Provost*

Ordered that what Expence Mr Renselaer & Mr Livingston shall be at towards the Expedition of the Indians shall be repaid them by the Governmt[1]

By order of ye Councill
/S/ Geo Clarke.

Instructions to be given to the two Indians to be Sent to Montreal and Quebek [*c. May 1709*]

Imp: That they take particular notice, what number of troops are in montreal, what Quantity of Provisions they can learn they have in the Place, and if Provisions be dear or Cheap in the place at ye time, and particularly to observe if there be any additionall fortification made to ye Town lately.

2. If they go from thence by way of Trois Riviers to take notice, what number of Troops are quarterd in that place, and if there be any late Improvements made as to ye fortifications of it.

3. When they come to Quebek they are to take Exact notice of ye fortifications of that Place, how many guns are mounted about it, and Particularly if the Stone wall, which they were drawing around ye Town towards ye Land Side of it be finish'd or not, what number of Troops are in it, how many they sent to newfoundland last fall, who took St. Johns from ye English, and if there be any more gone or a going thither this Summer, what Prise Provisions and ammunition are at, and how Soon they Expect their fleet from france, as Soon as they have Inform'd themSelves fully of these things, they are to make all possible haste to Albany, and deliver their account of their message to ye Persons who dispatchd them, who are to Transmitt ye Same by an Expresse to Boston or new york as yr Lordship [Lord Lovelace] shall order them hereafter

Signd
Sam: Vetch
ffr: Nicholson

[1] This and the succeeding documents refer to the Nicholson-Vetch campaign to conquer Canada.

Instructions for Mr Renselaer and Mr Livingston [c. May 6, 1709]

1. You are to go with the first opportunity to Albany, & so soon as you arrive there you are to find out four of the most Trusty and most Secret Indians you can get for the Expedition they are to go on, on Coll Vetch & Coll Nicholson's Instructions herewith given you.
2. When you have made your Choice of these Indians you are to cause the Indians Interpreter to Inform & fully to Communicate the said Instructions at the said Indians.
3. So soon as this is done you are to send the said Indians on their said Expedition (vizt) two to Montreale, and two to Quebeck, first dividing the Strouds Shirts, & powder you receive for this use among them; Charging them Strictly to obey those Instructions in every particular with all the Secrecy and dispatch Imaginable, promising them likewise an Ample and Sufficient reward if they perform the Injunctions you lay on them.
4. You are to be very carefull that the design of this Expedition be kept Secret from Every person whatever, and to Such persons as may be InquiSitive that they may not gues at the reale cause you are to say that we are apprehensive, the ffrench since the taking of st Johns will attempt something further on us.

/S/ Pr: Schuyler P[resident]

1709 *Account of ye negotiation of K: V: Renselaer & Robert Livingston who were sent Expresse to albany by ye President & Councill of N:York to dispatch Spys to Canada pursuant to ye Instruction of Col vetch & Coll nicholson.*

May

6 Friday Evening sett out fr: N: York in ye Sloop of Jan Van ness assoon as we had Receivd our Instructions

7 Saturday gott this Evening as far as Roeloff Jansens kill about 12 a Clok at night ye wind came about n west, So cast anker til morning

8 Sunday about 6 a Clok in ye morning with ye flood we turn'd it & gott about noon as farr as Loonenburgh, where we heard ye news of Corl. Vetches being come to Boston wth 25 officers, a Squadron of men of war With 2 bomb Catches & 4000 Red coats dayly Expected to Reduce Canada wh news was brought by 2 men fr n: England, we

got this Evening as far as Abr Staets but ye wind was So fierce there was no turning of it & so ankerd.

9 Munday ye wind blowing hard at north we went Early ashore & gott horses to kinderhook & fresh horses there to Albany all along we were ask'd about ye news of forces comeing to Canada wh. sd. 2 n: England men had brought, in 3 days fr Boston, with all its Circumstances wh we Endeavord to Stifle by design of Retaking of St Johns & Port Royall, alleadging yt must be Coll Vetches Errand & nothing else

This Evening assoon as we got to Alby an Expresse was Dispatch'd to Skachkook for 2 or 3 Trusty Indians to be Sent on a message to quebek

10 Tuesday John Baptist van Eps being Sent for from Shinechtady who arrived here this night was told ye necessity of his going to ye Mohogs Country to get 2 Trusty Indians to goe to mont Royall. The 3 Skackook Indians wth ye messenger yt was Sent came to Coll Shuylers farm this afternoon being discharg'd to come into Town.

11 Weddensday we dispatch'd Jan B: van Eps to Shinechtady & So to ye Mohogs Country & went then to Coll Schuylers farm 3 miles out of Town, agreed with 3 Skachkook Indians to goe to quebeck who were to have 105 bitts a *p*s., & Each 10 martins to buy Provisions, they are to *p*form ye journey in 35 days & for each day lesse they are to have 9s Extraordinary, & ye Capt of ym is to have a gratuity over & above if he brings a True & Exact account.

We gott those things ye Indians wanted in ye afternoon & hired a *p*son to goe along with ym to Skachkook & Soe yn Past Sarachtoge & not to lett ym Speak with any body.

12 Thursday we went to Shinechtady Jan Baptist van Eps telling us yt he would have ye Indians there from ye Mohogs Country about 2 hours Sun, & accordingly we found ye Sd. Jan Baptist Returnd from ye Mohogs Country who informd us he had gott Two Indians to our wish, who were Comeing by water & arrivd in less than an hours time, we agreed with them to goe to Montroyall & are to Inform themselvs of Such things mentiond in Coll Vetches & Coll nicholsons Instructions, they are to *p*form ye Journey in

24 days and are to have a Each 80 Bitts but if they doe it in 20 days are to have each 85 & if in 21 days 82: they furnish themselves with Provisions & oy[r] necessaries

13. friday Early in y[e] morning we dispatchd y[e] S[d]. 2 Mohogs Sending John Baptist van Eps with them to y[e] ael Place who see them over y[e] River Past all Christian Setlements, & we Return'd to Albany.

And asson as y[e] wind would ꝑmitt we took our Passage in y[e] Same Sloop we went up in & arrivd at n: york on y[e] 21th. of may 1709

K[iliaen] v. R[ensselaer]
R[obert] L[ivingston]

In y[e] woods neer y[e] flatts [near Albany] y[e] 11 of may 1709

Present
K: V: Renselaer
R[t] Livingston
Johannes kinneler baker Interpreter

Agreed with 3 Skachkook Indians called wappelowey alias Mattanas, Pakatoquascet and Paatkamp to goe

to quebeck and there to make Such discoverys as is mentiond in y[e] Instructions of Coll Vetch & Col nicholson w[h] journey they are to ꝑform in 35 days and are to have each 3 Bitts or 2s 3d. ꝑ diem, and for every day they ꝑform ye Journey lesse y[n] 35 days are to have 9d. over and above y[e] 2s 3d. besides Each 10 martins to buy Provisions. they Engage to be Sober Secret & Expeditious they desire to have a faddom of Strouds a Shirt and a p[r] of Stockings Each in Part of Payment w[h] is to be Sent them by a Trusty hand who is to Convey them above Sarraghtoge Past all y[e] Christian Setlem[ts].

Agreed with m[r] Dirk ten Broek for 15s: to Convey y[e] Said three Indians four miles above Sarachtoge & y[e] Strouds Shirts Stockings martins & some Tobacco was deliverd them accordingly.

Jan Baptist van Eps Interpreter

Shinechtady y[e] 12 may 1709
Then agreed with Two Maquas Indians calld kanerachtachere in Maquase but is babtizd Ezras, and

Tanechwanege to goe to Montroyal Pursuant to y[e] Instructions off Coll vetch & Coll nicholson who are to ꝑform y[e] journy in 24 days and are to have each Eighty Ryals or Bitts but if they doe it in 20 days are to have Each 85 bitts & if they doe it in 21 days 82 bitts a peece they furnish themselvs with Provisions & oyr. necessaries they went away on friday morning early being ye 13th of May ye Interpreter Seeing them over ye River Past all Christian Setlemts. ye sd Indians when they Return are to come to ye Interpreter who is to give directions to whom they are to give an act. of there journey & what discoverys they made.

K. v. R.
R. L.

Present
The honble. Coll Fr: nicholson
Commandr in Cheife of ye army wt goes by Land to Canada
Coll: Pr. Schuyler
Coll: Tho: wenham
Coll Kil: van Renselaer
Capt David Provoost } *of her Majes. Councell*
georg Clark Esqr.
Secretary of ye Colony
Capt. Evt Banker mayr
J: abeel Recordr
hend: hanse
henry holland
Johs. Cuyler } *Commissrs of ye Indian affares*
Myndt. Schuyler
Rt Livingston Junr
Johs Rooseboom
Nanning harmense } *aldermen*
Coll: Wm. Whiting
Coll: Pr Mathews *Majr D: wessels*
Majr John Livingston
Capt John Roberts
Commandr of her majes Ship SouthSea Castle
Rt Livingston Secry for ye Indian affares

Propositions made by the Honble. Coll: Richd. Ingoldesby Leut. govr. & Commandr in Cheife of her Majes. Provinces of new york ye Jerseys & Territories depending thereon in America to ye Maquase oneydes onnondages & Cayouges in Albany this 14 day of July 1709[1]

BRETHREN

It having pleased Almighty God to take to himSelf his late Excellency John Lord Lovelace, whom the Great Queen of Great Brittain my mistresse had been pleased to Constitute Governour of these Colonies, the Care and Government are by her Majestie Lodged in me, I was therefore willing to take ye first opportunity Possible to meet you to Renew the Covenant Chain on the behalf of all her Majes: Subjects on ye N: continent of america which

[1] Peter Wraxall's comment on this conference is "there is nothing material to be noted." McIlwain, 68.

I' think ought to be for ever kept bright, as it hitherto hath on our Part

BRETHREN

I have sent for you upon an Extraordinary occasion, to assist in an Expedition for ye Reducing Canada, wh. you have So much Long'd for, That neighbourhood you know hath been of a long time Very Troublesome to you, & many of here Majesties good Subjects In these Parts

We will not now Enumerate the many Perfidious and base actions they have been guilty off, we have whole Volumes full of Complaints which you have made to us of their Treacherous dealings. The French of Canada have killd Imprison'd, Carried away, and Transported your People, burnt your Castles, and us'd all means which lay in their Power to Impoverish you, and bring you to a low and miserable Condition.

They have not only Seduc'd your People, and Entic'd them away from your Country, but Incourag'd even your own Brethren to make war upon you, on purpose to weaken you,

They have Sett ye Farr Indians upon you and furnish'd them with arms and Ammunition in order to DeStroy you, The Pains they have taken to accomplish your Ruin hath been Indefatigable

They Incroachd upon your Rights and Libertyes by building Forts upon your Land against your wills, Possessing ye Principall Passes and hunting Places, whereby all your hunting (your only Support) was rendred not only Precarious, but dangerous.

Their treacherously murthering of Montour one of your Brethren, before your Faces, in your own Country this Summer is an Evident mark of their I'nsolence and how they Intend to use you. Most of these and other things having been truly Represented to ye Greate Queen of Great Brittain (who is victorious over ye French King in Europe) she hath taken them into her Royall Consideration and has been Graciously Pleased (notwithstanding ye vast Expence her Majestie is dayly at in Carying on this necessary just war against France in Europe) to Send over at a great Charge a Considerable Fleet, with men, Ammunition, Provision, and Artillery and other things necessary for ye Effectuall Reduceing of Canada, to Redeem you from that Bondage and Slavery The French deSignd to bring you under. I must therefore

Earnestly Exort you to be Cheerfull and Resolute in joyning with all your Strenth with her Majesties Forces which goe by Land on this Expedition, & you need not Doubt (with ye blessing of God) of a happy Issue, and of bringing yt Country under ye Obedience of ye great Queen of great Brittain, which of Right did belong to her Royall Predecessors.

This will be the only and Effectuall means to Procure a firm and durable Peace and quiet Possession of our Setlements for us, and for you and your Posterity for ever, There shall be all Possible Care taken to Supply those that have no ammunition and hope there shall be no want of Provision, this being also a good Season of ye year for hunting.

Brethren

I must tell you I am Concern'd to see none of ye Sachims of ye Sinnekes here in this Grand meeting,[1] I fear ye French Jesuits (whom they have so Long harbourd notwithstanding all ye Precaution to ye Contrary) have So far bewitchd ym, that they have forgot how ye French usd to Treat them formerly, how yt about 22 year ago in Peaceable times they designd to Destroy them, had not by meer Providence a Maquase Prisoner Escapd, and warnd them of their approaching Danger; however we will not wholly dispair of their Coming to themselvs again, and therefore shall keep their Share of this Present which her Majesty of her Royall Bounty has been pleasd to send you, not doubting but they will Soon be undeceiv'd, and find that ye Story of ye Farr Indians coming upon them now, is a meer Shamm, which they need not fear but that all ye Farr Indians assoon as the French are Subdued will be and Continue in amity with ym els the Brethren will be Assisted by her Majesty. I love to the See the Brethren all unanimous according to the ancient Covenant Chain, which has ever been kept Inviolable by us, having never had ye least Jarring or Dispute, but livd in Peace and Concord togather, since ye first Setlement of Christians in this Country

Brethren

I Esteem it a Very great happiness both to you and us, that the

[1] Wraxall noted that two Seneca were present who "doubted not but their Countrymen would be willing to join the 4 Nations in the present Expedition." McIlwain, 69. This and the documents that follow give evidence that no Seneca were present and that they refrained from participation in the expedition.

Honorable Coll: Francis Nicholson hath been pleased to accept of the Command of this army that goes against Canada whereof you are a Part, he is a Gentleman who has had the honour to be governour and Leut. Governour of most or all of her Majes. Colonyes on this Continent, and who out of a Reall affection to you and us, has offered his Service to ye great Queen my mistresse on this Expedition as a Volunteer at his own Expence which will be Very great

I must earnestly recommend to you to pay all ye Deference and Regard to him as your Commander in Cheiff, and Chearfully to obey all his Commands with ye utmost Diligence, which will Entitle you to the great Queen my mistresses further favour, and that on his death or absence you pay ye Like Obedience to Coll Peter Schuyler, who is in that case appointed to ye Command of this Land Army, Such of you as Signalize your Selvs in this Expedition your aforesaid Commander in Cheif will reward Suitable to ye Merit of ye action, which I hope will Excite every man to the performance of great and glorious Enterprize. When ye Indians heard that Coll Nicholson had tendred his service to her Maje. to goe as a Volunteer and had accepted of ye Command of ye army which goes by Land to Reduce Canada, They all gave a Shout, as ye Custome is among them when anything is Proposed that is Extream wel Pleasing and Gratefull Expressing ye great joy they had of so good & Experiencd a Souldier to be their great Capt. & Leader. The Brethren will Receive to morrow Four fatt oxen as a ꝑsent made to you by your Commandr in Cheife in order to hang over ye great kitle of war, yt you may Eat together according to your Custom, and will order you then four Barrels of Strong Beer to dring her majes. health & ye day following four Barels more.

Lastly I shall Conclude with this Exortation that your People take Especiall Care not to Destroy ye Christians Catle, but that they keep together and be obedient to Such Commands as they shall Receive from ye Commander in Cheiffe.

Orders being given to bring out the Presents Sadeganaktie Cheif Sachim of ye onnondages Rose up, & desired that the giving of ye ꝑsents might be deferr'd, till to morrow morning, because it was late, they would not have time to divide that night, & So were orderd to come Early in ye morning.

Assoon as ye Propositions were Ended, one of ye Cheif Capts. of ye Mohogs rose up & Sung a Song of warr, and took ye honble Coll: Nicholson by ye hand and walkd with him to and again, Severall times before all ye Indians Singing and Rejoycing yt so good and great a man had accepted of yt Command to be their Genll. in this Expedition wh. was approvd of by all ye 4 nations by Severall Shouts and aclamations. Promising to pay all ye Deference and Reguard to him they were Capable off, & to obey all his Commands with their utmost Diligence

Then a Capt. of oneyde Rose up and Sang a warlike Song in ye behalf of Coll: Schuyler aproveing and Rejoyceing that he had taken upon him ye Command under the honble Coll: Nicholson, and that he was to Succeed him in Case of his Death & absence. The Capt of onnondage rose up and Sang a Song of war and took Coll: Whiting by ye hand leading him to & again before all ye Indians & Rejoyced that he had brought Such Brave men under his Command from her Majes. Colony of Canecticut, and that there was So great Unity and Concord among all her majes. Christian Subjects, that they joyned as one man to Subdue the Common Enemy.

Then another Capt took Coll: Mathews by ye hand and led him to and again Singing & Expressing their Satisfaction and joy yt. So many brave officers were Imployed in this Expedition to Canada.

A true Copy Examind by me
Rt. Livingston Secry for the
Indian affaires.

Albany ye 17th of July 1709

Examination of Atheroghkoes an onnondage Indian Sent from his Castle by ye Sachims that were there, but without 7 hands of wampum as is Customary, Relates as follows

That a messenger came to onnondage from Cayouge five days ago with news, yt. a Sinneke had been Sent from ye Sinnekes Country with the following acct.

A Sinneke Indian who livd at TjughSaghrondie who is married there is come home to his oun Country, & gives ye following Relation, That he was come doun with a Party of Dowaganhaes as far as ochSwege, & when he came there, found it was a Place of

Randevous & many Indians got together, he See 3 Sinneke Squaes & 2 Sinneke Indians, and four onnondages Prisoners, who had been out a hunting, and heard yt it was Concluded by yt Party, to come and destroy 4 Castles Vizt two of ye Sinekes, & Cayouge & onnondage, and that it was talkd yt ye Enemy was Seen neer ye Sinnekes Country.
One of ye Dowaganhaes of yt Company Sd. he would fall upon 7 or 8 Indian houses belonging to ye 5 nations by Cadarachqui
Says further yt. an onnondage lately come from Cadarachqui says he heard of some French yt were come from Tjughsaghrondie yt ye Dawaganhaes were coming to DeStroy ye 5 nations, and therefore warn'd them to be upon their guard.
He heard also yt. 2 nations of Indians living in maryland calld Showanaes & Cachnawas were all dead of a Pestilentiall disease, only 3 of one & 2 of anyr Castle left alive.
The Leut. Govr. told them, that he knows not, how to give Credt: to this Story, Since it Comes from ye Sinnekes, who Declines to be Concernd in this Expedition, and they being of ye French Intrest are apt to beleeve any Story yt the french Putts into their heads.

A true Copy Examind ꝑ
Robt. Livingston Secy for
ye Indian affares.

At a Meeting of ye Commisrs. for managing the Indian Affairs in Albany this 17th day of July 1709

Present
Coll: Pr. Schuyler
Col: K: v: Renselaer
Evt. Banker
Henry holland
John Abeel
John Cuyler
Hend: hanse

The Honble. Leut. govr. Coll: Ingoldesby and Coll: nicholson have proposed to ye Commisrs. the necessity of Sending a Party of Christians and Indians to ye Sinnekes Country to Convince ye Sinnekes of ye lyes and Storys wch. are Spred among them by ye french of Canada, have desired ye Commissrs opinion in ye matter. The Comrs. are of opinion yt. it would be Convenient to send Capt. Abraham Schuyler with five Christians, to ye Sinnekes Country, to lye there during this Present Expedition to Canada, & if occasion Requires to Send two men at ye least Expresse to bring Letters from thence to this Place, with an account of what happens there.

Albany ye 19th. of July 1709

Four Sachims of onnondages called Carachkontie, Tejotderontore, awenagogare, & onnuwaroge, Communicated to Evert Banker Esqr. Mayer of Albany, that they had sent Two I'ndians called Carojadgegoe of oneyde & ajighwaghtha of onnondage to Canada 30 days ago, with Two Belts of wampum to tell ye Indians yt live near Mont Royall yt ye English had form'd an Expedition, by land, and by water, for ye Reduceing of Canada, & desired yt they should Return to ye Land of their ancestors, where they had been born and lived Vizt to ye 5 nations, & warnd them by no means to joyn wth ye french, or any ways Engage themSelvs with them, nor to quit their habitations, but to Stay in their Castles, and when ye army Comes into Canada to joyn her Majes. forces, & if they could not be pswaded to do this, they must expect no mercy, but to be Treated like open Enemies, ye Said two Indian messengers were directed, after they had desired this message to meet ye army at fort lamot, at a Creek where they would make some marks, and if ye army was not gott So farr they would come throu ye lake with a Cnoe with a flagg, wh. would be ye Sign & give an act. of their negotiation
this message was Sent in ye name of this government & of ye 5 nations, for Lawrence ye Interpreter was then at onnondage and Consented to ye Sending sd. Two Indians
This message was to be deliverd to Tatachquisero Sachim of Cachanuage neer Mont Royall, who is well I'nclin'd to ye English Intrest, for ye Indians are divided there as well as among ye 5 nations, ye one half is for ye English & ye oyr half for ye french, and lest ye govr: of Canada might Suspect any thing, ye 2 messengers had 2 other Belts wh. was to be Deliverd Publikly with this Proposition
1st That it was not probable ye govt. of N: York would concern themSelfs in Such an Expedition for they never had medled ali this while with ye warr that n: England was So deeply Engag'd in, altho they were their oun Countrymen, yt were murther'd dayly by ye french & their Indians
2. With ye 2d. Belt they were to Say, If it So happend yt ye

English did joyn their force and fall upon Canada, ye govr of Canada could blame no body but himSelf, for he had made it his Bussinesse to Stirr up ye I'ndians to goe dayly & kill & destroy ye People of N: England.

A true Copy Examind ꝑ
Robt: Livingston Secry
for ye Indian affares.

Present
Evt. Banker mayr
Johs. abeel Record
Myndt Schuyler }
Rt Livingston Junr }
hend: hanse } *ald*
Johs Rooseboom }
nanning harmense }
Johs mingrel }
Johs Sanders }
David Schuyler } *Justices*
Albt Rykman }
Johs Cuyler }
Majr. Dirk wessels

At a Meeting of ye Mayor aldermen of ye Citty of Albu ye Justices of ye Sd County, ye Commissioners for ye Expedition against Canada & Commissioners of ye Indian affarcs in albany ye 12 of augst 1709

The ꝑsent Expedition against Canada being taken into Consideration & yt ye Season of ye year is So farr Spent & no news of ye arrival of ye fleet yt her majes designd to Send from great Brittain for ye Reduceing of Canada,[1] it is feard yt. ye. fleet will come So late yt it will be impracticable to get up ye River of Canada this fall, by reason of ye northerly winds & oyr accidents yt may happen in their voyage & it being morally Impossible to Reduce Canada by ye Land army alone are therefore of opinion yt a Memoriall be draun to ye Leut govr: & Councill & assembly RepreSenting ye Deplorable & dangerous Condition these fronteers will be in this winter if Canada should not now be Reduced & to RepreSent that in Such Case

1. ye 3 new forts now built at ye Stillwater & both sides of ye great Carying Place may have a Sufficient garrison

2. That ye forts of Albany & Shinechtady who are Rotten & quite gone to decay may be Repaired & garrisond &

3. That they may be assisted in fortifying ye City of Albany wh. is weak & out of Repair

[1] The war in Europe having taken a bad turn, the sailing plans of the British fleet intended for the reduction of Canada had to be cancelled, leaving the colonial campaign temporarily suspended.

4. That there may be 200 Indians kept in Pay for Skouts & to hunt at ye Carying Place this winter
5. That Some measures may be taken to Secure the 4 nations who its feared Some of them will fall off from us, as ye Sinekes have done who are more numerous then ye oyr 4 nations
It is to be feared yt all ye forces Except ye Regular Troops yt are now Posted at ye wood Creek as wel those yt belong to ye neighbouring Colonys as those yt belong to this Colony wil all be Calld home & none Raisd to Supply their Rooms, when they see ye fleet doe not come or yt ye fleet comes too late, if Some Care be not taken to *p*vent it & therefore Propose
That for ye Security of her majes. sd. fronteers 400 Brisk men may be Raised out of this & ye neighbouring Colonys & Joyned to ye Regular Troops who are Computed about 200 fitt for Service, wh. wil make 600 & yt Such a number of ye forces now in pay may Secure ye Sd. forts till they be Releev'd
It cannot be Supposed yt that Vigilant Enemy ye french wil be idle this winter they wil make all Efforts to weaken these fronteers, & to deabauch our Indians, & assoon as they begin to murther ye farmers & burn their houses with their Smal partyes the People wil Desert, & ye County be quite Depleted, This wil desleatte us & Incourage ye Enemy & therefore all Imaginable Care ought to be taken to prevent it.
It is humbly Proposed yt her Majes. May be made acquainted with our miserable Circumstances & yt She wil be pleased to Send us Speedy Releeffe, Since it is wel known to ye world yt the People of albany have Spared no Pains nor trouble to forward the *p*sent Expedition, and yt ye genl may be addressed to keep So many of ye Troops now under his Command to Secure ye fronteers till a Sufficient number Come to Releev ym.

at a meeting of ye Comrs. appointed for managing ye Indian affairs in albany ye 28th June 1710

Present
Evt. Banker
H. Hansen
J. Cuyler
Myndt. Schuyler
P vn Brug
J. Roseboom

The Comrs. Considering his Excys. Letter to ym. dated ye 21th. Instant concerning ye Sachims of ye Mohogs, They have therefore Resolved to write a letter to Jan Baptist van Eps Interprr and ordr him forthwith to go to ye mohogs Country to desyre ye principall Sachims of yt Nation to come doun to Schinnechtady withall Speed, & yt they will meet them there assoon as they hear of their comeing thither.

Present
K: V: Renselaer
E. Banker
J. Cuyler
J. Roseboom

Shinnechtady 2d. July 1710
att a meeting of ye Comrs appointed for managing ye Ind affairs in albany.
Proposition made by ye Comrs to ye Sachims of ye mohogs being abt 60 in number, & consisting in 3 tribes of ye bear wolfe & turtel

Brethren

We are glad to Se yo here & have sent for yo. by order of his Exly. our govr., to acqt you yt her majes. hath been pleasd to send a great many familys who are arrived at n: York from great brittain, to go & Setle on ye Land at Skohere,[1] wh. is already purchased from you, ye Surveyor Genll. being come to Survey ye Same, but if yo. have yet any pretence thereon, we do assure that no Setlement Shall be made there, before it be Duly purchased & yu. Satisfyd

We do desire yu. to pitch on 4 or 5 of yr young men to go with ye Surveyr. Genll. on ye aforesd Land, to give their Best Information, & to See where a good Rhoad may be made from thence on this River for wagon or Cart, who Shall be well Rewarded for their trouble, by his Exly. our gov on his arrivall at albany.

The Sachims Sayd yt they would give an answer to morrow morning, and Desire yt in ye mean time they may have Some meat & drink, there men haveing brought nothing with them

It was orderd by ye Comrs that they Should have Provision dureing theire Stay

Shinnechtady 3d. July 1710
answer of ye mohog Sachims to ye Commissrs

Brethren

we have heard & Considerd on yr Proposall made to us yesterday & yt ye Queen has been pleased to Send a great many familys in Compe with ye Govr. who has orderd you to Speak to us con-

[1] This refers to the original design to settle the Palatinate refugees on the lands of Schoharie. The strong opposition of the Mohawks necessitated an alternative plan, their settlement on Livingston Manor.

cerning ye Land at Skohere wh. we had Sold; but my Lord Bellement Late Govr. of this province hath brooke ye Deed of Sale of ye Sd. Land & therefore it derives on us again

You told us yt ye Surveyor was come, to Survey ye Land and Lay out a Rhoad wh. we will not Suffer, do yo think to deal with us Like Children, the queen has been pleased to breake ye Deed, & we shall not be agt. her reqt to Let her have ye Land for Poor People.

we will not Suffer ye Land to be Surveyd before ye return of hendrick our Sachim & ye oyr Indians who are gone to great Brittain.

Wee had thoughts yt. Collo Nicolson should come with a great number of men to take Canada, but now we perceive ye 10 men, who are come, are Sent to take our Land from us

We are willing yt her majes. shall have ye Land at Skohere for poor people, & not one foot more, provided it be duely purchased

The Comrs. answerd ye sd Indians yt his Exly ye govr had Sent ye Surveyor genll to Survey ye Land & to See how much there is (who is now a great way from home) and assoon as his Exly comes at albany he shall Satisfy you for ye Land before any Setlement Shall be made thereon, & not in ye Least to Invade your property

Whereupon they answerd yt they would not suffer yt ye sd Lands should be Surveyd before ye arrivall of those Indians who are gone to great Brittain, & Roase up & went away very much Dissatisfyd.

The Comrs. used all possible Means to perswade the Sd. Sachims to give Liberty to ye Surveyor to Survey ye Sd Lands and to give their answer, who replyed yt they were gone to their Country to Consult with ye rest of their Sachims and young men, and would bring an answer in four days time.[1]

[1] On July 20 the Mohawks consented to the survey. *Cal. N. Y. Coun. Min.*, 239. Their consent was forthcoming only after Governor Hunter had acknowledged their title to the land. Then the Mohawks "resolved to make a present of those Lands to her Majesty which I accepted with thanks in Her Name and ordered them a suitable present." Hunter to Lords of Trade, c. October, 1710. O'Callaghan, 5: 171. However, the Palatines were settled on Livingston's lands since it was believed that they were better suited to the manufacture of tar and were more readily accessible.

Propos: by ye Showenoes Indians
to his Excel: Rt hunter gov genll.

Makadagqur in Behalfe of himselfe & the Rest of the Sachams his Speetch to his Excellencey Coll huntor viz

Fathor we have heard that you are Sent by the greate Queene of England: Thearefore we are sent by the rest of the Sachams to bid you welcom into this Goverment
Fathor when we did Cum first heare out of oure owne Cuntry we was permited to live at menessings undor the Glorius Son of the English Goverment thearefore we Cum to pay oure duty to our ffathor which is Sent by ye Greate Queen of England we are people yt Lives only uppon hunting to by English goods to Clothe oure Selves.
Fathor we let you Know yt all oure men is gon out a hunting. I thought by my Selfe & ye rest of ye Sachams of menessings & peyhoggicale to pay our Respects & duty to oure fathor: we are not Cum for any gifts but only out of a Love to oure fathor
New york ye 21 of octobr
1710

His Excel Answer

Children
I thank yu for yr kind Congratalotry welcom & visit
I am well Satisfyd yt a nation of Consequence Should come & Setle in her maje governmt where I doe assure yu yu Shall have all Protection imaginable & al necessary incouragemt as to a Trade in wh you shall be as kindly used as any oyr Indians in the govt.
I am wel Pleased yt yr young men are out ahunting & yt they Imploy their time So Innocently, and tho I know you are not come wth yt intention to get a gift, yet to manifest her maje. good will towards yu & my approbation of your good & quiet behaviour I do out of her majes. Bounty give yu. ye following Present vizt

a *p*s of Red Strouds
10 gunns
20 bags of Pouder
30 Barrs of lead
100 flints

A true Copy Examind
p Rt Livingston Secry
of ye Indian affares.

Albany pmo March 1710/11

Three Mohogs calld Tarigjoris Dotsigtade and Antony came from ye Mohogs Countrey, & told the Commissioners of ye. Indian affares, that they were Sent by the Mohogs Sachims to acquaint them that there was a generall meeting of ye Sachims at Tionondoroge in ye Mohogs Country, & deSird yt hendrik hanse (whom they call in their Language Sinnonquirese) might goe thither to be present with them, and hear what Should be Concluded among them, & to bring Jan Baptist van Eps along with him for Interpreter, & if any of ye other Commissioners would goe along it would be acceptable to ye Sachims, & laid doun Seven hands of wampum according to their Custom
Whereupon ye Commissioners Said if Sinnonquirese yt is hendrik hanse would goe they gave their Consent whereupon hend: hanse aforesd. undertook to goe, and departed ye 2d. thither.

At Sinnondoroge ye 5th. march 1710/11[1]

The Mohog Sachims in their Generall meeting Say as follows
Brother Sinnonquirese meaning hendrik hanse
We desired yu to come here and we are Rejoycd at yr Coming, & yt we See yu here.
Brother Sinnonquirese
our nation hath appointed you last fall to be ye head or Cheiff of a Fort yt is to be made by us, & desired then that this matter might be forwarded, That ministers might be sent into our Countrey to Instruct us in ye Christian Religeon, and have therefore Sent for you to Propose this the Second time
The Queen Promisd us yt if we deSired anything of her, that she would grant it, she Promisd us a Fort and a minister
Thus it is yt we have Concluded & made an absolut Resolution to Receive you as one of our own nation wherefore we will henceforth look upon you as one of us and we desire you that you will mannage our affares for we intrust all our matters in your hands, and desire further of you that you will come and live and dye with us.
Brother
What is now Said is ye firm Conclusion of both Castles, & shall

[1] Wraxall comments that "No furthe Acct of this Meeting Appears from the Records." McIlwain, 81.

be kept Inviolable, & wee will acquaint all ye five nations with ye Same
This Interpreted by me Jan Baptist van Eps.

New York Aprile 24th 1711

[Col. Peter Schuyler]
Sr
HAVEING this day reced a Letter from the Commissioners of the Indian affairs at Albany acquainting me that they had received a Message from onodage by Express telling them that three ffrench officers, one Interpreter, and thirty men were arrived there from Canada, and that thereupon the five Nations had sent seven hands of Wampum to desire you to Come to them, I have Communicated the said Letter to the Councill who are Come to a Conclusion that it is Necessary you go thither forthwith taking the Interpreters and such others with you as you shall think Convenient;
YOU are therefore on yor. arrivale there, to thank the Indians for this Notice they have given the Governmt. of ye arrivall of the ffrench in their Castles.
YOU are to tell them that I Expect from their allegiance to her Majty and their former promises that they will not permit any armed men, Priests or Emisarys from ye ffrench to Come among them.
YOU are also to acquaint ye Indians that I Expect they should have no private Consults with any of those ffrench who are now among them, but that you be present at all their Meetings and debates. That so soon as the ffrench have made their proposicons and the Indians have answered them, if they think fitt to make any answere thereto they oblige the ffrench to Leave their Country Assuring the Indians if any attempt be made against them from Kanada they will have all the Assistance the Government can give them.
Whilst you are at Onondage you are to send some Trusty Indians to the ffrontiers of Canada to discover The Motions of ye Enemy, and if any preperations are making by them either for their defence or for any Enterprise against her Majtys. Subjects.
THIS being done you are to send me by ye first opportunity an

Accot. of yor. proceedings and of the proceedings of ye ffrench and Indians.

I wish you a good journey and succes in what you go about. I am Sr yor very humble Servt

/S/ Ro. Hunter.

Albany 10th. february 1711/2
at 7 a Clock in ye Evening

Gentlemen

within this hour wee have Received Speedy Intelligence from our outskouts part thereof on there Return from Tionondoroga near ye Lake have discover'd Tracts of the Enemy four miles on this Side of the falls of the wood Creek wh. gives us Reason to beleeve the Enemy is approaching, have therefore thought fitt to give you notice thereof, Desireing you to detach two hundred men of the Palatines to be ready to march hither upon the next notice from us, in the mean time we desire you to Send fifty Palatines with all Expedition, we are with Respect

Gentlemen
Your very Humble: Servts.
/S/ Pr: Schuyler Corronll.

the Inclosed
to Collo Rutsen
we desire you
to forward with
all Expedition

[*addressed*]
on her majtys. Service
For Robt. Livingston Esqr. &
the other Comrs. for Regulateing
of the Palatine affairs at
the manor of Livingston.

an order from gov hunter dated ye 13 may [1712] to give an acct of ye number of Indians in ye 5 nations & what Part of Pouder & arms of her majs at albany and Shinnectady

Maquasen mit einige van Schagtkook		
Welke onder haer woonen[1]	180	Man
Onneyders	120	
Onondagers	350	
Kajoegers	150	
Sinnikers	1000	
	1800	

[1] Maquasen with those of the Schagtkook people who live among them.

This is besides a ConSiderable number of Sd. 5 nations who live neer Canastoge upon a Branch of ye Susquehanne River & at onnochquage upon a branch of Delawar River

There are above 2000 Indians to ye Southward & westward who are Tributaries of ye Sd. 5 nations & under their Command.

N york ye 14 of may 1712.

Ch: huddy's Letter to Coll Ingoldesby abt. Johs Luykasse
Fort Hunter 27th: feby 1712/13

Honble. Sr.

This comes to Acquaint yr. honr: that Johannis Lucas has been here & done a great deal of Mischief Among ye Indians, Told 'em yt. there Land would be Took from 'em pothering every house as he came in Telling 'em Soe upon wch acct. as Lawrence Tells all ye Schocticohe Indians are removing to Schocticote & Some gon ye Minister & my Selfe have assured ye Sachims to ye Contrary [(*torn*)] ye Indians here has been Cheated as they Say by ye N. Engld: people makes 'em faithless all ye men are well I' am with my humble Duty to yr honr:

Honble: Sr.
Yr Most Dutifull &
obedient humble Sert
/S/ Cha: Huddy

Copy
Letter of ye Comrs. to his Exly.
Albany ye 13th of May 1714[1]

May it Please yr Exly.

Wee Cant in duty omitt to acqt. yr Exly. yt mr. hansen Came yesterday from ye maquas Country where he has heard of a trusty Indian privately that there is to be a generall meeting at onnondage Speedily not only of the five Nations but of all ye Indians Liveing at the Jerseys Pensilvania marryland virginia Carolina &c. he that Revaild this Sayd that it is Resolvd & Concluded that if any privy to this Should acqt. any Christian Living in this governt. wth. ye Resolution of ys meeting Should Suffer ye pain of death in ye open meeting ye maquas Expect dayly a post to come to ye

[1] Wraxall dates this notice as May 20, but he gives an account of the meeting at Onondaga which followed. McIlwain, 96-97.

sd. meeting wee are afraid that this Lyes on no good buttom that they have Some bad Design agt. her majes. Subjects wh. may be of Ill Consequence.

wee have (with Submission) Resolved & thought proper to procure a good trusty Indian to go to onnondage & be ꝑsent at ye sd. meeting to take Speciall Regard on ye motions & Resolutions of ye Indians & dive unto their design and acqt. us of it assoon as ye meeting is broake up, wee shall promise him a good Reward for his trouble & fidility in this but we have not one farthing of ye publick in hands & it is Impossible for us treat with ye Indians without to be at some Expence So that we hope your Exly. will be pleased to take Care that we may have Some money to Defray ye Expence we are dayly at &a.

N: York the 13th. of June 1717

Dr. ffather

This goes pr Capt: Smith who is Agent for the Govermt of Virginia, to treat with the five Nations who have done abundance of damage in some parte of Virginia, he had been taken by a Pyrate at Sandy hook who detaind him some time, This Pyrate was a Tender to the Pyrate Ship that was cast away at Cape Cod & has ever since infested this Coast. . . .

/S/ Robt Livingston Junr.

[*Abstract in Robert Livingston, Jr.'s hand*]

Coll Spotswood governr of virginys Letter to gov hunter dated 30 may 1717

of an Insult made by ye 5 nations on ye Cattawba Indians who after a Rupture with South Carolina applyd to Virginy for Peace, and a Treaty being Set on foot they were to bring some of ye Cheiff mens Children for hostages wh they did at Christiana ye 9th. of april 1717 whither ye govr went in Person & having Surrendred their arms to ye English fort there ye next day Early a Party of ye 5 nations of 40 or 50 fals upon ym under ye wals of ye fort fires upon them kills 5 wounds 2 & Caryes Wittmannetaughkee ye Cheiftman & oyr 5 of ye Cattabaw Indians Prisoners, one of sd Prisoners after 11 days Escapes & brings the news yt ye Party were Sinnekes a Term wh. they give all ye 5 nations & about 40 in number among whom 5 or 6 were of anoyr nation, that Sd

Party deSignd to fall upon ye Tributaries of ye English calld Saponie Indians, & give out wil Return in a Short time & not only Cutt off ye sd. Saponie Indians but ye English Setled in their neighbourhood.[1]

That a Peace was concluded between virginy & ye 5 nations Ao 1685 virginy Indians being *p*sent, Sd. Peace is kept inviolable by ye English, ye govr being injoyned by ye King's Instructions to keep it, how far this action is Consistent with yt Peace & their frequent Professions they have made of their PreServing ye Covenant Chain (as they call it) he leaves our govr to judge. Ye Cattawba Indians thought them Selfs Safe Especially under an English fort but this treatment makes them Suspect ye English fidelity, ye gov had much adoe to *p*suade them of his Innocence, who at last *p*swaded ym to leave their hostages & goe away Satisfyd, but had never a harder task in his life.

ye sd Party Plunderd an English house on ye fronteers & used ye People Rudely they ound yt ye 5 nations had Robd ye virginy traders 1713 on Eno River & ye Reason they gave because they Refused to trade with ye Tuscarores while they were at war wth north Carolina, & Supplyd wth. amunition ye Southern Indians who were Enemyes to ye Tuscarores, they ound also of murdering 5 years ago majr winn agent of good act in virginy & Carried 2 Saponie Indians Prisoners, if these be ye fruits we are to Reap from their Confederacy wth. yr govt: & their Pretended Peace with this tis fit we should know it yt we put our Selvs upon our guard & not Suffer tamely ye lives of his majes Subjects to lye at ye mercy of these villains, while our hands are tyd up from doing our Selvs Justice by ye fallacious treatyes they made with us, and ye Reguard we have to their being under ye Protection of ye govt. of N york.

Desire yt ye Indian Captives may be Restored, & on what terms we are to be with these Indians for ye future, & because ye Sachims of ye Sinnekes or 5 nations may disoun this deed as done by some of ye Petty nations Inhabiting between virginy & them he hes Sent ye Bearer who can travel in ye woods to goe to those touns wth Some of ye Sachims to demand ye Prisoners & Conduct them hither.

[1] The problem of this attack on the Catawba Indians was dealt with by Governor Hunter in his conference with the Iroquois, June 16-17, 1717. O'Callaghan, 5: 490-492.

Desires he may Speak with ye 5 nations at alby & to Prevail with ym yt Some of their deputyes may come & treat in Virginy, or yt he wil meet ym in ye northern fronteers of virginy, & yt only to Secure ye Peace of ye kings Subjects

Recomends him ye bearer to ye govr for Credit to make Presents ye Rest of ye Letter was about ye Conversion of ye Indians wh. is thought Impracticable

yt Relating ye Pyrates was dashd out by ye Pyrat ye gent was taken with [*sic,* by] Coming from virginy.

Present
his Excellency
Coll Pr Schuyler
ye Commissioners of ye Ind. affairs mayr Recordr & aldermen & diverse oyr gent.
yt attended
his Excel to alby &
many of ye Inhabitants
Lawrence Claese Interpreter

Answer of ye 5 nations vizt ye Mohogs oneydes onnondages Cayouges & Sinnekes to his Excely Brigader hunter Capt Genl & govr in Cheiffe of his Majes. Provinces of N: York & ye Jerseys & Vice admiral of ye Same in Albany ye 14 of June 1717[1]

Dekanissore Speaker

Broyr Corlaer

You have acquainted us yesterday yt. we are come here by ye Command of yr & our great master ye king of great Brittain & yu have told us yt you Speak in his name giving us full assurance of his good will & affection & yt as Long as we Continue faithfull to ye Covenant Chain he will Protect us against all Such as shal dare to molest us as frinds to him for which we are Very thankfull; Say again yt we ye 5 nations we even as far as ye Shawenhes are thankfull for his majes. good Inclination & affection towards us, & hope shall never give any occasion of ye least Suspicion of any Breach of ye Covenant Chain, & yt what has been Said by our Broyr Corlaer is from ye bottom of his heart without any hypocriSy, for if we should deceive on anoyr. it would be Pernicious to us both did give a Belt of wampum

Broyr Corlaer

You have also Renewd ye ancient Covenant Chain wh. you declare Shall be kept Inviolable on ye Part of ye kings Subjects ye Christians & we Promise faithfully on our Part to doe ye Same yu told

[1] Hunter's initial proposition to the Five Nations of June 13, 1717, is given in O'Callaghan, 5: 484-485. The Iroquois answer, given here, is not included in that published version of the conference.

us also yt if any nation should attaque us yt yu would assist or Enable us by such methods as was in yr Power to Repell force by force, we hope we shall have no occasion to make use of yr kind Profer, but if there should be a necessity we Doubt not but yu wil be as good as yr words, for arms & amunition are ye Principall materials to be used in time of warr & we doe assure yu. yt ye 5 nations shall always live in Striktest frindship with all his majes. Subjects do give a few Bever Skins.

Broyr Corlaer

we are told also yt if any of ye Subjects of ye great king of Grt Brittain be attak'd by their Enemies we are to afford them ye Readyest & most Effectuall assistance in our Power Especially if ye English should be molested by their Indian neighbours wh we will be Ready & willing to doe to ye utmost of our Power but if ye English act of Pride or malice should be ye agressors & fall upon their Indian neighbours without a Cause we must first Consider of it before we offerd any assistance against those Indians.

You told us yt ye king of grt. Brittain has Sent us a handSom Present which we beleeve & are Thankfull to his majestie knowing & being very Senceible he has a great kindnesse for us we shall Endeavor by our duty full behavior to merit ye Continuation of ye great kings favour towards us, did give a Belt of wampum

his Excely Reply

Brethren

What I told yu yesterday was I can assure yu from ye bottom of my heart, & those assurances I gave yu is not only by ye Expresse Command of ye king my master but from my own Inclination & good wil to ye Brethren & if there be any vile base ill minded Persons among us Either Christian or Indian wh would make yu beleeve otherwise or Raise Jealousies among yu. I wish yu would diScover them that they might Receive their Deserts.

I am now to give yu ye Presents and I can assure yu yt all wh. has been Sent from great Brittain for ye Brethren while I have been in ye govt has been faithfully deliverd & nothing has been kept back but more has been added to it by this governmt. among ye Presents yt yu are now to Receive there is a Considerable quantity of Rom wh. I would advise yu not to touch but Secure it in Some of yr frinds houses till it be brought above Shinnechtady for fear by yr Peoples Intemperance Some Inconveniencys may happen.

Dekanissore answerd

That they Prayd his Excel would keep ye Rom in his oun Custody till ye waggons Should Cary it above ye Christian Setlements for if it were Put into ye Custody of Some of ye traders ye Rom might Probably loose its Strenth.

September 3, 1718
Governor Hunter's proposition to the Sachems of the Five Nations[1]

Our Commissioners here having sent notice that you did arrive here as deputies of our brethren of the five nations, as well as a message of what you have stated to them as a proposal in my absence, I have been willing, as a sign of the goodwill and affection I always have had for you and my friendship for you, to put all other matters aside and make haste to meet you here.

I am glad that we are assembled even though I cannot help but express some weariness about the suspicion and disloyalty you seem to possess. I hope it only seems thus, so that you will accept from us and our actions, after all the proofs that it is possible to give, the sincerity of our hearts and the declarations so many times renewed and repeated at the special orders of the great King, our lord and master and your very powerful protector and affectionate father.

You tell me that you have been informed of an action we have conceived to raid and cut off the brethren in order to get possession of your lands. I know that you do not believe it and therefore I have but little to say on this. You declare that you obtained these stories from your enemies, and whoever it is that whispers these things in your ears is certainly not your friend. Did we ever, in your, your father's, or grandfather's time, do anything that could evoke the least suspicion of such an underhanded procedure? Did we not on our side not only keep strictly to our covenant, which we have been known to renew many times, but refrain from becoming alarmed or distrustful by any part of your conduct which, to people less convinced of your true beliefs and honesty, might have seemed suspicious? And were we not willing to blame any misdeeds on the hotheadedness or carelessness of your young

[1] Translated from the Dutch. This document is referred to in *Cal. N. Y. Col. MSS.*, 2: 437, with the answer of the Iroquois. The latter item, however, is not found in the Livingston Indian Papers.

people rather than consider it as a breach of duty and obligation by our good brethren of the nations? You say that the Tuscarora Indians say that the Christians have raided them to get their land. But it is common knowledge, and you yourselves know it, that those Indians attacked the Christians, his Majesty's subjects of Carolina, at the time of a deep and quiet peace, and attacked and murdered them in their beds which evil and underhanded action you yourselves have offered to revenge, declaring that they were a mean and unbelievable people who had no truth in them and that there was no way to teach them but to destroy them. But it seems that they have quickly found credit or favor among you, or you or they have miraculously changed since those days, even though those Indians have now presented themselves and made peace with Carolina. For which reason I ask you to bury the hatchet that you took up against them on my request. Thereupon I give you this belt.

You say that you believe these rumors more readily because powder is so expensive. When I met you here on the last trip I gave you ammunition in a very large and liberal measure, and you were very well satisfied with it, which was not a sign of any conspiracy against you or of any raiding or anything similar by you against us. And what use did you make of it. Not that for which it had been given to you, to hunt and to protect yourselves against your enemies, but to harrass and attack some Indians who live far away from you and did not molest you, and I have reason to fear that they are some with whom you should not bother. But let them be who they may, what did you gain by it? You have lost a number of your swift young people, one of whom is worth a thousand Flatheads. Not only have you gone out without my advice, but you have also come back without letting me know. Nevertheless, I give this belt as a sign of my mourning for your loss.

And now, after all this, even though you have taken on this bad mood, in order to show that I have no evil conspiracies against you, nor intention to have any, nor expect them from you, I will give you a large quantity of ammunition. But only on the definite condition that you will use it only to defend yourselves against those who will invade or attack you and to hunt, the negligence of which has been so harmful to your whole group as well as to us.

We have yearly assemblies or public meetings and what has been done there is the making of laws and orders for the prevention of abuses and for the regulation of the conduct of the subjects towards each other and their neighbours. I would wish that you would do the same thing in your public meetings, for many times I receive complaints that your young people destroy the people's cattle in their coming and going. In order that there may be no reason to do that, I will, as I have done before, give you enough provisions to see you back home and expect that you will be responsible for any damage that you do to the common people in your coming and going. For if there is any, I will take it from your belts.

And now at last I here renew our old covenant. In his Majesty's name I assure you of his protection as long as you keep to your covenant and remain within the limits of your duty. In accordance, I give this belt.

[*Received on January 1, 1720/1*]

Dear Sr

I have writ about your affair in a pressing manner To the Lords of Trade & recommended your Son as you desire and when I close my packet will Send your memorial in it.[1] I have acquainted them with my design about Niagara and Therefore must desire you to inform me if what I hear be true That the Sinnekees did make a formal gift of the Land about Niagara to the English in Coll Dungan time before the French as they call it conquered that country. if you dont know this let your Son inquire among the old books of the Board where they keep the propositions made to the Indians & the Indians Speeches to them. I am told it is in one of These Indian Speeches that they made this Solemn declra-tion. Pray either your Self or by your Sons means clear me up as much as you can in this matter because it is of consequence.
I am

Dear Sir
Yours entirely
/S/ W. Burnet

Mr Livingston

[1] Refers to Robert Livingston's desire to have his eldest surviving son, Philip, succeed him in his local appointive offices, including that of Secretary for Indian Affairs.

Albany June ye 16, 1721

Honored Sr[1]

I make bold to Give you the trouble of a Line and to Send you a Small Paper Relateing to the Indian Trade which is most Certainly Carried on by the handlers[2] in an Unfair Way by Sending off their Goods to the Mohacks Country & placeing them Amongst the Indians in their Indian houses the way that it is done they send the Indians with their Goods from Albany to the Indian Country and then it is out of the Power of Any officer to Discover them Now if it be possible to obtain An Act that all Traders be Obliged to Exonorate themselves on Oath that are or may be Suspected to trade against any Law that is in force is the only way to make the trade to go in the Right Channell

Sr. I hope that you will Excuse me for giving you this Trouble and beleive that I am Sr

Your Obliged humble Servt.
/S/ Henry Holland

Ye 4 of Sepr 1721 in alby[3]

His Excel told ye 10 Sachims of ye 5 nations yt he beleeving them to be as he knew true frinds to this governt. Sent for ym to discourse of some heads yt are to be Proposed in ye Publick Propositions.

That its their Intrest to be Steady to ye English nation who are a free People & So very Jealous of their liberty & yt ye king who was too great a frind to ye french was deposed Since he would infringe ye liberties of his Subjects

That tho we are in Peace wth. ye french yet ye Subjects of great Brittain are not to be familiar wth ye french or have any [(*torn*)] them, or goe to Canada without leave from this government

If non of ye Brethren did Correspond with ye french or Suffer ye french to come & Trade among them or to Treat wth ye 5 nations I' dout not but Some of our People would be inclind to

[1] Not addressed, but probably sent to Livingston.

[2] *Handlaers,* or Dutch merchants. The paper referred to is not found in the Livingston Indian Papers and was probably forwarded to Governor Burnet.

[3] Draft in Robert Livingston's writing. This was a prelude to the public conference of September 7-9, 1721, given in O'Callaghan, 5: 635-640.

come & Setle among ye Brethren who would be able not only to Strenthen yu but also to Supply yu with Such necessaries as yu want

I understand yt ye Brethren have Sufferd ye french to make a Blokhouse on this Side of ye Lake & by yt means wil incroach upon yu wh. wil be of Pernicious Consequence for ye future, & as long as yu Suffer that our People wil be discouraged to come & Setle among yu

altho it be Peace now with france it wil be dangerous to Suffer ye french to make any Such Storehouse or Trading house wh. if a warr Should break out they Soon can turn into a fort & So perplex ye Brethren & hinder their hunting.

The french have many Souldiers wh. they keep to Enslave their oun People & would if they could make ye brethren Slaves likewise, but we being a free People have no Such aim or Intention, but upon occasion of a warr al our People are willing & ready to offend ye Enemy as wel as Defend their Country

The Brethren must not halt between two & think to be Equally [*(torn)*] & dependence upon us & ye french there wil always be a jealousy and mistrust of one Side or oyr & Since this govt has been always true to them & they true to us, Pray Consider which of ye 2 they are to Chuse.

I desire to know if ye Brethren be not inclind to forbid ye french coming to yr Countrey & ye Demolishing of ye Trading house ye french have built on this Side ye Lake of Cadarachqui.

Ye 10 Sachims answerd yt ye matter yt his Excely pleasd to Communicat were of Such moment that they could not readily make answer now but desird leave to make answer to morrow morning His Excely said he was well Satisfyd they should Consult together till to morrow & give him their opinion of ye matter without Communicating ye businesse to ye rest of ye Sachims, and yt he had oyr things to discourse with them but would not bother their memories with too much at one time & assurd them yt what he told them was for their oun good, and from ye tender Regard he had for ye wellfare of ye 5 nations and therefore warnd them to prevent those mischieffs yt might follow thereupon.

At a Councill held in Albany the 8th. of Septembr 1722[1]
Present
His Excell Willm Burnet Esqr
Capt Genll and governour in Chief
The Honble. Coll Alexander Spotswood
govr of virginia
Rip van Dam }
John Barbary } *Esqr.*
Cadwalleder Colden }

His Excely. having sent for two Sachims of each of ye 5 nations said

I have sent for you to discourse with you about the affairs of New England, the Governr of Boston has writ me yt. ye Indians to ye Eastward have broak their Treaty that they made with ye English and have committed severall murders on ye kings Subjects there taken their vessels burnt their houses and Committed severall outrages, I desire that you will tell me what you know of that affair, and if those Indians have Sent any messages to any of ye 5 nations.[2]

The said 10 indians answer by Hendrik a mohog their Speaker on this occasion & said

We are Sorry to hear of ye mischieffs that are don to ye Eastward, we know nothing of yt affair but ye Reports we hear here, neither do we know of any Belt that was sent to any of ye five nations lately by those eastern Indians but acknowledge yt about a year and a half ago ye Mohogs received a Belt of Blak wampum from ye onnagingues or eastern Indians by which they said to ye mohogs. Fathers, we are designd to make warr upon ye English to ye Eastward and desire you to ConSider of it, and to assist us in ye proSecution of yt warr, and before we begin we will acquaint you with it, and Say further we acquainted ye Commissioners therewith, and Stopd ye Belt, and would not Suffer ye Belt to go further to ye oyr 4 nations but Smotherd it, and have heard nothing from them Since, but nothing hereof appears upon the

[1] This was one of a series of conferences held by Burnet, Spotswood, and Keith with the Iroquois, August 29—September 12, 1722. All the other public transactions are published in O'Callaghan, 5: 657-681.

[2] Burnet commented that the Massachusetts authorities wanted to engage the Iroquois in a war with the Eastern Indians. "But finding a great averseness in the [New York] Council . . . & the Government of New England not agreeing to send commissioners to treat with us previously upon the heads to be proposed to the Indians, I found no way but to take this matter wholly upon myself." Burnet to Lords of Trade, November 21, 1722. *Ibid.*, 655.

Commissioners minutes, only one of ye Comrs. Says, he heard such a Report of a maquase Indian from Sarachtoge, yt a certain Belt had been sent to ye Mohogs from ye Eastern Indians telling them they were apprehensive there would be a warr between them and ye English, and Since they were all Indians and of one Cullour they hoped they would have their assistance if yt So happend

His Excely told them

Do you not Remember that ye Covenant Chain which has been So often Renewed included all ye kings Subjects as well as those of new England as the rest of Kings Provinces, and whether you do not think that ye Eastern Indians have don wickedly in falling upon ye English.

and Said further

The governr. of Boston has sent a ꝑsent in order to Treat with you, and to desire you to go to those Eastern Indians to putt a Stop to this warr, but I would not do any thing till I heard how you were inclind, and I desire to know whether you are under any Engagement to those Eastern Indians whereby you are hinderd from going upon any message relating this affair if requird.

who answer

That we maquase made no Such Engagment, nor did not so much as answer those Eastern Indians yt brougt ye Blak Belt, but Stifled it and Rejected it, not likeing or approoving of ye Proposition neither would we so much as Lett the oyr 4 nations know of any Such thing, and further added they could not give an ansser to his Excely Propositions till they had Consulted ye Rest of ye Sachims

Wm Burnet Esqr. Capt Genl.
To Leiut. harme Vedder

I Reposeing Special trust and Confidence as well in the care diligence and CircumSpection as in ye Loyalty and readinesse of you to do his majes. good & faithful Service have nominated constituted and appointed and I do by vertue of ye Power and authority to me given by his majestie under ye great Seal of great Brittain hereby constitute nominate and appoint you ye Sd. Harme

Vedder Leut. to Majr Abr. Schuyler who is now going with some Young men to abide in ye Sinnekes Country for a twelve month, you are therefore during yt Term to Obey observe & follow such orders & Directions as you shall from time to time Receive from him ye sd Majr Abr. Shuyler Pursuant to ye trust Reposed in you, & for so doing this Shall be your Sufficient warrant & Commission given under my hand & Seal at arms in albany this 8th day of Septembr 1722 in ye 9th year of his Majes Reign &ca.

Instructions for Major Abraham Schuyler

You are with all Expedition to go with that Company of young men that are willing to Setle in the Sinnekes Country for a twelve month to Trade with the farr Indians that are come from ye upper Lakes, and endeavour by all Suitable means to perswade them to come and Trade at Albany or with this new Setlement
You are not to trade with ye four hithermost Nations, (except for Provisions in your passage to and fro) but to carry your goods as far as ye Sinnekes Country, and to trade with them or any other Indian nations that come thither.
Since there is a Setlement or Trading house built by yt Company yt went with Capt Peter Schuyler Junr.[1] who are now expected home at a Place calld by ye Indians Caniaterundaquanat belonging to ye Sinnekes you are to make use of ye same if you think it Conveniently Seated or els make another in Some more Convenient place on this Side ye Cadarachqui Lake either at ye Sinnekes Castle or elswhere, and use all lawfull means to draw ye farr trade thither by Sending notice to ye farr Indians that you are Setled in ye Sinnekes Country for their ease and Incouragement by my order, and that they may be assured they shall have goods cheeper here than ever the French can afford them at Canada, for the French must have the Principall Indian goods from England not having them of their oun.
You are also to acquaint all ye farr Indians that I have an absolut promise and Engagement from the five nations that they will not only Suffer them to passe freely and Peaceably throu their Country, but will give them all due Incouragement, and Sweep and keep

[1] The instructions to Peter Schuyler, Jr., September 11, 1721, are given in O'Callaghan, 5: 641-642.

ye Path open and Clean whenever they intend to come and trade with this Province.

Altho ye Place where you Setle be Land beLonging to ye Croun of great Brittain, both by ye Surrender of ye Indians and the Treaty of Peace with France, neverthelesse you are to Send out Skouts and Spys and be upon your guard, the French not to be trusted who will use all means to prevent ye farr Indians comeing to Trade with you or their Coming to Albany.

You are to keep an Exact Dyary or Journall of all ye Proceedings of any ConSequence & Keep a Constant Correspondence with the Commissioners of the Indian affairs at Albany, whom I will order to give me an account thereof from time to time, and whenever you shall receive directions frome me to treat with the Sinnekes or any of ye five nations, you are to be Carefull to minute doun your Proceedings and their answers and to send them to me with the first opportunity, incloseing them to the Commissioners of ye Indian affairs who will forward them with all expedition, and if any matter of great moment and fitt to be kept very Secret do occur, you are to Send an account thereof to me in a letter Seald, wch. may be inclos'd to the Commissioners in order to be forwarded, and you are not obliged to mention Such matters in your Letter to the Commissioners

When you come to ye Sinnekes Country you are to give them a Belt of wampum in token that they are to give Credit to you, as my agent to Treat with them of all matters relating to ye Publik Service and the benefit of ye Trade, and at your desire to furnish you with such a number of their People as you shall want for your assistance and Safety on Such Conditions as you and they can agree upon.

When you have Pitchd upon a Convenient place for a Trading house, you are to endeavour to purchase a Tract of Land in ye kings name, and to agree with ye Sinnekes for it, wh. shall be paid by ye Publik in order yt it may be granted by Patent to those yt shal be ye first Setlers there for their incouragement.

You are not to hinder or molest any other British Subjects, who are willing to trade there on their oun hazard and account for any Indian goods Rom only Excepted.

You are to Communicat to the Compe Such articles of your Instructions as shall be proper for their Regulation from time to time.

If you judge it necessary you may Send thre or four of your Company either among ye farr Indians or to come to Albany as ye necessary Service of ye Company shall require, but yt. not above four of ye said Company of which yourSelf may be one be Permitted to be absent at one time.

Before you absent your Self from ye Said Setlement which you are not to do for above two months during the whole year, without particular leave from me for so doing you are to leave a Copy of Such part of these Instructions with your Leiutenant as you judge necessary for his Regulation.

All ye goods and merchandise that you and ye said Company shal take along with you, are to be upon one joynt Stock & account, and all your Profit and Losse to be ye Same.

and whereas it is thought of great use to ye British Intrest to have a Setlement upon ye nearest part of ye Lake Erie near ye falls of Jagaro and also below ye falls and upon ye Confines of ye Lake ontario you are to endeavour to purchase in his majes name of ye Sinnekes or oyr native Proprietors all Such Lands above ye falls of Jagero fifty miles to ye Southward of ye said falls which they can dispose off, and also below ye sd great falls towards ye Sinnekes Country & on this side of ye great Lake ontario.

You are to have a Copy of my Proposition to ye five Nations and their answer, and to use your utmost Endeavour that they *p*form all that they have Promist therein, and that non of these Instructions be Shown to any *p*son or *p*sons, but what you shall think necessary to Communicat to the Leiut. and ye rest of ye Company. Lett what agreement you make with ye Sinnekes or any oyr of ye nations of any Land, be to be paid in Pouder & Lead & in no oyr Commodities.

You are to Demand of Capt Peter Schuyler Junr. all Such blank deeds or Conveyances that were deliverd to him in order to be made use of upon ye Purchase of any Tracts of Lands of ye Indians wh. you are to make use of when you shall have Purchased those great Tracts of Land both above and below ye great Falls of Jagaro and on ye Sides of ye great Lakes calld ontario and Erie.

Given under my hand and Seal at arms in albany ye 8th day of Septembr in ye 9th year of his Majes Reign Ao 1722.

[William Burnet]

Present

William Tailer / *Spencer Phips* — *Esqrs. members of his Majes. Council of The Province of the Massachusets Bay*

John Stodder — *Esqr member of the house of Representatives of said Province*

Peter Schuyler
Henry Holland
Peter van Brugh
Evert Bancker
Phil Livingston
Johs Wendell
Johs. Bleeker — *Esqrs. Comrs.*

Interpreted by Lawrence Claese after it was Translated into Dutch by Philip Livingston

Proposition made by William Tailer Spencer Phips and John Stodder Esqrs. Commisrs appointed by his Majes. Governt. of the Massachusets Bay to the Sachims of the five Nations (to witt) the Mohoggs, Oneydes, Onnondages, Cayouges & Sinnekes as also to those of Tusquarora in albany the 28th. day of May 1723

The Sachims being Conveen'd Said first

Brethren

YEHOWANNE and KINSIE the first in the Indn. Tongue is a broad Way and the last Signifies Pingon which they take from Coll. Pingon[1] who has formerly treated with them in behalf of the Governt. of Boston.

YOU have Invited us to come here. We the Sachims of the five Nations & of the Tusquaroras being Eighty in Number and Impowered by the Several Nations to treat with you are arriv'd here, and now ready to hear what you have to propose, but we are first to beg a favour of you, & acquaint you that as it has been from Antient Time the Comon Practice of all Governrs. to get our guns Hatchetts & Kettles mended which we desire you may also order to be done now.

THE GENTLEMEN Replyed that as they are Sent by the Governt. of Boston to treat with them they desire to Speak first and shall take Notice of what they say afterwards.

BRETHREN

We are well pleased that after our & your long Travail we are mett together, and have the Satisfaction of Seeing one another & Congratulating each other on our safe arrival.

[1] John Pynchon of Springfield, Massachusetts.

Friends & Brethren

The Government of the Massachusetts bay, recalling to mind that ffriendship that hath (long Since) been contracted, often renewed & Inviolably maintained between them and your Tribes, and Considering that by Reason of your great Distance from them they have not frequent Opportunity of Conversing with you and thereby Encreasing mutual Respect and Friendship, therefore they thought proper to Send three Gentlemen about a year and half Since to make you a visit, and to renew that amity that hath Continued almost time out of mind, and to negotiate Some other affairs with you, but you being then lately returned from hence to your own Country they had not the Opportunity to Speak with you

Since which Several of your Chiefs (being delegates from their Respective Tribes) have taken a Journey to Boston which was very acceptable and pleasing to that Governt. and gave them an Opportunity of Expressing their Respect to you and we doubt not but they have been so Just as to acquaint you with the kind Reception & friendly Entertainment they met withal.

THE GOVERNMENT being Sensible of the disappointment of their former Comrs. Resolved upon Sending us hither (partly) on the Same Errand. We are accordingly come by order & in Name of that Governt. to brighten the Chain of ffriendship (into which they have put their hands from which they neither can nor desire to withdraw them) and to give you the outmost assurance of their Respect & Friendship & that they will Endeavour by all proper Methods to Cultivate a good Understanding between them and your Tribes & Endeavour to Continue the Same to future Generations. And as a Testimony of their Regard to you & Evidence of their Sincerity they have Sent you this present which we in their Name deliver to you

WHEN you have Considered of what we have said, and Returned your answer we Shall have Something further to offer to you.

THAT the *p*sent now delivered you is given you by the Governt. of the Massachusets Bay and is a Token of their ffriendship & Renewing the Antient Covenant Chain which has always been kept Inviolable on their Side.

This being the Birth day of our Soveraign Lord King George we have ordered a barrel of Beer for you to drink his Health.

THERE are also fifty Keggs with Rum filled which you can See and are to be brought up above Schinectady where you are to receive them which you may carry to your own Castles to drink with the rest of your Sachims.

A True Copy Examind ꝑ
Philip Livingston Secr
for Indian affairs.

GLOSSSARY OF SHORT TITLES CITED IN FOOTNOTES

Brodhead: John R. Brodhead, *History of the State of New York* (2 vols., New York, 1853-1871).

Cal. N. Y. Col. MSS: Edmund B. O'Callaghan, ed., *Calendar of Historical Manuscripts, in the Office of the Secretary of State, Albany, N. Y.* (2 vols., Albany, 1865-1866).

Cal. N. Y. Coun. Min.: Berthold Fernow, ed., *Calendar of Council Minutes, 1668-1783* (*New York State Library Bulletin, 58, History 6,* Albany, 1902).

Colden: Cadwallader Colden, *The History of the Five Indian Nations of Canada* (2 vols., New York, 1922).

Duane Report, 1780: James Duane, "Report of a Collection of Treaties &c with the five Nations remaining among the Papers of Robert Livingston & Philip Livingston Esqrs deceased; formerly Secretaries of Indian Affairs, in the hands of Col. Robert Livingston their Descendant and Heir at Law." Submitted to the New York State Senate and Assembly, March 30, 1780. (Duane Papers, The New-York Historical Society.)

McIlwain: Charles H. McIlwain, ed., Peter Wraxall, *An Abridgement of the Indian Affairs . . . From the Year 1678 to the Year 1751* (Cambridge, 1915).

O'Callaghan: Edmund B. O'Callaghan, ed., *Documents Relative to the Colonial History of the State of New York* (11 vols., Albany, 1856-1861).

Smith: William Smith, *The History of the Late Province of New-York, From Its Discovery, to the Appointment of Governor Colden in 1762* (2 vols., New York, 1829).

GLOSSARY OF INDIAN TRIBAL NAMES

NO UNIFORMITY existed during the colonial period in the spelling of Indian tribal names. The forms most often used in the Livingston documents are listed here, each followed by the generally accepted modern version (if any) and the tribal location in that period.

IROQUOIS (THE FIVE NATIONS)

Maquase—Mohawks

Oneidas

Onondagas

Cayugas

Sinnondowannas—Senecas

Tuscaroras: Moved by slow degrees through Pennsylvania (by way of the "Tuscarora Path") to New York as a result of the Tuscarora War of 1711-1713, and became a Sixth Nation under the aegis, first, of the Oneidas, later of the Senecas.

LAURENTIAN TRIBES

Cahennajages—Caughnawagas: Settled on the St. Lawrence River near Montreal; composed primarily of Mohawk and Oneida converts to Roman Catholicism who had moved to Canada in 1668.

Rondackses—Adirondacks: An Algonquian tribe settled at Three Rivers and Oka in Quebec.

RIVER TRIBES

Mahikanders—Mahicans: Settled on the upper Hudson River between Albany and Lake Champlain.

Wawyachtenokse—Wawyachtonoe: Band of the Mahican confederacy in Dutchess and Columbia Counties, N. Y., and Litchfield, Conn.

Warrencockse: Group of Esopus Indians settled on the west bank of the Hudson River near Kingston (Esopus), N. Y.

Menessings—Minisinks—Munsees: A division of the Delaware Indians (Lenni Lenape) settled on the upper Delaware River, with outlying communities on the Hudson below the Warrencockse.

Catskills: A branch of the Munsee Indians; settled on Catskill Creek west of the Hudson River.

Scaghkook—Scaticook: Originally a Mahican village on the east bank of the Hudson River at the Mouth of the Hoosic River, but later occupied mainly by New England Indians who fled to New York after King Philip's War (1675) and who took their name from this village.

EASTERN TRIBES

Onnagonques—Abnaki: Members of an Algonquian confederacy centering in northern New England.

Aurages—Pennacooks: Members of an Algonquian confederacy on the Merrimac River.

SOUTHERN TRIBES

Piscataway: A Conoy village situated in Prince Georges County, Maryland.

Appamatocks: A small tribe in Prince Georges County, Virginia; extinct by 1722.

Chickahominy: A tribe on the Chickahominy River in Virginia.

Cachnawas—Conoys: A tribe near the Potomac River in the 1670's, which later came into Pennsylvania and moved slowly north up the Susquehanna Valley, stopping for a time at Conejohela, near the old Susquehannock Fort; later at modern Bainbridge, Harrisburg, Shamokin (Sunbury), Wyoming, Owego, and Chenango (near Binghamton).

Saponi: A Siouan tribe living in south central Virginia.

Flatheads—Catawbas: A Siouan tribe living in Carolina, with whom the Iroquois had been at war for many years.

Schowaenos—Shawnees: A scattered, highly migratory tribe of Algonquian stock who appeared on many of our early frontiers after 1690. They are believed to have originated in the upper Ohio Valley. The migration of Ohio remnants to the Munsee country in 1694 has been thoroughly discussed by Hanna in *The Wilderness Trail.*

Susquehannas—Conestogas—Minquas: A tribe of Iroquoian stock on the lower Susquehanna River in Pennsylvania and Maryland. In 1675 they were defeated by the Iroquois and dispersed.

WESTERN TRIBES

Twightwees—Miamis: A tribe concentrated near what is now Chicago, by the end of the seventeenth century. They are thought to have come from the Wabash.

Dionondadoes—Tionontati—Petun or *"Tobacco Nation":* At this time living near Mackinaw, Lake Michigan; formerly southwest of the Georgian Bay, adjoining the Huron territory.

Dawaganhaes—Waganhaes—Ontwaganha: An epithet applied by the Iroquois to the various northern and western tribes of Algonquian stock (Chippewa, Ottawa, Miami, Shawnee, and the "Far Indians").

Ottawawas—Ottawas: An Algonquian people of the Upper Lakes, noted as intertribal traders.